The
Norman
Commanders

The Norman Commanders

Masters of Warfare 911–1135

PAUL HILL

Pen & Sword
MILITARY

First published in Great Britain in 2015 by
Pen and Sword Military
an imprint of
Pen and Sword Books Ltd
47 Church Street
Barnsley
South Yorkshire S70 2AS

ISBN 978 1 78346 228 5

A CIP record for this book is available from the British Library

Printed and bound in   alta
by Gut nb r Pr   Ltd

Typeset in Ehrhardt by Chic Graphics

Pen & Sword Books Ltd incorporates the imprints of
Pen & Sword Archaeology, Atlas, Aviation, Battleground, Discovery,
Family History, History, Maritime, Military, Naval, Politics, Railways,
Select, Social History, Transport, True Crime, Claymore Press,
Frontline Books, Leo Cooper, Praetorian Press, Remember When,
Seaforth Publishing and Wharncliffe.

For a complete list of Pen and Sword titles please contact
Pen and Sword Books Limited
47 Church Street, Barnsley, South Yorkshire, S70 2AS, England
E-mail: enquiries@pen-and-sword.co.uk
Website: www.pen-and-sword.co.uk

Contents

List of Illustrations vii

Introduction 1

   A note on the sources..2

Part 1 The Rise of the Normans

Chapter 1   Establishment and Expansion in Normandy 7

Chapter 2   Legitimacy in the South..14

Part 2 The Commanders

Chapter 3   Robert Guiscard, Duke of Apulia, Calabria and Sicily
         (d.1085) 25

Chapter 4   William the Conqueror, Duke of Normandy (1035-
         1087), King of England (1066-1087) 34

Chapter 5   Richard I, Count of Aversa and Prince of Capua (d.1078) 47

Chapter 6   Roger I, Count of Sicily (d.1101) 53

Chapter 7   William II Rufus, King of England (1087-1100) 63

Chapter 8   Robert II Curthose, Duke of Normandy (1087-1106) 80

Chapter 9   Henry I, King of England (1100-1135), Duke of
         Normandy (1106-1135) 88

Chapter 10 Bohemond, Prince of Antioch (d.1111)......................100

Part 3 Battles and Campaigns

Chapter 11 Introduction 116

Chapter 12 In the North..117

   Val-ès-Dunes 1047 117

   Hastings 14 October 1066 120

   Tinchebrai 28 September 1106...133

   Alençon December 1118 137

   Brémule 20 August 1119 138

   Bourgthéroulde 26 March 1124 142

Chapter 13 In the South 145

The Three Battles of 1041 145

Civitate 17 June 1053 149

Cerami, June 1063...157

Misilmeri 1068...161

Dyrrhachium 18 October 1081 162

Part 4 The Norman Way of War

Chapter 14 The Nature of Warfare across the Norman World 172

Chapter 15 Recruitment, Organisation and Mercenaries 175

Obligated Troops 176

Stipendiary/Mercenary troops 180

Chapter 16 The Normans and their Horses 184

Chapter 17 Logistics and Supply 188

Chapter 18 Training 192

Chapter 19 Leadership and Discipline 194

Chapter 20 Strategy 196

The Role of Castles and their Garrisons........................196

The Nature of Sieges...199

Ravaging and Harrying 206

Using the Landscape..208

Stratagems and Ruses 214

Chapter 21 Tactics on the Battlefield 216

Command and Control...216

Mounted Tactics: Shock Cavalry, Stirrups, Couched Lances
  and the Feigned Retreat 218

Infantry Tactics: Heavy and Light Infantry 226

Infantry Tactics: Archers and Crossbowmen 228

Conclusion...231

Bibliography..234

Index 238

List of Illustrations

Photographs (Black and White)

1. Jumièges Abbey, Normandy, France. © Rene Drouyer. Dreamstime.com
2. Falaise Castle, Normandy, France. © Bridgeman Images
3. Church at Santissima Trinatà at Venosa. © Danilo Mongiello. Dreamstime.com
4. Statue of William the Conqueror at Falaise, France. © Ancient Art and Architecture Ltd
5. Abbaye aux Hommes at Caen, Normandy, France. © Paul Hill. Author Collection
6. Abbaye aux Dames at Caen, Normandy, France. © Julie Wileman. Author Collection
7. The Estuary at Saint-Valery-Sur-Somme, France. © Paul Hill. Author Collection
8. William the Conqueror's tombstone at Abbaye aux Hommes in Caen, Normandy, France. © Paul Hill. Author Collection
9. Coin of Roger I of Sicily. © Ancient Art and Architecture Ltd
10. Cape Milazzo, northern Sicily. © Michele Mondello. Dreamstime.com
11. A fanciful depiction of the death of William II Rufus. Private Collection © Look and Learn/Bridgeman Images.
12. The Vestiges of Bishop Gundulf's work at Rochester Castle, in Kent, England. © Paul Hill. Author Collection
13. The early Norman Motte at Tonbridge Castle, in Kent, England. © Paul Hill. Author Collection
14. The early Norman Motte at Tonbridge Castle, in Kent, England from outside the gatehouse. © Paul Hill. Author Collection
15. Pevensey Castle, Sussex, England. © Charlotte Leaper. Dreamstime.com
16. Gisors Castle in the Vexin, France. © Philippehalle. Dreamstime.com
17. Gloucester Cathedral, England. Tomb of Duke Robert II Curthose. © Elizabeth Hill. Author Collection
18. Statue of Henry I, Rochester Cathedral. © Paul Hill. Author Collection
19. Statue of Queen Matilda, Rochester Cathedral. © Paul Hill. Author Collection
20. The Phare de Gatteville at the tip of Barfleur, Normandy. © David Lamb. Dreamstime.com

21. Mausoleum of Bohemond Prince of Antioch. Canosa Cathedral, Puglia, Italy. © Bridgeman Images
22. Walls of Antioch, 1894 engraving. Private Collection. Bridgeman Images
23. Duke William's Flagship the Mora, from the Bayeux Tapestry. © Ancient Art and Architecture Ltd
24. E.A. Freeman's map of the Battle of Hastings
25. The site of the High Altar at Battle Abbey. © Paul Hill. Author Collection
26. Oakwood Gill, to the north of Caldbec Hill, near to Virgin's Lane. Battle, Sussex. © Paul Hill. Author Collection
27. Duke William is presented with his horse at Hastings, from the Bayeux Tapestry. © Jorisvo. Dreamstime.com
28. Palermo, Sicily, from Utveggio Castle. © Angelo Giampiccolo. Dreamstime.com
29. Norman Cavalry attack the English shieldwall at Hastings, from the Bayeux Tapestry. © Jorisvo. Dreamstime.com
30. The preferred method of a mounted attack on an infantry line, from the Bayeux Tapestry. © Jorisvo. Dreamstime.com

Photographs (Colour Plate Section)
1. The Castle at Melfi, Italy. © Danilo Mongiello. Dreamstime.com
2. The Sanctuary of Monte Sant' Angelo, Gargano, Italy. © Valeria Cantone. Dreamstime.com
3. The Abbey at Monte Cassino, Italy. © Myszolow. Dreamstime.com
4. The Natural Defences at Enna, Sicily. © Goran Bogicevic. Dreamstime.com
5. Gerace, Calabria, Italy. © Quanthem. Dreamstime.com
6. Paternò Castle in Catania, Sicily. © Sebastiano Leggio. Dreamstime.com
7. Hastings Castle, East Sussex. England. Paul Hill. Author Collection
8. Mont-Saint-Michel, France. © Martin Pegler. Author Collection
9. Fiskardo Bay, Cephalonia. © Dinosmichail. Dreamstime.com
10. Abbey of Santissima Trinatà at Venosa, Italy. © Milla74. Dreamstime.com
11. Church of San Giovanni Dei Lebbrosi, Palermo, Sicily. Photograph: Nilde. ©123RF.com
12. Ruined Keep of Domfront Castle, Normandy. © Musat Christian. Dreamstime.com
13. Chepstow Castle, Monmouthshire, Wales. © Richard Hill. Author Collection
14. Bayeux Tapestry. Norman Supply Cart. © Ancient Art & Architecture Collection Ltd
15. Miscellany on the Life of St. Edmund. The Pierpont Morgan Library, New York. MS M.736, fol. 7v. Purchased by J.P. Morgan (1867-1943) in 1927
16. Roger II is crowned king of Sicily in 1130. Santa Maria dell' Ammiraglio, Palermo, Sicily. © Ancient Art & Architecture Collection Ltd

17. Bamburgh Castle, Northumbria, England. © Darren Turner. Dreamstime.com

18. The traditional battlefield site of Hastings at Battle Abbey, East Sussex, England. © Jakich. Dreamstime.com

19. Rochester Castle, Kent. England. © Paul Hill. Author Collection

20. Exchequer Hall at Caen Castle, Normandy, France. © Paul Hill. Author Collection

Illustrations

Fig. 1. Early Rulers of Normandy (Family Tree)

Fig. 2. The Hauteville Kin – Robert Guiscard (Family Tree)

Fig. 3. Robert Guiscard – Duke of Apulia (Family Tree)

Fig. 4. William the Conqueror, Duke of Normandy, King of England (Family Tree)

Fig. 5. Richard I Count of Aversa, Prince of Capua (Family Tree)

Fig 6. The Hauteville Kin. Roger I Count of Sicily (Family Tree)

Fig 7. Roger I Count of Sicily (Family Tree)

Fig 8. William II Rufus (Family Tree)

Fig 9. Duke Robert II Curthose (Family Tree)

Fig 10. Henry I, King of England (Family Tree)

Fig 11. Bohemond, Prince of Antioch (Family Tree)

Fig 12. Possible deployments for the Battle of Tinchebrai 1106

Fig 13. The Battle of Brémule 1119

Fig 14. The Battle of Bourgthéroulde 1124

Fig 15. The Troop Pools from which the Norman Commanders drew

Fig 16. Duke William's 'order of march' before Hastings

Maps

1. Map of Normandy showing bishopric boundaries and battle sites (after Douglas)

2. Map of southern Italy showing principal ports and towns

3. Map of England and Normandy (after Douglas)

4. Map of Sicily

5. Map of the 1088 rebellion against William II Rufus

6. The First Crusade in Anatolia

7. Map of Bohemond's Illyrian Campaigns

8. The Region of Antioch, Northern Syria

9. Map of the Battle of Val-ès-Dunes 1047

10. Map of the 1066 coastline of East Sussex (After Morillo)

11. Map of Central Southern Italy Showing the Campaigns of 1041

12. Map of the Civitate Campaign – the approach

13. Map of the Battle of Civitate 1053
14. Map of the Campaigning before Dyrrhachium
15. Map of the Battle of Dyrrhachium 18 October 1081
16. Map of William II Rufus's march to Le Mans, June 1098

Tables
Table 1. Probable combatants at Hastings

Introduction

The Norman Commanders is intended to introduce readers to a number of the main characters in the history of Norman warfare and to show how these men approached the art of war. It is not a social or administrative history, nor is it an ecclesiastical one. The political history of the era, as recorded by churchmen and others, plays a huge part in framing the context of what we have to say about the military capability of the Normans, so that context is brought to the reader's attention throughout this book.

There are some key military themes to explore. The basic question of what warfare was really like in the period is examined. How often for example, were there pitched battles or strategic campaigns? Were our Norman commanders influenced by the classical manuals of warfare, such as Vegetius's great work *De Re Militari*, or any of the great Byzantine military manuals of the ninth and tenth century? The evidence is sometimes enigmatic, but as we shall see, there is an explanation for why it is a strange sort of question to ask in the first place.

How the commanders recruited their armies is examined. The training of troops, how they were supplied and kept cohesive on the campaign trail, is also explored. But it is with the strategies and tactical capabilities of the commanders that we are blessed with real hard evidence. The Normans achieved their military and political goals in a number of ways, from the strategic ravaging of an area of land, down to the more localised tactic of the 'feigned flight'; a much discussed topic in recent decades. The famous Norman knight and his much-vaunted cavalry charge is discussed. Here, as the mounted knight found himself facing enemies in England, southern Italy, Sicily and the Holy Land, was a tactical response which brought admiration from one easily impressed Byzantine observer. But was this a particularly 'Norman' trait? Were the Normans any different in their approach to war than the other contemporary Western cultures which they melted into, like the Anglo-Saxons, Franks (with whom they are closely identified in a number of Byzantine references) and the Lombards of Italy? Certainly there were differences between Norman warfare and that of the great imperial states such as the Byzantine Empire. The Normans never had the resources (not even when they were the kings of England) to run a professional standing army with infantry drilled, barracked, paraded and regimented in the way that their Byzantine counterparts were, but this would not make the Normans any less of a threat to the Byzantine world.

Throughout this book there are examples of Norman military prowess. There are also examples of how and why things could go wrong. Immediately apparent is the importance of personal leadership skills. By understanding the character of the men who led armies to remarkable successes or conspicuous failures, we can get to the heart of these events.

The men under consideration here were complex human beings. Despite the propensity of military history to offer a dry picture of events and developments, it is hoped the reader will enjoy a very human story. So many of the Normans' achievements were driven by the personalities of their leaders. Before we look at the men, their characters and methods of approach, we need to heed a warning from the scriptorium. We base our observations on the historical evidence we have to hand. Frequently, we refer to certain medieval writers, whose works provide fascinating but sometimes frustrating detail about Norman warfare. The background, motivations and character of some of these writers is important.

A note on the sources
Documentary evidence exists in a variety of forms. There are charters, writs, pipe rolls and legal codes which give us hints about Norman military organisation and supply arrangements. We also rely on narrative accounts provided by contemporary and near-contemporary commentators. Some of the material we draw upon is biased, inaccurate or downright lies. Sometimes, the military terms used by the chroniclers and biographers of the medieval age are drawn from classical references and give us misleading ideas about technical equipment and army organisation. However, there is a wealth of material to draw on and some of it contains some remarkable revelations.

Our knowledge of the story of the Norman adventure south of the Alps is based around the work of three main writers. For the invasion and conquest of Sicily and southern Italy one of the sources is Geoffrey of Malaterra's *Deeds of Count Roger of Calabria and Sicily and of his brother Duke Robert Guiscard*. Malaterra had been brought to Sicily and was established as a monk by Count Roger after the last phases of its conquest in 1091. It was Roger who asked Malaterra to write this work and so it contains some remarkable accounts of Roger's achievements, many of which are written to cast Roger in a good light. Written at the turn of the century, Malaterra's work is a homage to its sponsor, with predictable tales of Christian supremacy and the power of God's work. This is especially true in the accounts he gives of the Battle of Cerami in 1063 (pages 157–160) and other aspects of the conquest of Sicily (1060–72).

Malaterra has far more strengths than weaknesses for those wanting to study the military aspects of the age. However, those weaknesses that do exist are frustrating. Rarely does he give us the combatant numbers in his accounts of battles and campaigns and, when he does, they are usually – but not always – so huge on the side of the Saracens as to immediately provoke scepticism in the modern reader. Nor are those Saracen armies ever described in terms of their troop types or capabilities. Battle accounts soon lose their authentic feel when Malaterra slips into the realms of the supernatural, citing the appearance of a saint as a saviour in one of them. But Malaterra shines when he tells of Count Roger's motivations, and of his struggles with his stingy brother Duke Robert Guiscard. He is also able to draw from the oral history of Sicily and elsewhere, which he heard being told around him. He chose to use that material to glorify Count Roger and the Normans, whom he often refers to as 'our men', and he presents examples of the behaviour of commanders and their knights which are not given elsewhere and which help bring colour to the picture.

Amatus of Monte Cassino provides much detail about the slow conquest by the Normans of southern Italy, but is not as detailed as Malaterra on the subject of Sicily. He wrote in about 1080 and clearly had access to the archives of Italy's famous monastery, which had a relationship with the Norman lords of the Mezzogiorno that fluctuated from open hostility to adulation. The surviving version of his colossal work *The History of the Normans* was copied in a later century into medieval French with useful additional commentary added by the translator. However, the chronology of the work is infuriating, jumping around from event to event and place to place. There are some detailed accounts of sieges, particularly those of Bari, Salerno and the Norman Prince Richard I's assault on his own city of Capua. Amatus makes no secret of the pain and agony of warfare for those who were besieged. His harrowing accounts must be taken to be something near the truth. Despite the fact that it is believed Amatus had no military background, his battle descriptions reveal some interesting details about battle signals and tactics which can only come from the quill of a man who knew what could also be achieved with the sword.

William of Apulia was a layman in the court of Duke Roger Borsa (the son of Duke Robert Guiscard and his successor to the dukedom of Apulia). William's work *Gesta Roberti Wiscardi* (*The Deeds of Robert Guiscard*) was written between 1096 and 1099 in hexameters. It covers the period from the arrival of the Norman adventurers in Italy in around 1016 to the death of Robert Guiscard in 1085. The work is silent on the early events of the invasion and conquest of Sicily in the 1060s. However, it is clear that William had a great deal of military knowledge, as he provides a detailed account of the Battle of Civitate in 1053 (pages 149-157) and the sieges of Bari and Dyrrhachium (pages 202-204 and 205). William, who would have spoken to veterans and may even have been one himself, revels in the detail of troop types and dispositions.

Of the northern writers William of Poitiers is the most important. He was William the Conqueror's military chaplain. However, he is very sycophantic. Once we accept that Poitiers could not portray William the Conqueror in anything other than a heroic light, we are still left with an invaluable work in his *Gesta Willelmi ducis Normannorum et regis Anglorum* (*The Deeds of William Duke of Normandy and King of England*). For the Battle of Hastings, Poitiers provides realistic accounts of the deployment of the Anglo-Saxon and Norman armies and he also tells of the troops' different capabilities.

Notoriously unreliable (though some believe this to be an unfair assessment) is the work of Dudo of Saint-Quentin. There is so little historical material for the early history of Normandy that sometimes Dudo is the only source. This dean of Saint-Quentin was asked by Duke Robert I of Normandy (1027–35) to write his *Historia Normannorum* which he composed from 996–1015. He seems to have used few written sources for his account, preferring to rely upon oral tradition handed down to him by knowledgeable men, including Raoul, count of Ivry. For this reason, the dates and people's names and actions are often called into question. He is the only source, for example, for the famous Treaty of Saint Clair-Sur-Epte of 911, which is taken by many to be the founding moment of the duchy of Normandy. Without Dudo we would survive only on scraps of information. William of Jumièges, William of Poitiers, Master Wace and others all used his work.

William of Malmesbury is another whose writings owed much to what he heard around him in an ancient West Saxon town where the memory of good kings was stronger than anywhere else in England. Half Norman and half English, his Anglo-centric comments provide a counter-balance to the expected pro-Norman views of his day.

Jumièges Abbey, Normandy, France. William of Jumièges wrote his famous Gesta Normannorum Ducum (Deeds of the Norman Dukes), basing part of it on an earlier work by Dudo of Saint-Quentin.

There are numerous other sources, of course. The *Anglo-Saxon Chronicle* provides a contemporary – if occasionally brief – account of the tumultuous events of the years around 1066. The *Annals of Bari* assist with events in Byzantine-held Apulia, where other sources are weak. Then there is Hermann of Reichenau, who gives valuable German information around the build up to the Battle of Civitate (1053) in which the Pope found himself stricken. In fact, even the Pope – in this case Leo IX – provides written material to support his claims against the Normans in Italy in the form of a surviving letter (pages 154).

For the attack by Duke Robert Guiscard on the Byzantine Empire between 1081 and 1085, and for his son Bohemond's Illyrian campaigns in later years, we have Anna Comnena's *Alexiad*, written in the mid-twelfth century. This remarkable woman was the daughter of the emperor Alexius Comnenus (1081–1118). She wrote about events which occurred earlier in her lifetime and she even met some of the Normans about whom she writes. Her bias is obvious, but her words are invaluable when she talks of numbers, troop movements and battles.

One final word must go to a man whose personal background straddles the painful divide between the Anglo-Saxon and Anglo-Norman period in England. Orderic Vitalis was born in 1075, the son of a French priest and an Englishwoman. At the age of eleven he was sent to the abbey of Saint Evroul in Normandy. He would go on to write the *Historia Ecclesiastica*, a grand history with novel components including a remarkable commentary on the struggles between the sons of William the Conqueror (Duke Robert II Curthose of Normandy, and kings William II Rufus and Henry I of England). Orderic is important for his detailed histories of a number of Anglo-Norman families, his interesting contemporary interpretation of the role and value of the Norman castle, and his general revelations as to how Norman warfare was conducted.

All the events and campaigns of the Norman era mentioned by these writers happened long after the great Viking invasions of northern Europe. It was here amid the burning fires of the villages and monasteries of Northern France that a new age would be forged. Somehow there arose from these ashes leaders such as Robert Guiscard, William the Bastard (the future William the Conqueror) and Richard, the first Norman Prince of Capua. Such fantastic riches and power cannot have been imagined by many men in later ninth-century France. These were aspirations above the reach of most, even the nobility. But the predatory warriors who descended upon the shores of Carolingian Francia in the ninth century had a tireless desire to buy into the societies they invaded. They would take for themselves the things they wanted; raiding at first and then settling within enemy domains. Most of all, these Vikings – the ancestors of the Normans – would wish for legitimacy, for territory and power in their new lands. Their sons and grandsons would make few mistakes in finding it.

Part 1

The Rise of the Normans

Chapter 1

Establishment and Expansion in Normandy

The monks of Noirmoutier were among the first to suffer the violence which the swollen Atlantic Ocean served upon the shores of their remote island at the mouth of the River Loire. These devoted followers of Saint Philibert fell prey to Viking adventurers hungry for portable wealth. The community built a church as a place of refuge from the pagan marauders between 814 and 819 on the mainland nearby, but by 836, after repeated raids, the followers of the saint gathered their relics together and transferred them to a mainland site at Déas. It was not enough. A raid on Déas in 847 heralded the beginning of a melancholy exile for the community, which saw the monks cart their revered casket across France from one monastery to another. This tale of upheaval and hardship was repeated along the western and northern seaboard of France, with similar tales of woe coming from communities in England and Ireland.

The great river networks of Russia, England and France were penetrated by the renowned shallow-draft Viking ships. In France, the Seine, the Loire, the Garonne and the Rhône were all violated. In 841 Rouen was sacked. In 843 the Vikings – ever knowledgeable about their victims' calendar – descended upon the summer feast of St John and attacked the festival crowd at Nantes, allegedly killing the bishop and taking away numerous human prizes as slaves. In 845 Paris was sacked by a fleet of 120 ships and the resulting payment of silver made by the king of the Franks Charles the Bald (840–877) to the Viking leader (possibly Ragnar Lothbrok) was of humiliating proportions. Soon, the exaction of tribute would not be enough for the Viking leaders. They began to over-winter in their victims' countries, hovering menacingly in the great river estuaries of Europe. Always looking for opportunities to exploit political discord, the Vikings began to settle in these new lands. They would even be prepared to adopt the Christian religion and customs of the cultures they came into contact with as they sought the prizes that the rulers of their ancestral Scandinavian homelands could not afford to give them. Successes in England led to the establishment of a whole region north of the line of the ancient Roman Road of Watling Street. Only the kingdom of Wessex under Alfred the Great (871–900) held out. Success in Ireland led to the

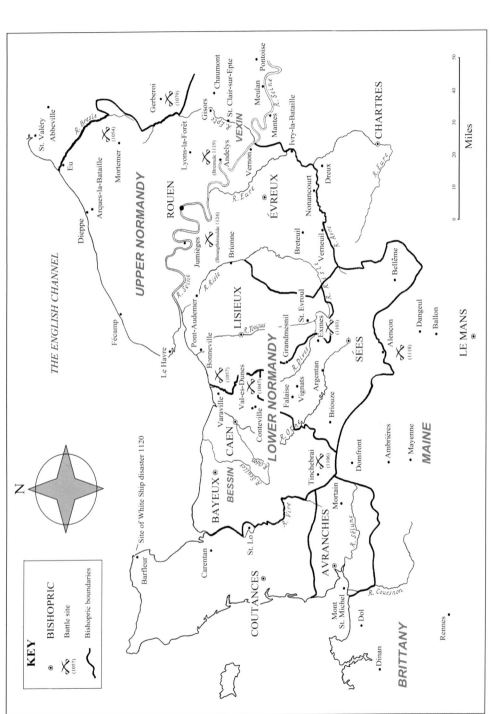

Map 1: Map of Normandy showing bishopric boundaries and battle sites (after Douglas)

KEY

BISHOPRIC ⊙

Battle site ✗

(1057)

Bishopric boundaries

N

THE ENGLISH CHANNEL

UPPER NORMANDY

LOWER NORMANDY

BESSIN

VEXIN

St. Valéry
Abbeville
Eu
R. Bresle
Arques-la-Bataille
Mortemer ✗ (1054)
Gerberoi ✗ (1079)
Lyons-la-Forêt
Gisors
Chaumont
St. Clair-sur-Epte
R. Epte
Meulan
Pontoise
Dieppe
R. Seine
Bremule ✗ (Bremule 1119)
Andelys
Vernon
Mantes
R. Seine
Ivry-la-Bataille
CHARTRES ⊙
Fécamp
Jumièges
Bourgthéroulde ✗ (1124)
Brionne
ÉVREUX ⊙
R. Eure
Breteuil
Nonancourt
Dreux
R. Eure
Le Havre
R. Seine
R. Risle
Pont-Audemer
LISIEUX
R. Touques
Bonneville
Grandmesnil
St. Evroul
Exmes ✗ (1103)
Verneuil
R. Avre
Bellême
Varaville ✗ (1057)
Val-ès-Dunes ✗ (1047)
Conteville
R. Dives
Argentan
SÉES ⊙
Alençon ✗ (1118)
Dangeul
Ballon
LE MANS ⊙
Falaise
Vignats
Brionze
R. Orne
Site of White Ship disaster 1120
CAEN
BAYEUX ⊙
R. Seulles
R. Odon
Tinchebrai ✗ (1106)
Domfront
Ambrières
Mayenne
MAINE
Barfleur
Carentan
St. Lô
R. Vire
Mortain
AVRANCHES ⊙
R. Sélune
COUTANCES ⊙
Mont St. Michel
Dol
R. Couesnon
Dinan
Rennes
BRITTANY

0 10 20 30 40 50
Miles

establishment of a Scandinavian kingdom based at Dublin and the control by the Vikings of other major ports along the eastern and southern seaboard of the island.

Although these Viking successes would be temporarily reversed by some gifted English and Irish rulers, the long-term effects were inevitable: Scandinavian settlers had come to stay. They had brought their fighting styles, and their commercial and political acumen, with them. One place where the fusion of Scandinavian and indigenous political and military cultures bore the greatest fruit was in the ancient region of Neustria, in northern France, established many centuries before by Merovingian kings in the sixth century. A particular region within this huge stretch of land would come to bear the name of the men of the north who created it. These 'Normans' would be greater even than their Viking forebears, and they took some of their ancestors' tenacity, hunger, cruelty and guile with them on what was to become European medieval history's greatest adventure.

The area of northern France which was to become Normandy was more of a political idea than a geographical one. We owe the amusing story of the foundation of the duchy to Dudo of Saint-Quentin. At Saint-Clair-sur-Epte, in the autumn of 911, the Scandinavian adventurer Rollo placed his hands between those of the French king in a ceremony which marked him as the king's man. The Frankish bishops present demanded that a further token of humility be asked of the man who had recently brought so much destruction to the province of Neustria. Rollo was to kiss the king's foot. An indignant Rollo chose one of his own men to perform the task and, as this chosen warrior raised the king's foot to his lips without bending, Charles the Simple (893–922) was catapulted backwards in his chair and fell to the ground. Everyone held their breath until laughter on all sides broke the silence. The famous treaty of Saint-Clair-sur-Epte, ratified and extended at this great gathering, could well have ended in a bloodbath and the future duchy of Normandy might never have been created. As it was, Rollo was baptised, took the Frankish name of Robert and had the land in which he and his followers were already settled formally recognised and extended. The 'Northmen' of the Rouen area in the valley of the Seine would give rise to the 'Normans' of the next generation.

Rollo won some concessions from the French king in return for his protective military service. He extended an original agreement and chose to rule lands between the Epte and the sea. He also made the French king aware that the land he was to hold was already ravaged after years of warfare. He wanted a land to plunder as well as a land to rule. He was offered Flanders, but finally accepted Brittany. The story of the Norman counts who came after Rollo was one of a gradual westward expansion and inevitable conflict with the Bretons to the west. The Bessin was acquired in 924 and Avranchin in 933. With this expansion came the graduation in prestige of the leaders, whose title evolved from count to duke.

Rollo's son and successor William Longsword (c.933–942) was brought up as a Christian. His westward expansion was held up by other groups of Scandinavians who preferred not to recognise the authority of this new count of Rouen. But his military capability was up to the task. He defeated a rebellion led by a man named Riouf. Also, he expanded his influence northwards to Montreuil, bringing him into conflict with Arnulf, the count of Flanders, which led to William being ambushed at Picquigny on the Somme where he was killed on 17 December 942.

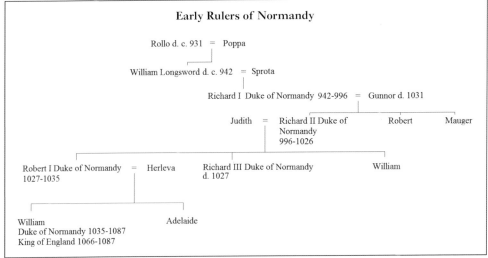

Early Rulers of Normandy

Rollo d. c. 931 = Poppa

William Longsword d. c. 942 = Sprota

Richard I Duke of Normandy 942-996 = Gunnor d. 1031

Judith = Richard II Duke of Normandy 996-1026   Robert   Mauger

Robert I Duke of Normandy 1027-1035 = Herleva   Richard III Duke of Normandy d. 1027   William

William Duke of Normandy 1035-1087 King of England 1066-1087   Adelaide

Fig. 1

After William Longsword's death, Normandy was ruled for almost fifty years by his son Richard I (942–996). An inevitable struggle for power took place at the beginning of the reign, but Richard held firm and later allied himself with the Capetian dynasty of French rulers. During this period the Norman church flourished against a relatively peaceful backdrop. However, this was the beginning of a new era of Scandinavian incursions into northern Europe and relations with the king of England, Ethelred II Unræd (979–1016), became strained when the English king accused the Norman duke of harbouring England's Danish enemies in Norman ports. The tension was so severe that the Pope had to intervene and negotiate a treaty in 991.

Duke Richard I had no children with his official wife, Emma, but had raised many with a Danish concubine named Gunnor. She bore him another Richard, who became Duke Richard II (996–1027). Richard II was very active militarily. He assisted the Capetian French king Robert the Pious (996–1031) in his conquests of Burgundy and reversed the earlier policy of hostility with the Bretons by allying himself through marriage to the Breton duke's daughter. But it was another alliance that had a seismic effect on the destiny of both Normandy and its larger neighbour, the kingdom of England. The difficulties with King Ethelred had not gone away. In 1001– 02 the English king launched a military expedition against the Normans on the Cotentin, which had to be repulsed in what was probably an early English experience of fighting against the mounted Norman knight. The result of this conflict was a marriage between the duke's sister Emma and Ethelred himself, a union from which two half-Norman boys, Edward and Alfred, would issue. There then began a long and famous Norman interest in the destiny of the kingdom of England. William the Conqueror would use this alliance as a basis for his claim to the English throne. Emma would go on to marry Cnut, the Danish king of England (1016–36), but the seeds of Norman interest were already sown.

Richard II died in 1026. His son Richard III succeeded him. His reign was to be desperately short – just one year – but even in this short space of time he had shown himself militarily capable. He had been sent into Burgundy at the head of a large army by his father, to help Count Renaud who was held prisoner there. His reputation was therefore in the ascendancy when he came to power. But there was unrest from his younger brother Robert. Unhappy with his limited power in the county of Hiémois, Robert rebelled against Richard III. Robert's base was at Falaise (where he would meet Herleva, a beautiful tanner's daughter and future mother of William the Conqueror). The duke besieged Robert at Falaise and secured his surrender, subsequently treating him with relative compassion. However, within a year Richard III was dead. Rumours of poisoning were widespread, but nothing was proved. The Duke's younger brother Robert was the beneficiary, and he became Duke Robert I (1027–1035).

Falaise Castle, Normandy, France. Birthplace of William the Conqueror. From these walls Duke Robert I (1027-1035) is said to have spotted William's mother, Herleva.

Private wars and instability marked the beginning of this tempestuous youngster's rule. It was also a period of wanderlust as sons of the noble families of the duchy looked elsewhere to gain riches and power, such as Italy and Spain. As these men headed out on new adventures abroad, Duke Robert I began his rule by attacking two churchmen. Hugh of Ivry, who might have harboured thoughts of exercising some sort of regency over Robert, was besieged at Ivry and the late arrival of the French king's forces could not prevent him from surrendering and subsequently being sent into exile. Robert's uncle, Robert archbishop of Rouen and count of Évreux, was also besieged and exiled but fought back by excommunicating the duke and issuing an interdict preventing the saying of mass and distributions of the sacraments, all of which must have spread further discontent among the nobility. Duke Robert then continued his onslaught against the church by seizing some of the key properties of the abbey of Fécamp.

Roger I de Tosny

Roger de Tosny, or 'Roger of Spain' was the son of Raoul de Tosny, seigneur of Conches. He fought in the wars of the Iberian Peninsula. Called to assist Ermesinde of Carcassonne (972–1057), the Regent-Countess of Barcelona, Roger got involved in the wars of the Reconquista. He gained notoriety as a result of his cruelty. His style of warfare included a psychological approach, even if the tale seems far-fetched. Daily, he chopped a Saracen prisoner into two pieces in front of the other prisoners and boiled one part of the victim, then served him to the others. He would let others tell the tales of horror to their comrades, thus spreading the rumour of barbarity. Roger returned to Normandy in the 1020s. He founded Conches-en-Ouche castle in 1035 and became embroiled in the struggles during the early years of William the Conqueror's minority. He was killed in battle during campaigns against his neighbour, Humphrey of Vieilles, in 1040.

By about 1028 there was a reconciliation between the duke and the archbishop and Archbishop Robert was reinstated. Duke Robert's rule took on a more mature and constructive tone. Both men set about restoring church lands and by 1034 the duke had restored most of Fécamp's estates. However, it was outside Normandy that Duke Robert flexed his muscles most. He proved himself to be militarily successful. The French king Robert the Pious died in 1031 and his son Henry was forced to flee, since Queen Constance of Provence was supporting her second son Robert instead. Duke Robert I of Normandy, however, gave Henry refuge at Fécamp and lent him important military support against his brother at Villeneuve-Saint-Georges. The victorious Henry ascended the French throne as Henry I. He rewarded Duke Robert with sovereignty over the French Vexin, an area over which the dukes of Normandy and the kings of France would quarrel for centuries to come. Further afield, Duke Robert intervened on behalf of the ageing count of Flanders, Baldwin IV, who faced a rebellion from his own son, capturing the castle at Chocques and restoring the count to his seat. Robert was no less energetic in putting down a Breton revolt led by his cousin, Alan III of Brittany. He built a border castle and ravaged the territory by land and sea, forcing Alan into submission.

It was the Norman fascination with the kingdom of England that provoked Duke Robert's most enigmatic military effort. In 1033 the duke is thought to have launched an invasion of England, which was still being ruled by the Danish king Cnut. This was designed to restore the son of Emma, Edward (soon to become Edward the Confessor) to his paternal kingdom. William of Jumièges says that Robert's requests for the restoration of Edward had been refused by Cnut, or at least Robert had received an unfavourable offer in return. An invasion fleet was assembled at Fécamp (with Edward on board), but when it set sail it was apparently blown off course and arrived not in England but at Mont-Saint-Michel via the island of Jersey. It is a curious diversion for an invasion fleet, but there may be some truth in it. Charters drawn up around this time, possibly dating to when the invasion fleet was at Fécamp, refer to Edward as 'king'. We can only guess at what would have happened if this fleet had arrived on the south coast of England.

At the height of his power Duke Robert left Normandy to go on a pilgrimage to Jerusalem. Whether he ever intended to revisit the English succession problem is open to question. However, he never returned. In 1035 he died on the return journey at Nicaea after falling ill. He left behind him a young son and heir, William, whose own relationship with the kingdom of England would become the stuff of legend. Duke Robert's rule lasted only eight years, but in this short time he embodied a characteristic that would become a hallmark of Norman prowess. There was a boundless energy in his military efforts. It was supplemented by an extraordinary knack of winning almost every conflict he got involved in. We cannot know what was said between father and son on the eve of Robert's departure for Jerusalem, but we can be certain that the boy inherited the tenacity of his father and possessed similar leadership skills. He would need them. As the young Duke William began his minority and more noblemen left the duchy for adventures in Italy, the hulks of his father's invasion fleet lay rotting at Rouen. Any dreams William might have held of the military conquest of an ancient and powerful kingdom must have seemed a long way off.

Chapter 2

Legitimacy in the South

Wearing a long robe and curious headwear in the Grecian style, a Lombard nobleman stepped out of the flickering shadows at the shrine of the Archangel Michael at Monte S. Angelo (Monte Gargano). As he approached some forty or so Norman pilgrims, he revealed himself to be Melus of Bari, a dispossessed yet driven man. The year, according to William of Apulia, was 1016 and Melus was at war with the Byzantine Empire. He told the Normans of his desire to regain former Lombard territory in southern Italy and he appealed for their help with promises of great rewards for their military service. But Melus had caught his visitors by surprise. They were not equipped for the military adventure they were offered, despite its obvious attractions. They promised to return to Italy the following year, bringing with them the men and equipment they would need.

William of Apulia's vivid tale of the beginning of the Italo-Norman story does not exist in isolation. Amatus of Monte Cassino has a tale in which forty or so Normans came to Salerno from the Holy Land on a ship from Amalfi. The Prince of Salerno, a man named Gaimar III (999–1027), received them with open arms and, whilst they were with him, the Normans flung themselves at a besieging Saracen force and defeated it, greatly impressing Gaimar. The year, however, was 'before 1000'. Gaimar asked the Normans to stay at his side, but they refused and said they must return to Normandy. They were packed off with riches and promised that they would speak to their kinsmen in Normandy and return. They went with tales of the Mezzogiorno being full of milk and honey.

There was a recorded raid on Salerno by Saracens in 1016, and there is a less reliable mention of the same for 999, the first year of Gaimar's rule. Amatus tells an enticing tale, but he squeezes together many events when he describes the advent of the Normans in Italy, including the exile by Duke Robert I of Normandy of a man named Gilbert Buatère, who came to Italy with his four brothers. However, he neatly forgets that Robert was not duke of Normandy until 1028. As if these stories were not different enough, Leo Marsicanus, when describing the revolt of Melus against the Byzantines, tells of forty Norman pilgrims coming not to Salerno or Monte Gargano, but to Capua. They had fled their homeland because of the anger of their lord, the 'count' of Normandy.

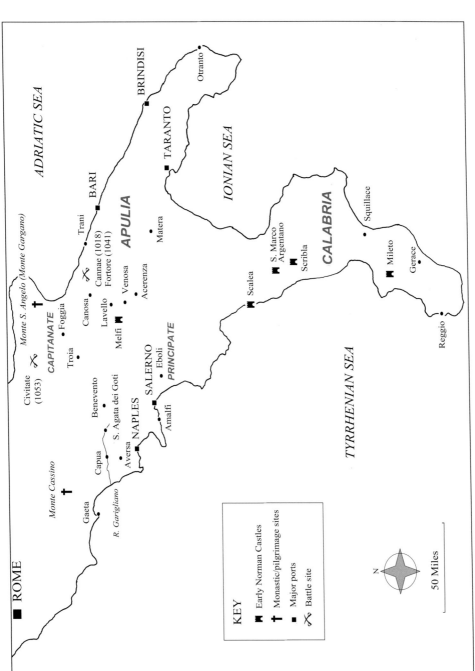

Map 2: Map of southern Italy showing principal ports and towns

KEY

▇ Early Norman Castles

✝ Monastic/pilgrimage sites

■ Major ports

✗ Battle site

50 Miles

N

ROME

ADRIATIC SEA

Monte S. Angelo (Monte Gargano)

BRINDISI

Otranto

TARANTO

BARI

Trani

IONIAN SEA

APULIA

Cannae (1018)
Fortore (1041)

Matera

Canosa

Foggia

Lavello

Venosa

Melfi

Acerenza

CAPITANATE

Civitate
(1053)

Troia

CALABRIA

Scalea

S. Marco
Argentano

Scribla

Squillace

Mileto

Gerace

Benevento

Eboli

SALERNO

PRINCIPATE

Reggio

Monte Cassino

S. Agata dei Goti

NAPLES

Capua

Aversa

Amalfi

Gaeta

R. Garigliano

TYRRHENIAN SEA

Melus asked them to join him in his attack on Greek-held Apulia. In this version of his chronicle of Monte Cassino, Leo goes on to list these Normans. There was Gilbert 'Botericus', Rodulf of Tosny, Osmund, Rufinus and Stigand. The invasion date of Melus's force is later given as 1017.

Radulf Glaber is another contributor to the evidence. He was a Burgundian monk writing during the first generation of Norman incursions into Italy. He says there was a man who had angered the Norman count Richard II (996–1027). The man, one Rodulf, travelled with others to Rome. Here, Pope Benedict VIII (1012–1024) asked him to attack Apulia. Glaber recounts how the news of early successes attracted other Norman families to Italy and how – in a manner which became all too familiar – the Normans forced their way through the Saint Bernard Pass, refusing to pay tolls.

At this time the principal Lombard strongholds into which the Normans arrived as mercenaries were Salerno, Capua and Benevento. These places held the balance of power in the centre of the peninsula. To the east the remnants of the old Byzantine Langobardia still held out, although part of it was now remodelled into the 'Catapanata' (under a ruler called a catapan), which nominally stretched from modern-day Foggia in a line down to the tip of Calabria in the south west. Apulia, Calabria and the Otranto region in the heel of the peninsula were in Greek hands. Centuries of Byzantine influence had led to Greek culture being adopted in merchant cities such as Gaeta, Naples and Amalfi. These cities retained a degree of independence, but were closely tied politically and culturally to Constantinople. Moreover, the Holy Roman Emperor of the West also had his part to play. He looked to gain wide control south of the Alps, just as his predecessor, the western Emperor Charlemagne, had done centuries before him. The Pope, with territorial interests at Benevento, also had a keen eye on developments. It was upon this colourful stage of competing loyalties, jutting into the Mediterranean Sea, that the mail-clad Norman knight, with his spear, shield, horse and sword, made his entrance. His performance would change the course of the history of medieval Italy.

Amatus has five military successes for the Norman mercenaries in these early years. By 1018 they had helped the Lombards penetrate to Trani, just a day's march north of Bari. But there was to be a setback. The Byzantine catapan Basil Boioannes had called for help from his emperor Basil II (976–1025). The result was that Boioannes fielded an army of considerable size, reinforced by a unit of the Varangian Guard. They met the Normans at the Battle of Cannae in October 1018. We know that the Normans fought bravely at the battle, but we also know that Gilbert Buatère, the probable commander of a Norman contingent of a small force, was killed. Only ten of 250 Normans survived. Melus escaped and found refuge at Bamburg under the protection of the western Emperor Henry II (972–1024).

It was Rainulf, the brother of Gilbert, who led the Normans through the wilderness in the wake of Cannae. Still the immigrants came from France and found favour, not only with Rainulf and the Lombard princes, but also with the Byzantines. The catapan Boioannes even installed a force of Normans at Troia, a fortress town about thirty miles northeast of Benevento. There then followed an unsuccessful papal appeal to the German Emperor Henry II and also the death of Melus, whose brother Dattus soon found himself holed-up in a tower on the banks of the Garigliano with a group of attendant Normans. But Prince Pandulf IV of Capua, a notoriously scheming man known as 'the wolf of the Abruzzi', betrayed him to the Byzantines. In June 1021 Dattus and his handful of Norman mercenaries could not withstand Boioannes, though they held out for two days. Pandulf took the defeated Dattus and seems to have been bribed to hand him to the Byzantines, whose emperor, after parading him through the streets of Bari, organised a horrible drowning. The Normans, however, were spared. Boioannes began to fortify the periphery of Apulia in the months that followed Dattus' execution. Hilltop sites were naturally chosen and among them were Civitate and, further south, Melfi. Both these places would be forever linked to the Norman story.

Between 1021 and 1022 a great German army came into Italy under Henry II. The Norman contingents in Italy played only a minor part in the episode, but those at Capua betrayed Pandulf to the emperor, who had Pandulf imprisoned. The giant army besieged Troia before deciding to return north of the Alps, leaving an exhausted but defiant fortress behind them. Soon, a new Holy Roman Emperor released Pandulf and he quickly sought out his beloved Capua, appealing for help to Rainulf, Gaimar of Salerno and even to the Byzantines. It took eighteen months to complete the siege of Capua between 1024 and 1025 and restore Pandulf to his city. During this time there had been Norman mercenaries on both sides of the walls.

Pandulf now fell upon nearby Naples, in the wake of the departure of the large part of the Byzantine army. In Naples Duke Sergius IV had harboured the man who had taken over from Pandulf in Capua. Sergius fled into the arms of Rainulf. He gave to Rainulf the town of Aversa, about nine miles north of Naples.

According to William of Apulia, there was no place more pleasant than Aversa. Rich and fertile, it lacked very little in terms of resources. Futhermore, the widow of the duke of Gaeta was Sergius's own sister and he offered her hand in marriage to the Norman warrior. The significance of this colossal achievement, a properly granted legitimate fiefdom in a land he could now call his home, was not lost on Rainulf. Other Normans had been successful elsewhere. Some had gone to Benevento, others were placed by archbishop Atenulf of Monte Cassino at Pignetaro and still more went to Comino with the sons of Melus. Aversa, though, was different. The newly built fortress there would come with a right to levy tribute from the surrounding district. We cannot be sure of the numbers of Normans wandering Italy in search of a paymaster at this time, but they were out there in significant numbers. Rainulf of Aversa's success must have had a huge effect on the Norman warriors of the south, providing at once a centre of political gravity and a stark example that more was to be had in this land than they could possibly have imagined.

Rainulf would switch allegiances in his new role as fortune waxed and waned for Pandulf of Capua. One particularly sizable Norman family, in the form of the first set of the sons of Tancred de Hauteville, soon fetched up in the area. William, Drogo and Humphrey de Hauteville had arrived in Italy by 1035 and their contribution, along with that of the numerous siblings who followed in their trail, would eclipse that of all the Normans who had preceded them, including the Drengot family to which Rainulf belonged. All this came at a time when another German military intervention had seen Pandulf run off to Constantinople and a dashing new Gaimar (IV) rise to power in Salerno. For the Normans, the German visit had brought a legitimacy to their holdings. The Holy Roman Emperor Conrad II (1027–1039) confirmed Rainulf of Aversa in his position by way of an investiture in 1038. Henceforth Aversa would be held from Salerno, not Naples. Rainulf was awarded a lance and gonfanon, symbols which the Normans held dear for years to come.

The first generation of de Hautevilles to arrive in Italy found themselves bound up in a curious campaign to recover Byzantine Sicily from the Saracens in 1038–40. The Byzantine emperor Michael IV (1034–1041) sent his finest commander, George Maniakes, to lead an army into Sicily. The army comprised the usual Lombard pressed recruits (referred to by Amatus as 'feeble hands'), the Greeks themselves and a force of Bulgars. A Varangian Guard contingent, which also went with Maniakes' army, was led by a Norwegian who would later play a part in the tumultuous campaigns of 1066 in northern England: Harald Sigurdsson, later known famously as 'Hardrada', or 'the ruthless'.

The Byzantine fleet, commanded by a well-connected but ineffective admiral named Stephen, sailed not directly to Sicily, but to Salerno. Gaimar, who now looked after more Normans than he could count, gladly released 300 of them to join with Maniakes, along with numerous local levies. The Byzantine writer John Skylitzes spoke of 500 'Franks' who took part in the great expedition. Another important character who went with the force was a Lombard commander who led the Salerno forces. He was called Ardouin, and was a Greek speaker who may have acted as an interpreter. He was close to the Normans throughout the campaign. The imperial army made slow progress through Sicily. It reached Syracuse in 1040 and began a siege at which the Norman commander William 'Iron Arm' de Hauteville apparently acquitted himself well.

There were disputes over the share of the spoils. Ardouin protested loudly on behalf of the Normans and it all reached a flashpoint when the Lombard wished to keep for himself a prized Arab horse he had won in battle, which Maniakes had confiscated from him. Maniakes, displaying an unfortunate style of leadership for which he was to be long remembered, had the Lombard whipped around the camp. Maniakes' control of his troops in the aftermath of Syracuse soon fell to pieces. The money dried up for the mercenaries and the Varangian Guard made an early exit from the theatre, along with the disgusted Normans. To compound the misery Maniakes, on hearing the news that the hapless admiral Stephen (whose job it was to blockade Sicily) had actually let a Saracen fleet slip through, proceeded to physically assault Stephen. George Maniakes was a widely renowned man-mountain, and Stephen was not. Surviving a beating by Maniakes was the first step in Stephen's recovery; revenge was the second. Stephen got a message through to Constantinople and George Maniakes was re-called in disgrace, being replaced by an ineffective eunuch called Basil. And so the Sicilian campaign petered out.

Hervé Frankopoulos of Grumento

Hervé Frankopoulos, (or Phrangopoulos) had a colourful career in Italy and the east. Originally one of twelve Norman commanders granted lands at Melfi in 1042, Hervé was given Grumento, to the south of the new Norman capital. He campaigned in George Maniakes' Byzantine invasion of Sicily in 1038–40. In the early 1040s he campaigned in Apulia and gained the city of Avelino.

Hervé rose to great heights as a mercenary commander in the pay of the Byzantines. By 1050 he was in command under Nicephoros Bryennios the Elder, becoming one of the Byzantine general's two chief lieutenants. He suffered a defeat to Pecheneg horsemen in 1050, however, and in 1056–57 Hervé fell out with the emperor after he was refused an important title. He took off with 300 of his cavalry to the east around Lake Van, but any dreams of founding a patrimony were smashed by the wars he found himself involved in. Encounters with Armenians and Seljuk Turks were ended when Hervé was sent back in chains to Constantinople by the emir of Ahlat. After reconciliation with the emperor Hervé finally got his coveted title of Magistros plus other military and symbolic offices. The circumstances surrounding his decline and eventual execution are unclear. However, Matthew of Edessa states that in 1063 the Turks of Amida were able to bribe a certain 'Frankabol' not to give battle. The emperor Constantine X Doukas had Hervé executed.

As the Normans returned to the Italian mainland they found Apulia in uproar. The Lombard communities, which had been taxed by the Byzantines and coerced into supporting the Sicilian expedition, had simply had enough. Melus, the man who had appealed to the Norman pilgrims at Monte Gargano in 1016 or 1017 had left a son, Argyrus, who had suffered imprisonment in Constantinople. He, like his father, was a rabble-rouser. He would soon come to Bari, where for a while at least, he acknowledged the overlordship of Constantinople. But it was not difficult to light the torch of rebellion. Several leading Byzantine figures in Apulia had been killed in recent years and, with the assassination of the catapan Nikephoros II Doukeianos in 1040 at Ascoli, the revolt began in earnest.

The Byzantine emperor Michael was fading fast. A well-known epileptic, his fits were on the increase and his hold on power was slipping. It was his brother, the Orphanotrophus, who appointed the new catapan Michael Doukeianos. This catapan had the strength lacking in some of his predecessors. The intensity of the Apulian revolt was subsequently reduced by his actions, if not entirely quelled. But Doukeianos knew he still had a problem. He set out to Sicily to recall some of the remaining Greek forces. On his way back, however, he stopped at Salerno. If he ever had time to reflect upon it, he might have wished he had gone somewhere else.

Ardouin was nobody's fool. His flight from the Greek army after the indignity of his whipping at Reggio had involved a small battle with a Byzantine detachment and he escaped from it victorious. Perhaps it was by way of apology that Michael Doukeianos offered Ardouin a position as the commander (topotorites) of Melfi on the Byzantine–Benevento borderland, or perhaps they just got on well together. Maybe it was the impressive Norman contingent, so recently tried and tested, which appealed to the catapan. Soon Ardouin began inciting his citizens against their Byzantine masters. Tales of Greek cruelty poured into his hall from the hard-pressed people and he lapped it all up. In March 1041 he travelled to Aversa, spinning stories of Greek effeminacy and cowardice. It was a masterpiece of propaganda and the Normans loved it. It was not difficult for Ardouin to persuade Rainulf and Gaimar to once again release 300 knights into his service. Gaimar was always worried when his Normans were idle. The result was the creation of twelve future Norman counties of southern Italy, which were to redraw the political map. The exact timing of the establishment of these territories is unclear. It seems to have been set in the minds of the Normans before it became a reality on the ground. These counties were to be Civitate, Siponto, Ascoli, Melfi, Lavello, Cannae, Trani, Minervino, Venosa, Acerenza, Montepeloso and Monopoli.

Tristan of Montepeloso

Tristan was one of the twelve commanders who received divisions of land at the Melfi meeting of 1042. He had come to Italy with other northern French warriors in around 1030, but was in fact a Breton. Like many of the distinguished 'twelve commanders', he went on campaign to Sicily in 1038–40 with the Byzantine commander George Maniakes. We do not know anything of Tristan's military capability, but the region of Potenza which he held, deep in the central southern part of Italy, was clearly of strategic value and he seems to have held his own there. Tristan married the sister of Norman leader 'William 'Iron Arm' de Hauteville.

The Normans took on the Byzantines in a series of battles during 1041 (pages 145-149). They won them all. And yet at Melfi, after the second battle, it was a man named Atenulf, a member of the ruling family of Benevento, who seems to have bribed his way into the leadership of the Lombard revolt at the expense of Ardouin. Just when the revolt appeared to be gathering an unstoppable momentum, a split developed between the many leaders. Gaimar, by now ruler of both Capua and Salerno, was deeply suspicious of Atenulf. The Normans were pulling apart too. Troia, which had already experienced a generation of Norman settlers, was somewhat distant from Melfi, at least in outlook. Gaimar's Norman friends from Aversa also had their own motives, seeing their fortunes linked to the Salernitan prince. Moreover, despite the fact that they had acknowledged their western cousins' role in the revolt so far, the Apulian Lombards favoured the son of Melus, Argyrus. Atenulf, however, did not help himself. He had sold the captured catapan to the Greeks and, according to some, pocketed the money from this and other ransoms. Argyrus was winning the moral high ground, and the Normans had no choice but to throw in their lot with him by acknowledging him formally at Bari in February 1042.

Events in Constantinople prompted the return of the larger-than-life George Maniakes as catapan. The Byzantine Emperor Michael IV died in December 1041 and, after a fast-moving power struggle, it was Constantine IX who became the new Emperor. Maniakes went to Italy to rescue what was rapidly becoming a nightmare for the empire. He landed in Taranto in April 1042. After an unsuccessful Norman siege attempt was withdrawn, Maniakes began a punitive campaign along the eastern coast of Apulia in which he dealt terror and reprisal everywhere he went. By June Matera and Monopoli were recovered. And then Maniakes learned he was to be re-called once again. He resolved to sever allegiance with Constantine and proclaim himself emperor instead. After torturing the man sent to tell him about his re-call and replacement, Maniakes seems to have tried to treat with Argyrus and the Normans, to no avail. He left Italy and met his death in battle against the Byzantine emperor, falling at the very moment of his victory.

While palace intrigue was beginning to define the fate of Maniakes, the Normans and their allies were besieging the loyal Byzantine town of Trani under Argyrus, having already retaken Giovenazzo. It was a curious event. We read in the *Annals of Bari* that Argyrus and the Normans had brought with them a huge wooden siege tower 'the like of which the human eye has never seen in recent times'. With this engine, and after thirty-six days of besieging, it seemed Trani would fall. Amatus has the city capitulating to Argyrus at this point; but whether it did or did not fall to the siege engines of the allies, all accounts agree on what happened next.

Argyrus suddenly ordered the siege machines to be burned. The *Annals of Bari* say that he had received an imperial letter offering him 'the titles of patrician, catepan [sic] and vestatus'. And so the son of the great Melus, the staunch Lombard nationalist, went over to the Greeks. For the Norman contingent, it was all utterly bewildering. They fell back into the countryside, seething to the last man, as Argyrus went back to Bari via Otranto to plot again. One of the twelve Norman commanders, Peter, son of Walter, vowed to kill Argyrus and had to be restrained by his comrades. They had been selling themselves to the highest bidder in Italy for a generation, but even the Normans had never seen anything like this. It was an event which marked the beginning of the next phase of Norman expansion. They would slowly turn their back on supporting the Lombard nationalist dream. The Normans elected their own leader, a tested hero who could at least be trusted to promote their own interests. At Matera William 'Iron Arm' de Hauteville was acclaimed as the new count of Apulia. It was September 1042.

The Normans knew they could not invent a political leadership without proper bonds of lordship, so they turned to a natural sponsor, Gaimar of Salerno. They went to his court at the end of 1042. Here, in a great ceremony, in the presence of Rainulf of Aversa, Gaimar received the Normans 'as sons'. This prince of Salerno, who was soon to be styled 'Duke of Apulia and Calabria', gave William the hand of his niece, Guida. The bonds were now strengthening and legitimacy was once again established. The Normans had indicated to Gaimar that they wished for Rainulf to take the figurehead role over all of their kind. They all rode to Melfi, where amid great rejoicing the future of the whole region was outlined. Amatus tells us that Rainulf was to receive Siponto and the region of Monte Gargano and the 'castelli' around it. One could hardly imagine a more symbolic gift for a Norman warrior than this, the very spot upon which the Normans' most coveted warrior-saint, the archangel Michael, had made his earthly appearance. There was more symbolism to come, as Gaimar handed out the parcels of land to the Normans: intriguingly, some of them had yet to be conquered. But this was a vision held not only by Gaimar, but by every Norman in Melfi. Amatus records it as follows:

> The remaining lands which they had acquired and which they would acquire the Normans divided among themselves in good will, peace and concord. In this manner William received Ascoli; Drogo had Venosa; Arnolin had Lavello; Hugh Toutebove had Monopoli; Rodulf had Canne [sic]; Walter, Civitate; Peter, Trani; Rodulf, son of Bebena, Sant' Arcangelo; Tristan, Montepeloso; Hervey, Grumento; Asclettin, Acerenza; and Rainfroi, Malerbine (which is Minervino).

Amatus goes on to drop a line into his work to remind us who started this Melfi business in the first place. It was Ardouin, whose name is conspicuously absent from the sources throughout this period of burgeoning Norman power. Nobody knows what finally happened to him; whether he died, fell for a Greek bribe, or was murdered. Amatus says 'they also gave Ardouin his half according to the oath they had made with him'. And then he is gone.

At around the same time as Maniakes was boarding his ship for his fateful voyage across the Adriatic, Gaimar and his Normans attempted a siege of Bari in January 1043 which lasted for five days. The city did not fall, and curiously this was one of Gaimar's few strategic military adventures in the region with the Normans at his side, another being an expedition to northern Calabria in 1044 with Count William in which they established what proved to be an important base at Scribla. But the Normans were now learning to prevail without Salerno's help.

Melfi then, became 'common to all' the Normans. At last, their presence in the south of Italy was a political as well as a physical reality. The days of playing to the most promising paymaster were nearly over. All that was needed was someone to pull it all together, to bring a sense of all-conquering purpose to the Norman adventure in Italy. He was not long in coming. His name was Robert Guiscard.

Part 2

The Commanders

Chapter 3

Robert Guiscard, Duke of Apulia, Calabria and Sicily (d.1085)

Timeline of Robert Guiscard

1048	Arrives in Italy. Joins retinue of Lombard Prince Pandulf IV of Capua but falls out over unfulfilled promises. Receives castle at Scribla from count of Apulia but sets up later at San Marco Argentano
c. 1049 –51	Marries Alberada, aunt of Gerard of Buonalbergo
1053	Battle of Civitate
1057	Acclaimed by Normans at Melfi as count of Apulia
1057-58	Uprising in Apulia
1058	Falls out with brother Roger de Hauteville at Gerace. Reconciliation and concessions to Roger. Widespread Calabrian famine Marriage to Lombard noblewoman Sichelgaita
1059	Council of Melfi and investiture by Pope 'by the grace of God and Saint Peter Duke of Apulia and Calabria, and in future, with the help of both, of Sicily'
1060	Siege of Reggio with his brother Roger
1061	Campaigns around Milazzo and Rometta in Sicily. Messina taken and re-fortified. Battle of Enna. Relief of Melfi on mainland.
1062	Falls out with his brother Roger de Hauteville. Incident at Gerace
1064	Campaign around Palermo thwarted by spiders at Monte Tarrantino
1068 – 71	Siege of Bari
1067 – 68	Apulian uprising
1072	Apulian uprising. Siege and capture of Palermo
1073	Siege of Cisternino and humiliation of Peter II of Trani
1076	Siege of Salerno
1079-80	Apulian uprising. Conference at Ceprano in which the Pope lifts Robert's excommunication
1081	Battle of Dyrrhachium and campaigns against the Byzantine Empire
1082-83	Apulian uprising
1084	March upon Rome to expel Henry IV, enemy of the pope
1085	Dies on 17 July and is succeeded as duke by son Roger Borsa

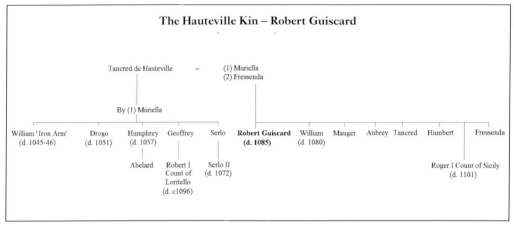

Fig. 2

Character and Career

This Robert was Norman by birth, of obscure origin, with an overbearing character and a thoroughly villainous mind; he was a brave fighter, very cunning in his assaults on the wealth and power of great men; in achieving his aims absolutely inexorable, diverting criticism by incontrovertible argument. He was a man of immense stature, surpassing even the most powerful of men; he had a ruddy complexion, fair hair, broad shoulders, eyes that all but shot out sparks of fire. In a well-built man one looks for breadth here and slimness there; in him all was admirably well proportioned and elegant. Thus from head to foot the man was a fine specimen, and I have often heard from many witnesses that this was so. Homer remarked of Akhilles that when he shouted those in earshot had the impression of a multitude in uproar, but Robert's bellow, so they say, put tens of thousands to flight. With such endowments of fortune and nature of soul, he was, as you would expect, no man's slave, owing obedience to nobody in all the world. Such are men of powerful character, people say, even if they are of modest background. *The Alexiad I, 10*

This description was written by Anna Comnena, the daughter and biographer of the Byzantine emperor Alexius I (1081–1118). There is no small hint of admiration when Anna writes about Robert, despite the fact that he had been the arch enemy of her father.

Robert arrived in southern Italy in around 1047–48, to be met with a rebuff from his kinsman Drogo de Hauteville, the count of Apulia. He did not get the fiefdom he sought. Instead, Robert offered himself into the service of the Lombard Prince Pandulf IV of Capua. Robert fell out with Pandulf over a broken promise of both a castle and the hand of Pandulf's daughter. Thus, after Pandulf's death in 1049, Robert returned to Drogo with cap in hand and was duly packed off to Calabria, barely conquered by the Normans, where he established himself at the castle at Scribla in the valley of the Crati. Here Robert dwelt in the malaria-ridden low-lying valley, picking off victims in the Cosenza and scarcely accruing enough wealth to survive. Scribla was so bad for the health of his men that Robert established another castle about fifteen miles to the southwest, at S. Marco Argentano, on higher ground. From here he began a career of brigandage and acquisition, but it was still a life of hardship. He lived off the land and even kidnapped people in order to ransom them for bread and wine. He again approached his half-brother, but was turned away. Robert Guiscard, however, was a charismatic man, able to inspire his followers even in these hard times.

Robert acquired riches using stratagems which seem to have been especially suited to his character. Malaterra has an amusing, though sinister, story of the prearranged capture of Peter, son of Tyre, the wealthiest man in Bisignano. Robert usually met with Peter on the plain outside his 'castrum' at Bisignano. On one occasion he suggested that they meet away from the crowds of supporters, lest another of their frequent disputes get out of hand. This was agreed, but when the appointed time came Robert's men were closest. When Robert physically seized Peter around the middle and carried him off towards his own men, the Calabrians were powerless to intervene. Peter was held at S. Marco by Robert until he paid an enormous sum of money. With this newly acquired wealth Robert was able to attract a large following to his military household, which already included sixty Slav warriors. Malaterra explains:

> Learning of the cunning Guiscard had displayed in this and similar enterprises, the Calabrians (a most timid people) were all absolutely terrified of him: indeed they said that there was nobody who could equal him, either with weapons, in strength, or in craft.

Drogo de Hauteville

Drogo succeeded William 'Iron Arm' de Hauteville as the second Norman count of Apulia. He campaigned alongside William in the Byzantine Sicilian campaigns of 1040. Drogo was another of the twelve commanders who had met at Melfi and from this meeting he was given Venosa to hold. He later seized Bovino. Drogo married the daughter of the prince of Salerno, but it was the German Emperor Henry II who invested Drogo with the title 'Duke and Master of Italy and Count of the Normans of all Apulia and Calabria'. The end came for Drogo in 1051 amid a climate of distrust of the Normans who had ravaged the land. He was assassinated, probably at the instigation of Argyrus, the former rebel turned Byzantine catapan. Drogo was succeeded by his brother, Humphrey de Hauteville.

Robert acquired the sobriquet 'Guiscard' around this time. Amatus (III.11) says it was Gerard of Buonalbergo who first coined this phrase, which meant 'the cunning'. Gerard was clearly impressed by Guiscard's character. He offered the hand of his aunt Alberada in marriage to Robert. The offer came with a promise of 200 of Gerard's knights and a pledge to help him conquer all Calabria. Gerard seems to have had sizable resources in terms of men. He brought with him the services of the men of Telese (only a day's march to the northwest of Benevento) as well as those of Buonalbergo. And so Robert's *familia*, or household, grew larger. His already high reputation was enhanced by the marriage to Alberada, who would soon bear him a quite remarkable boy (pages 101–102).

Robert would marry again, however. He discovered, apparently to his chagrin, that his union with Alberada had not been a legitimate one in the eyes of the church. Alberada was a distant relation. Robert soon repudiated Alberada and left himself free to marry a woman called Sichelgaita. She was a formidable Lombard, a sister of Prince Gisulf II of Salerno, who would fight at the side of her husband in the years to come. Robert took her into Calabria, first providing generously for Alberada and her infant son. Alberada seems not to have born a grudge against her former husband.

During the period in which Robert Guiscard's fortunes began to improve, there was general hostility in Italy towards the Normans, which had the backing and active support of the Pope. Abbot John of Fécamp even wrote to the recently consecrated Pope Leo IX complaining that Italian hatred of the Normans had reached such levels as to make it impossible for a Norman pilgrim to travel without fear of assault or imprisonment.

Tension culminated in the tumultuous Battle of Civitate in 1053 (pages 149–157), at which Robert Guiscard acquitted himself admirably under the command of Humphrey de Hauteville, the new count of Apulia, who had replaced his murdered brother Drogo. But Robert's relations with Humphrey were not always cordial. He was even incarcerated by him at one point. After Civitate and Robert's subsequent campaigns in the heel of Italy against a retreating Greek enemy, Humphrey knew that Robert was a force to be reckoned with. Humphrey put Robert back in Calabria, where he continued to thrive, and then, on his deathbed, Humphrey appointed Robert guardian of his son Abelard. Robert wasted no time in seizing his nephew's lands and, in August 1057, after Humphrey's death, Robert Guiscard was acclaimed by the Normans as Humphrey's successor. A bigger confirmation was to follow at the Council of Melfi in August 1059, at which Pope Nicholas II (the papacy now reconciled with the Normans) invested Robert 'by the grace of God and Saint Peter Duke of Apulia and Calabria, and in future, with the help of both, of Sicily'.

The arrival of Robert's brother Roger de Hauteville in the Mezzogiorno revealed a different side of Robert Guiscard's character. Their relationship was close and together they would conquer Calabria and Sicily, but Robert's stinginess towards his brother led to a serious rift, which saw the latter leave his service for another de Hauteville brother, William. After a successful siege of Reggio in Calabria and the taking of Messina in 1061, the brothers Roger and Robert would fall out again, this time over Guiscard's failure to assist Roger in enfeoffing his new wife. This led to an incident in which Robert stole into Gerace in disguise and only managed to escape from an angry mob through skilful oratory and the mercy of his own brother (page 56). The story, recounted by Malaterra, gives the impression of an audacity of spirit and extreme self-confidence, which in this case nearly cost Robert Guiscard his life. Duke Robert never seems to have been afraid to create enemies.

Much of Robert's time in the later 1060s was spent dealing with various Apulian insurrections. It seemed that these revolts from within his own patrimony could only be crushed when Guiscard himself was present; the force of his personality was on his side. He and Roger continued to work together, cooperating at the siege of Bari (1068–71) and then again at the siege of Palermo in 1072. Such were the duke's Apulian concerns that after the fall of Palermo in 1072 he never returned to Sicily. The island was linked to his vassal and brother Count Roger for some time, and not to its overlord the duke of Apulia.

Robert's relationship with the papacy blew hot and cold in the 1070s. Rumours of Guiscard's death spread after he suffered an illness in 1073, and it was clear that Pope Gregory VII thought that Robert's son Roger Borsa (by Sichelgaita) should succeed the duke. However, after learning of Robert's survival and recovery, the Pope fell out with him over continual Norman incursions into papal territory, which he felt the duke could have prevented. In 1074 Robert Guiscard was excommunicated by the Pope. It took two years for the relationship to mend, but ten years later, in 1084, Guiscard marched on Rome to support the Pope and force the Pope's enemy, Emperor Henry IV, to retreat. The cost to Rome was immense. Saracens from Count Roger's Sicilian army, who were accompanying Robert Guiscard's forces, had run amok for days. The Roman citizens turned on Robert, who was only saved in the nick of time by his own son and heir Roger Borsa, whose well-timed entry into the city brought with it 1,000 warriors.

The mid-1070s saw the duke of Apulia conduct the siege of Salerno, finally confronting Gisulf II, his wife's brother, whose power had been on the wane, but who had constantly stood up to the Normans. Robert Guiscard had his eye on a greater prize, however: the Byzantine Empire itself. He was nothing if not ambitious. In March 1081 he sent a fleet under the command of his son Bohemond (by Alberada) to attack Corfu and secure bases on the Albanian mainland. By 17 June that year Robert was laying siege to Dyrrhachium (pages 162-170) on the Albanian coast. The expedition may even have been designed as a campaign of conquest to secure a new patrimony for his son Bohemond, rather than to secure further riches for the duke of Apulia. The battle at Dyrrhachium was a success, despite the efforts of the redoubtable and gifted Byzantine emperor

Alexius Comnenus, who went on to learn from his mistakes. However, subsequent campaigns were not as successful and the duke, as we have seen, was needed back in Italy, not only to quell further uprisings, but also to support the Pope against Emperor Henry IV.

Robert Guiscard's second expedition to Illyria was fraught with difficulties. Bad weather and heavy naval defeats took their toll. In the end, illness caught up with him. On his way to meet up with his son, his ship was forced to put in at a small bay either on the north of the island of Cephalonia, a place which still bears his name, Fiskardo, or on the beach at Atheras further south. Here, in a tranquil place, the great Norman commander died on 17 July 1085. William of Apulia, who reported these final moments in his great poem, said of him:

> So, in exile, the soul of this mighty prince left his body. The man who had never allowed his men to show fear in his presence and who had been accustomed to raise the spirits of others now rendered up his own spirit.

The Commander

There are several key stages in Robert Guiscard's military career. First, there was the service he offered to others, such as Pandulf IV of Capua, which he would have provided from his *familia*, or household men. This household grew bigger when he became richer on the back of his acquisitions in Calabria. For some years Robert conducted small-scale operations of reduction around Salerno, denying his enemies control of the landscape's resources. He then had the means to conduct wars of conquest of his own, before taking the title of count of Apulia held by Humphrey de Hauteville. His wars of conquest in Calabria and Sicily were followed later by the great sieges he undertook at Bari, Palermo and Salerno. After reconciliation with the Pope the duke was able to launch his great enterprise against the Byzantine Empire.

Robert Guiscard was spectacularly charismatic. He had an ability to inspire his troops with enthusiasm, which may explain why he was successful in putting down the many revolts he faced. Anna Comnena describes a giant of a man, capable of great words and deeds. But from Amatus we learn of a commander able to foment religious enthusiasm in his soldiers, which was beginning to become an important aspect of campaigning in the non-Christian world in the immediate pre-Crusading era. Before the Battle of Enna in central Sicily in 1061 Robert gave a speech to his troops in which he told them it was not the size of the forces which mattered, but God's favour. Citing Matthew 17:19 he allegedly said 'if you have faith as a grain of mustard seed, ye shall say unto this mountain remove hence to yonder place, and it shall remove'. To be worthy of divine aid Robert's men had to cleanse themselves through penance and confession. It was all rousing stuff, and there is no reason to suppose that Amatus was exaggerating Guiscard's motivations.

Guiscard had personal leadership qualities in abundance. However, his cunning came into play on a number of occasions when campaigning. One famous example is recalled by William of Apulia and has the ring of the apocryphal about it:

> While he plundered hither and thither, he was unable to capture any castrum or city, and so he resorted to a stratagem to enter a certain place, which was very difficult of access since there were many inhabitants, and the monastic community which was living there would allow no stranger to enter. The cunning [Robert] thought up an ingenious trick. He told his people to announce that one of their number had died. The latter was placed on a bier as though he were dead, and on Robert's order was covered with a silk cloth which concealed his face (as it is the custom of Normans to cover bodies). Swords were hidden on the bier under the 'body's' back. The 'body' was carried to the entrance of the monastery to be buried there, and this pretended death deceived those who could not be taken in by living men. While a simple funeral service was being conducted the man who was about to be buried suddenly sprang up; his companions seized their swords and threw themselves on the inhabitants of the place who had been deceived by this trick. What could those stupid people do? They could neither fight nor flee, and all were captured. Thus, Robert, you placed your first garrison in a fortress!

The accounts of Robert Guiscard actually fighting in pitched battle are as praiseworthy as one might expect. But pitched battles were not the norm for the duke. The siege was a far more common form of warfare, and Robert Guiscard spent much time beneath the walls of one town or another in southern Italy, putting down insurrections and denying his enemies freedom of movement in the landscape. Not least among his enemies were the Norman kin group centred on 'the sons of Amicus', whose frequent tussles with the de Hautevilles usually saw them come off second best. Besides the great sieges of Bari, Palermo, Salerno and Naples, which were on an altogether different scale, Robert Guiscard undertook sieges at Reggio (1059); Troia (1060); Messina (1061); Mileto (1062); Otranto (1064–65); Ajello (1065); Montepeloso (1068); Trani (1073); Cisternino (1073); Corato (1073); Andria (1073); Lacedonia (1073); Canne (1073); Aquino (1073); Santa Severina (1075) and Taranto (1078), to name just a few. This compares to just two major pitched battles at Civitate (1053) and Dyrrhachium (1081).

Robert Guiscard realised the importance of naval power at a relatively early stage in his career. The Sicilian expedition of 1060–61 was commanded (at Robert's behest) by Geoffrey Ridel, a Norman from the Pays de Caux, whose responsibility covered both naval and land forces. But it was when Robert and his brother Roger gazed helplessly at the merchant ships coming in and out of Palermo in 1064, that they realised that such glittering prizes as this great city could only be taken by joint land and sea enterprises on a massive scale. Thus, pressing into service the sailors of Calabria and the Apulian coastal cities, the duke embarked first on the great naval blockade of Bari in 1068–71 and then Palermo in 1071–72 (pages 202-204).

The campaigns against Byzantium illustrate Robert Guiscard's strategic and tactical capability, as well as his ability to organise such large-scale enterprises. A conference at Ceprano was held in 1080 between Pope Gregory VII, Robert Guiscard and the Norman Prince Jordan of Capua, at which hostilities between the papacy and the Normans were put to an end and Robert's excommunication (recently reimposed) was lifted. He was therefore free to plan his Illyrian campaign. This he did in Salerno, using as a political excuse the restoration of the deposed emperor Michael VII, to whose son Guiscard's daughter Helena had been betrothed. But there were good practical reasons for such an expedition. The recent Apulian revolts had been sponsored by the Byzantines, even though their power in southern Italy was on the wane. The governor of Dyrrhachium, Perenos, had even provided money for the revolt of 1067–68. Joscelin of Molfetta and Roger Toutebove had sought refuge at the Byzantine court and Abelard, Robert Guiscard's rebellious nephew, was very close to Constantinople. A strike at Dyrrhachium and a subsequent conquest of Illyrian lands would achieve the two-fold result of knocking out a sponsor of home-grown rebellions and establishing a landed base with which to reward loyal barons such as Robert's own son Bohemond.

In preparation for the expedition Robert appears to have called out the *arrière-ban* (a full-scale feudal summons, for which see below, page 178) to man his campaign across the Adriatic. The first Illyrian campaign, which culminated in success at Dyrrhachium, is examined below (pages 162-170). It was followed by another campaign in which Bohemond, for a while the master of Thessaly, lost his territories. With 120 ships, the ageing Duke Robert set about rebuilding his Illyrian conquest from the start, planning once again for the capture of Corfu. He took with him his sons Bohemond, Roger Borsa, Guy and Robert. But in November 1084 he was held at Butrinto due to bad weather. When he finally crossed the sea, he was pounced upon by a combined Greek and Venetian fleet and defeated twice in three days. This would have been enough for most commanders, but Guiscard was able to do more than recover, although Anna Comnena reports that he was depressed by the defeats. The Venetians had sent their smaller vessels home to bring news of the victories, but Robert chased the enemy with his fleet and engaged in another sea battle near to Corfu harbour. The heavy Venetian galleys, which had been deliberately lightened and consequently stood tall in the water, capsized when their warriors rushed from one side of the vessel to another. Anna Comnena, who tells of a probably exaggerated 13,000 dead, has this to say about the duke's treatment of his prisoners after the battle:

> After this signal victory Robert in a fit of harshness treated many of the prisoners most cruelly, for he had the eyes of some gouged out, the noses of others cut off, and some he deprived of their hands and feet, or both.

Old Church of Santissima Trinata at Venosa, Italy, showing the tomb of Alberada, mother of Bohemond, in the background.

Corfu fell, but as 1084 gave way to 1085, typhoid gripped the Norman force. It was more devastating than anything the emperor Alexius could throw at them. By spring some 500 Normans had succumbed to the disease and even Bohemond had sailed back to Bari to recuperate. Robert turned to his other son, Roger Borsa, heir to the duchy of Apulia, and sent him out to Cephalonia. It was then that the sickness took Robert Guiscard himself. This great man – energetic, charismatic, almost mesmerising in his leadership qualities and an ever-present commander – had been symbolic of the fire at the heart of the warlike Norman character.

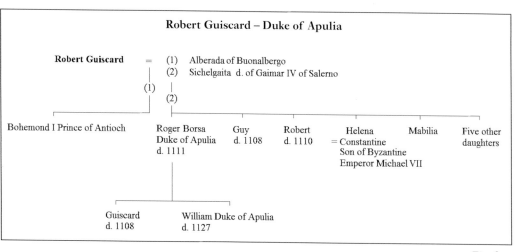

Fig. 3

Chapter 4

William the Conqueror, Duke of Normandy (1035–1087), King of England (1066–1087)

Timeline of William the Conqueror

1035	Death of Duke Robert I of Normandy and beginning of minority rule
1036	Murder of half Norman Alfred the Ætheling in England and beginning of Norman hostility to the English House of Godwin
1040	Death of William's guardians Count Alan III of Brittany, Count Gilbert of Brionne and Osbern the Steward
1042	Edward the Confessor becomes king of England
1046	Revolt in Normandy of the western vicomtes and Guy of Burgundy causing Henry I, the king of France to intervene
1047	Battle of Val-ès-Dunes
1051-52	Marriage to Matilda, daughter of Baldwin V count of Flanders. Campaigns around Alençon and Domfront against Geoffrey Martel count of Anjou
1053	Capture of Arques by William
1054	Battle of Mortemer
1057	King Henry invades Normandy. Battle of Varaville
1060	Death of King Henry I of France. Succeeded by Philip I, a minor
1063	Duke William invades and conquers Maine
1064	Earl Harold Godwinson visits Normandy
1066	Death of Edward the Confessor, King of England. Election of Harold Godwinson as king. Battles of Fulford Gate, Stamford Bridge and Hastings. William crowned king of England
1067	Eustace of Boulogne raids in Kent
1068	Campaigns around Exeter and York. Warwick, Lincoln, Huntington and Chester occupied
1069	York rebellion. Loss of Le Mans in Maine. Invasion of Yorkshire by Swein Estrithson, king of Denmark and gathering of rebels supported by king of Scots. York occupied by rebels and re-taken by William

1070   The Harrying of the North. March over the Pennines. Lanfranc
         becomes archbishop of Canterbury
1071   Battle of Cassel and death of William FitzOsbern, trusted Norman
         magnate. Danish force leaves England. Fenland uprising under
         Hereward the Wake
1072   Anglo-Norman invasion of Scotland
1073   Norman re-conquest of Maine
1075   Earls' revolt in England
1076   Earl Waltheof executed in England. Campaigns in Brittany and defeat at
         Dol for William
1077   Attack on La Flèche by Fulk of Anjou
1078   Rebellion of son Duke Robert II Curthose
1079   The Battle of Gerberoi. Scottish raids in Northern England
1081   Fulk attacks La Flèche again
1082   Odo, bishop of Bayeux and earl of Kent imprisoned
1083   Duke Robert II Curthose further rebels. Death of Matilda
1085   Cnut IV of Denmark prepares to invade England with Flemish support
         probably prompting the compilation of the Domesday survey
1086   Cnut is murdered. Assembly at Salisbury and oaths sworn to William by
         his tenants-in-chief
1087   King Philip I of France invades Évreçin and William invades the Vexin
         and sacks Mantes. William dies on 9 September at Saint-Gervais

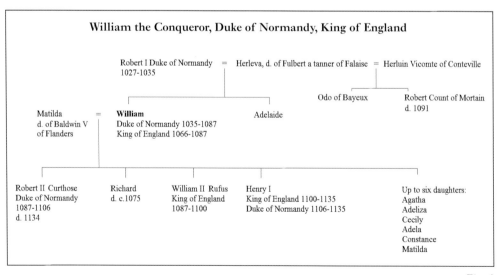

William the Conqueror, Duke of Normandy, King of England

Robert I Duke of Normandy = Herleva, d. of Fulbert a tanner of Falaise = Herluin Vicomte of Conteville
1027-1035

Odo of Bayeux   Robert Count of Mortain
                 d. 1091

Matilda   =   **William**   Adelaide
d. of Baldwin V   Duke of Normandy 1035-1087
of Flanders   King of England 1066-1087

Robert II Curthose   Richard   William II Rufus   Henry I   Up to six daughters:
Duke of Normandy   d. c.1075   King of England   King of England 1100-1135   Agatha
1087-1106   1087-1100   Duke of Normandy 1106-1135   Adeliza
d. 1134   Cecily
                                                                                         Adela
                                                                                         Constance
                                                                                         Matilda

Fig. 4

He was of just stature, ordinary corpulence, fierce countenance; his forehead was bare of hair; of such great strength of arm that it was often a matter of surprise, that no one was able to draw his bow, which himself could bend when his horse was in full gallop; he was majestic whether sitting or standing, although the protuberance of his belly deformed his royal person; of excellent health so that he was never confined with any dangerous disorder, except at the last; so given to the pleasures of the chase, that as I have before said, ejecting the inhabitants, he let a space of many miles grow desolate that, when at liberty from other avocations, he might there pursue his pleasures. *William of Malmesbury. A History of the Norman Kings III. 279*

Character and career

There are not many visual depictions of William the Conqueror to support what the people of his time said about him. The Bayeux Tapestry and William's personal seal are both somewhat artistically 'representative', as opposed to real portraiture. However, there are enough comments to help us imagine the

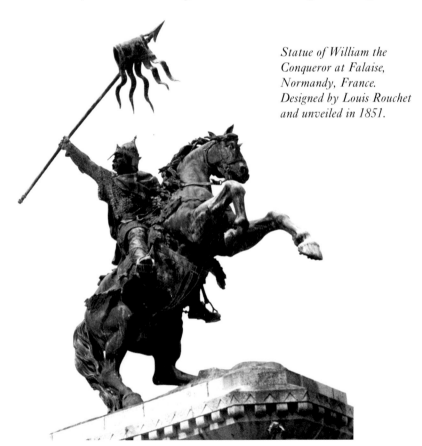

Statue of William the Conqueror at Falaise, Normandy, France. Designed by Louis Rouchet and unveiled in 1851.

appearance of the man. A monk of Caen knew him as a burly warrior with a harsh guttural voice, great in stature but not ungainly. This same monk mentioned William's moderation in eating and drinking as he apparently abhorred drunkenness in others, but the monk may have drawn from classical precedent here. William's immense physical strength and stamina were frequently observed. His physique was famously 'confirmed' after the opening of his tomb at Caen in 1522, when observers saw a body with long arms and legs. Later, his one surviving femur – if indeed it was his – was measured and was said to indicate a man of about five feet and ten inches in height.

Texts mainly speak of a wise and powerful ruler, but the English writers, or at least those with sound knowledge of the suffering William brought on Englishmen, speak of a man with a bent for cruelty. By the standards of his day, William was perhaps able to instil fear into his subjects and enemies more than some of his contemporaries and predecessors.

It could be said that the childhood makes the man. If so, William the Conqueror is a seductive candidate for such a theory. One cannot easily imagine how vulnerable a child of seven years old feels when he inherits power in a violent world. In 1035 the young duke had around him those who had supported his father, Duke Robert I: the ageing archbishop Robert of Rouen, Count Alan of Brittany, Osbern the steward and Turold or Turchetil, one of the boy's personal tutors. The death of the archbishop in 1037 led to a period of chaos during which the young duke was forced to look over his shoulder almost constantly. Alan of Brittany died in 1039 or 1040 and Count Gilbert of Brionne took over the guardianship of the boy. Within months he was murdered. Then Turold was murdered, and then, to ram home the violence of the age in the mind of the young boy, Osbern, while sleeping in the duke's bedchamber at Vaudreuil, was murdered too. Walter, William's maternal uncle, was said to have whisked the boy from place to place, even hiding the duke in the houses of local peasants. It is inconceivable that these events did not affect William's outlook on the world.

Turbulent years followed. William's relatives William and Mauger, both the sons of Duke Richard II (996–1026) rallied to the young duke's cause. The former became established in the county of Talou at Arques and the latter became the archbishop of Rouen. Also in the mix were Ralph of Gacé, who had been responsible for the murder of Gilbert of Brionne and Guy of Burgundy, a grandson of Duke Richard II. William lived through this cycle of vengeance and retribution that swept across the duchy and possibly shared the experience with his cousins William FitzOsbern (the son of his former steward), Roger de Beaumont and Roger of Montgomery. These young men would go on to play important roles in the years after the conquest of England.

The repeated interventions of the French King Henry I (who regarded William as his vassal), were of great significance in William's career. The king viewed William as under his protection. When an open revolt of the western Norman vicomtes against William erupted in 1046, the king came to the support of the young duke. The result was a battle in the following year fought at Val-ès-Dunes, at which the victorious young William came of age (pages 117-120). After the battle, a 'Truce of God' was agreed, which prohibited private warfare from Wednesday evening until Monday morning and during Advent, Lent, Easter and Pentecost.

A long period of internal and external threats against the duke followed, including a switching of sides by the French king and the rebellion of William of Talou. More happily, William then married Matilda, daughter of Count Baldwin V of Flanders, in around 1051. Pope Leo IX seems to have forbidden the marriage, probably on the grounds of prohibited degrees of kinship, but the marriage went ahead and it was a happy one for the most part. Four sons and perhaps six daughters were the result. Matilda, a diminutive person by all accounts, was also a strong woman. William and Matilda lost Richard, their second son, in around 1075 in an accident in the New Forest, a phenomenon which seemed to plague the hunt-loving Normans after the conquest of England. There is some evidence that Matilda stayed supportive of her son Duke Robert II Curthose through his struggles with his father in later years (pages 81-82). Interestingly, in a stark contrast to his other son, the future Henry I of England (1100–1135), William the Conqueror does not appear to have had any illegitimate children.

By 1060 William had eliminated the threats to his dukedom through significant battles at Mortemer (1054) and Varaville (1057), and had also benefited from the deaths of the French King Henry I and the Angevin Count Geoffrey Martel, who had been a powerful thorn in his side. The complex evolution of events on both sides of the English Channel from around 1051 to 1066 is the subject of much debate, but it is clear that William was a consummate politician. He handled his relations with the House of Godwin – the most powerful family in pre-Conquest England – with near mastery and was also able to keep his political allies together in a long and protracted build-up to the invasion of England in 1066.

The changes the Norman Conquest brought to England were profound, and William's administrative skill is manifest in the great Domesday survey, which he initiated. The survey may have been prompted by the serious Danish threat his kingdom faced in the 1080s, and yet it displays a grasp of government not seen in England since the days of King Alfred and his sons. The Conqueror was perhaps a less flamboyant character than his illustrious contemporary Robert Guiscard, but no less able to enthuse his followers with the promise and delivery of great rewards. It is arguable that he delivered more in this respect than Guiscard did. His lack of flamboyance, perhaps even a dourness of character, coupled with the suffering of the people whom he conquered, colours an otherwise impressive reputation.

Abbaye aux Hommes at Caen, Normandy, France (top) and Abbaye aux Dames (bottom), both originally built in atonement for Duke William's marriage to Matilda against the Pope's ruling.

Map 3: Map of England and Normandy (after Douglas)

The Commander

William's military career falls into three phases. The years between the successful Battle of Val-ès-Dunes in 1047 and 1060 mark a defensive struggle with both internal and external enemies. Then, between 1060 and 1075, there is a remarkably expansive period leading to the conquest of England and its subsequent aggressive consolidation. Later there is a return to the defensive stance, which was not always successful. In fact, William experienced setbacks at Dol (1076), Gerberoi (1079), La Flèche (1081) and Saint Suzanne in 1084–85. Orderic Vitalis even says that in the last thirteen years of his life William the Conqueror did not once take a fortress he besieged or put an army to flight. This period marks a decline in his effectiveness as a military leader, although his earlier colossal achievements somewhat eclipse the mediocrity of these later years.

Warfare in Normandy was dominated by the fortified place. William quickly learned that speed was of the essence when his enemies installed themselves in their castles. His approach to the growing power of Count Geoffrey Martel of Anjou showed an early sign of strategic awareness, quickness of action and the brutality for which William became renowned.

Geoffrey Martel had obtained control of parts of Maine to the south of Normandy, much to the concern of William and his overlord the French King Henry I. But it was when the count of Anjou took the fortresses at Domfront and Alençon that William was stung into action. William approached Domfront through the lands of the strategically important lords of Bellême with the king's permission. Initially, he tried to take the place by surprise, but when this failed he built four siege towers around it and conducted an active scouting regime. Geoffrey Martel brought an army up to the region to relieve the siege. However, William advanced to meet him, leaving behind a force large enough to continue the siege. Martel chose not to fight William. Instead, he remained close enough to stop him ravaging Maine. William then turned with remarkable speed upon the other fortification at Alençon. William had learned through his scouts that Alençon was in a poor state of readiness, so he rode through the night and torched the fort on the other side of the river and took numerous prisoners. From the walls of Alençon the garrison hurled personal insults at Duke William. They insulted him for his illegitimacy, reminding him of his grandfather's occupation as a tanner (or more likely an embalmer). They intimated that the pelts and hides they were hanging over their walls were those of the dead of his own army. William subsequently cut off the hands and feet of his prisoners. Not surprisingly, the barbarism of this stratagem had its effects on the defenders at Alençon and the place surrendered after the citizens were warned that this same horrific fate would befall them. Word of the atrocity followed William's victorious army to Domfront, which fell through fear alone.

William FitzOsbern

William FitzOsbern was a great magnate of the immediate post-Conquest period in England. He had been close to Duke William since childhood and fought at Hastings in 1066. His skill won him a very early title after the Conquest as Earl of Hereford, but not before he had already established himself on the Isle of Wight. So trusting was William the Conqueror of FitzOsbern's loyalty that he left the running of the English kingdom in his hands (held jointly with Odo of Bayeux) when he went to Normandy in the summer of 1067. FitzOsbern accompanied the king on his subsequent campaigns in the west of England, and in 1069 he was given the castle at York and campaigned against English uprisings in the West Midlands.

FitzOsbern's castles perhaps define him the best. His drive into the Welsh territories was based around a strength provided by fortifications at Chepstow (the keep of which was built in stone from the start), Monmouth, Wigmore, Clifford and Berkeley castles. A succession crisis in Flanders and the offer of the hand of the widow of the deceased duke of Flanders lured FitzOsbern to his doom and he was killed at the Battle of Cassel on 22 February 1071.

After William's success at Domfront and Alençon, Geoffrey Martel remained strong in Maine. But King Henry's changing of sides presented a real dilemma for the duke. The king, now reconciled with the Angevin count, lent his support to the rebellion of William of Talou, count of Arques, who had deserted the duke and set himself in the impressive castle at Arques-la-Bataille. The duke had heard news of the stand at Arques while at his base in the Cotentin. He rode with great speed across Normandy, sending his milites (knights) ahead to intercept the king's supply carts, with limited success. However, the subsequent investment of Arques and a skirmish a mile from its walls which went in favour of the duke, led to its capture and the banishment of William of Talou. Here, it seemed that swiftness had been the key in the duke's response.

William still faced hostility from the French king. How he dealt with it is revealing. Just a few months after Arques in 1054, he suffered a two-pronged invasion. One force assembled under the king at Mantes and probably included Geoffrey Martel. The other came from the north east and brought with it Odo, the brother of the king, Rainald of Cleremont and Guy of Ponthieu, who had lost his brother in the action outside Arques the year before. This second force ravaged the east of the duchy while the first came up from Mantes. The two forces were probably destined to meet near Rouen. William rallied support from within his duchy. He split his forces into two, either side of the Seine. On the north side William's army was led by Count Robert of Eu, Hugh of Gournay, Walter Giffard, Roger of Mortemer and William de Warenne. The duke himself headed out to oppose the French king's force. Near to Mortemer in the far northeast corner of the duchy Odo, Rainald and Guy's forces were caught by surprise by Count Robert, who attacked them while some of their force were out foraging and others were sleeping off the effects of the previous night's drinking. Casualties were numerous and Guy was captured. On hearing the news, the French king withdrew his own forces. The Battle of Mortemer, as it has become known, is an example of what must surely have been William's good use of prior intelligence. His strategy had been a highly defensive 'shadowing' one. The duke had positioned his forces 'so that he neither came to a close engagement nor yet allowed his land to be devastated', according to William of Malmesbury. His growing support within the duchy had provided him with a force of sufficient size that he could be confident in splitting his forces. More than this, it was becoming clear that the duke of Normandy was a master of surprise. This would become his most consistently rewarding stratagem.

Walter Giffard

Walter Giffard was the son of the lord of Longueville and Avelina, the sister of the duchess of Normandy. He was therefore the cousin of William the Conqueror. He was a loyal supporter of William and had an active role to play at the siege of the rebel Count William of Talou at Arques and in the Battle of Mortemer. Giffard's military career extended to Spain where he fought at the siege of Barbastro in 1064. Tradition has it that Giffard brought back from Spain a gift for Duke William, a magnificent horse which the duke rode at Hastings in 1066. Giffard remained close to William the Conqueror and played a key part in his preparations for invading England, providing him with thirty ships for the fleet. He refused to carry the standard at Hastings, preferring to have his hands free to fight. The reward for his loyalty was immense. He received over a hundred lordships, many of which were centred on Buckinghamshire. He died before 1085. His son, also called Walter, was the first earl of Buckingham.

Despite a reconciliation between the duke and the French king, Henry I turned once again to the count of Anjou and attacked the Normans. The campaign of 1057 saw the allied army enter Normandy from the south, coming up through the Hiémois towards Bayeux and Caen. The same shadowing game was played by William, only this time, with a small and fresh force of men, he was able to seize upon a golden opportunity. The invasion force was trying to cross the River Dives at a ford at Varaville. Part of the force had crossed the river when the approaching tidal surge made it impossible for the rest of the force to follow. Thus the rear of the invading army was exposed and William's force cut it to pieces in a well-timed attack. All of this was viewed with dismay by the French king from the nearby Bassebourg hill. Breaking off the campaign, he returned home and never invaded Normandy again.

As a commander on the offensive William was, in one respect, no different than the defensive William. Seeking battle was not a desirable option. William's campaigns in Brittany in 1064 (on which he was accompanied by his future English enemy, Harold Godwinson) was a cautious affair. His arrival at Dol forced Conan of Brittany to abandon his siege there, but there were no pitched battles in the subsequent campaigning. In Maine in 1063 and again in 1073 William's rapid reduction of the countryside was preferred to the seeking of battle, and this policy was brutal in its execution. The strategic goal was the surrender of Le Mans. William adopted the same policy of burning and destruction when he approached London in 1066, and the city surrendered. These are two examples of the strategic thinker at work.

William's role as commander of the Hastings campaign is considered below (pages 120-133). The logistical challenge was huge. Estimating numbers is always controversial, but some basic points serve to show that the duke was up to the task. While it was stationary for a month at Dives-sur-Mer, the Norman invasion force, which may have included up to 3,000 horses, required in the region of 9,000 cart loads of grain, straw and firewood. This fact alone raises the problem of the horse excrement and urine, let alone the additional problem of feeding and watering the horses and the troops, and indeed paying the men. This difficult situation presented a headache of logistical and political management which William clearly overcame.

The estuary at Saint-Valery-Sur-Somme, France, where up to 700 vessels were moored prior to the invasion of England in 1066.

Once William had subdued the English in the years after Hastings, his style of warfare shows the same concern to avoid pitched battles except where the odds were in his favour. The strategy of castle building was widely employed and among the first built were Nottingham, Lincoln and York (where two were built and manned by 500 troops). These strongholds provided bases for operations in otherwise hostile territory. This is not to say that William did not seize his opportunities to fight, however. There appears to have been a battle at York in 1069, which may have been a reprisal for the killing by rebel forces of the Norman Robert de Comines. Here, William came up from the south and caught the English rebel Edgar the Ætheling and his forces by surprise and routed them. Several hundred men who were unable to get away were killed, according the *Anglo-Saxon Chronicle*. We know little about the fighting, but the punitive sacking of York which followed presaged what was to become William the Conqueror's most controversial military campaign, the 'Harrying of the North'. Here, in a personally led march across the Pennines, the ultimate strategy of landscape reduction and human destruction brought consternation even from contemporaries who would otherwise have supported William. It was another example of the brutality of William the Conqueror, which seems to have been so effective.

The Conqueror's approach to warfare was sophisticated and organised. He did not fling himself into battle. He clearly had a strategic grasp superior to many of his enemies. His use of intelligence and scouts was extensive, and like Robert Guiscard he seems to have preferred on occasions to conduct his own reconnaissance (an example being at the siege of Exeter in 1068). He realised the need to act quickly and attack enemy supplies when countering sieges. But it was William's adoption of the psychological aspect of warfare which marks him out as particularly of note. The events at Alençon and the 'Harrying of the North' bear this out. They were both forms of measured cruelty, designed with military and political goals in mind.

Discussion of the military achievement of William the Conqueror is always dominated by the Battle of Hastings and England's subsequent conquest. However, it is arguable that as a commander of a pitched battle, William was not as assured as he was on the strategic front. He managed to coordinate his army at Hastings only at the eleventh hour in the face of stubborn resistance, and had to show himself to his troops after losing his mount more than once. The encounter with his son Robert at Gerberoi in 1079 was another case in which, in the heat of battle, William nearly paid dearly with his life.

It is unfair to highlight the failures of later years. William the Conqueror met his end after the siege of Mantes in the disputed Vexin region. Since the arrival of the Normans the old 'pagus', or territory, of the Vexin had been divided, with the area between the Epte and Andelle in Norman hands and that between the Epte and the Oise in the hands of the French. Simon, the last count of the Vexin had

William the Conqueror's tombstone at Abbaye aux Hommes in Caen, Normandy, France.

been brought up in the court of William the Conqueror but had retired from secular life in 1077. Thereafter, the French king had made his move on the Vexin. William had reacted with some of his old energy. Through burning and ravaging he reminded the king of France how effective his style of warfare could be. Whether he fell ill during this action, or was injured by the pommel of his saddle (as Orderic Vitalis contends), is a disputed matter. What is not disputed is the effect William's warfare had on the people of his domains. For this, we turn again to Orderic Vitalis, who places a deathbed speech into the mouth of the Conqueror. Orderic, we may recall, was half-English himself, and can be forgiven if these words were never actually spoken. For him, however, they rang true:

> I treated the native inhabitants of the kingdom with unreasonable severity, cruelly oppressed high and low, unjustly disinherited many, and caused the death of thousands by starvation and war, especially in Yorkshire... In mad fury I descended on the English of the north like a raging lion, and ordered that their homes and crops with all their equipment and furnishings should be burnt at once and their great flocks and herds of sheep and cattle slaughtered everywhere. So I chastised a great multitude of men and women with the lash of starvation and, alas! was the cruel murderer of many thousands, both young and old, of this fair people.

Chapter 5

Richard I, Count of Aversa and Prince of Capua (d. 1078)

Timeline of Richard, Prince of Capua

1045	Arrives in Italy with forty knights. Becomes lord of Genzano. Falls out with Drogo de Hauteville and is imprisoned. Death of Rainulf II of Aversa
1048	Herman, son of either Asclettin or Rainulf II rules Aversa under tutelage of William Bellabocca
1050	Expulsion of Bellabocca. Richard rules alongside Herman who is not heard of after 1050
1051-52	Marriage to Fressenda, sister of Drogo de Hauteville
1052	Besieges Capua
1053	Takes leading part in Battle of Civitate
1058	Capture of Capua. Becomes prince of Capua. Received at Monte Cassino by Abbot Desiderius with full honour
1059	Provides three hundred knights to Pope Nicholas II. Attends synod of Melfi
1061	Swears fealty to Pope Alexander II
1062	Besieges Capua again, ensuring the town surrenders its citadel to him. Captures Teano
1063	Gains control of Gaeta. Revolts of counts of Teano and Gaeta aided by William of Montreuil
1066	Richard's troops invade Roman Campagna. Intervention of Godfrey of Lorraine
1067	Plundering expedition into county of Marsia
1072	Reneges on promise to Robert Guiscard to provide 200 knights for Palermo expedition. Supports Apulian rebellion against Robert
1073	Swears fealty to Pope Gregory. Probable death of wife Fressenda
1076	Siege of Salerno. Campaigns in papal Campagna
1077	Siege of Naples
1078	Dies Thursday 5 April

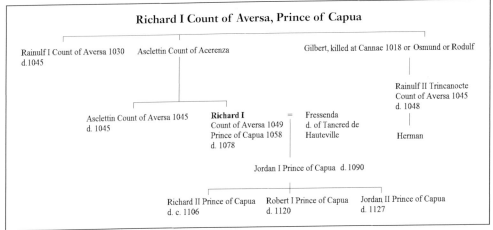

Fig. 5

During this time arrived Richard, the son of Asclettin, who was a fine figure of a man and a lord of good stature. He was a young man of open countenance and strikingly handsome, and he was loved by everyone who saw him. He was followed by many knights and people. By deliberate choice, he rode a horse so small that his feet almost touched the ground. He was loved and honoured by everyone for his youth and extraordinary good looks as well as for the love the people bore his uncle and brother. *Amatus II. 44*

Character and Career

Richard Drengot, the son of Asclettin, is another character upon whom the sources allow us to shed some light. In 1054 he arrived from the Pays de Caux region of Normandy, coming into southern Italy at the head of a forty-strong following. Amatus gives us an almost beatific image of the man who would later provide so much support for the monastery at Monte Cassino. But this man, who would come to displace the last Lombard Prince of Capua, would have to work hard to get what he wanted, and he certainly possessed the vaulting ambition needed to achieve it.

Richard's uncle Rainulf, the first Norman count of Aversa, had died in the late spring or summer of 1045. He had been a hugely successful member of the first generation of Norman adventurers. Rainulf I's successor was his nephew, who carried the popular family name of Asclettin. This new count of Aversa was Richard's own brother. However, Asclettin died soon after Rainulf. There followed a struggle between a new man (also called Rainulf) and a pretender called Rodulf. The new Rainulf prevailed in this struggle and became Count Rainulf II of Aversa.

Rainulf II saw Richard as a direct threat and he gave him a frosty reception. Soon, Richard went elsewhere looking for gain. He quickly found service with

Humphrey de Hauteville and then, at the invitation of Sarulus of Genzano, established himself there as the successor to Asclettin. Richard's acquisitive style saw him quickly become strong enough not only to challenge Rainulf II, but also to somehow incur the wrath of the Norman count of Apulia Drogo de Hauteville, who threw him straight into prison. It was during this period of incarceration that Count Rainulf II of Aversa died and Richard's fortunes reversed. Drogo de Hauteville had kept Richard imprisoned so that the young heir to Aversa – a boy named Herman who was probably Rainulf II's son – could be brought up under the guidance of William Bellabocca, a de Hauteville relative. It was not a happy arrangement in the eyes of the Aversans, who wanted a man of the line of Rainulf I to rule instead. And so, with the help of the powerful Prince Gaimar of Salerno, Richard was released from prison and brought to Aversa, clad in silk robes, to be greeted by a joyous population. Richard, son of Asclettin, whose achievements it could be argued were often augmented by sheer good luck, would now rule alongside the boy Herman. It is not clear how comfortable this joint arrangement was for Richard of Aversa, but by the early 1050s the boy, whose name appeared on charters alongside that of Richard, becomes conspicuous by his absence. He is never mentioned again. Richard, the new count of Aversa, now embarked on a typically Norman approach to political acquisition.

These early years of Richard's rule are characterised by the rise of the Normans in southern Italy in general. It was not always a happy experience for the people of the countryside, whose vineyards would frequently feel the flames of Norman torches, nor, as we have observed, was it happy for the Pope, whose flock complained to him of the depredations of the Normans.

After the showdown at Civitate in 1053, at which he acquitted himself admirably, Richard's eyes fixed on Capua and perhaps had been from the start. The city's illustrious Lombard rulers had lately ruled not as counts but as princes. Pandulf IV, our scheming 'wolf' (with whom we might recall Robert Guiscard tried to find favour), was one such ruler. However, Pandulf's son Pandulf VI [sic] could not hope to match his father's political acumen. Richard seized his opportunity in 1057 after the death of Pandulf VI and the accession of a new prince, Landulf. He had already intimidated the people into giving him 7,000 gold bezants back in 1052; now in 1057 he besieged the town, eventually winning their recognition of him as the new prince of Capua.

Richard provides us with perhaps the best – and worst – example of the Norman predatory kinship strategy in action. To modern eyes he seems a brutal character, but his exploits are a stark example of how Norman political success could be won. Richard brokered a marriage between his daughter and the son of Duke Atenulf of Gaeta, but the intended husband died in 1058, not long before the wedding. According to the Lombard law of morgengab, one quarter of the husband's fortune would become the property of the wife after marriage, payable after its successful consummation. Richard demanded from Duke Atenulf the morgengab due his daughter, despite the fact that the intended husband had died. Atenulf understandably refused. There followed an ugly military campaign of reduction and misery carried out around the town of Aquino by Richard's men. Although Richard was soon received at the abbey of Monte Cassino by its abbot Desiderius, amid great pomp and ceremony, the events around Aquino must surely have made men question the motives and methods of this great Norman warlord. The only intervention made by Desiderius however, was to broker the morgengab deal by forcing Richard to accept a slightly reduced payment from Atenulf on the grounds of the latter's poverty. Morality, it seemed, came a poor second to business in the prince of Capua's world.

Richard also involved himself in papal politics. In 1059 the papal advisor Hildebrand (who would later become Pope himself), resulted in the release of 300 of Richard's knights to assist Pope Nicholas II against his enemies. At the Synod of Melfi in 1059 Richard was recognised by this pope as prince of Capua and possibly even invested as such. It was a remarkable change in papal attitude to the Normans from the days of tension before Civitate. Later, in 1061, Richard's knights would enthusiastically support the claim of Alexander II against an anti-Pope, but once again, when Richard broke his bonds of vassalage in 1066 and marched on Rome, it is difficult to avoid the conclusion that he intended to acquire for himself the temporal rule of the Roman aristocracy.

The fluidity of Richard's relations with Robert Guiscard, alongside whom he had sworn an oath to the Pope at Melfi, would ebb and flow across the dusty Italian landscape in the early 1070s and would range from genuine antagonism to seemingly complete reconciliation. At its lowest point Richard reneged on a promise to supply Robert with 200 knights under his own son Jordan for the duke's Palermo expedition, and he probably threw this same resource into an Apulian rebellion against Robert. Nevertheless, by the time he fell ill and died in Capua in 1078, Richard son of Asclettin had become one of the most powerful men in Italy. It had taken him thirty years.

The Commander

What evidence we have of Richard's capabilities as a commander points to a man who, like other military men of his time, was perfectly capable of a variety of approaches to warfare, demonstrating knowledge of the basic principles which people often assume were missing in medieval commanders. Like many other Normans, he was master of the ambush. For example, after he had been rebuffed by Prince Gisulf of Salerno in the early 1050s, he arranged a classic ambush early in the morning. His men pretended to flee from the slingers and archers of the Salernitan Prince, who had provided himself with an armed escort. Consequently, the Normans drew them into an ambush from which they had no means of escape. Some were cut down, while others threw themselves into the sea. Here, Richard

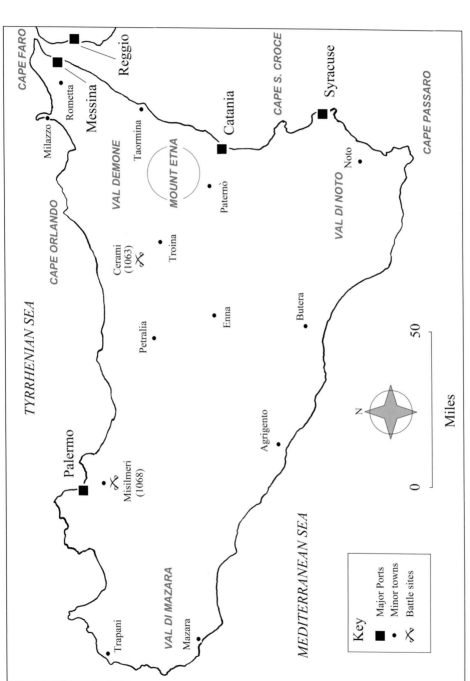

Map 4: Map of Sicily

demonstrated the use of a stratagem (the feigned flight) frequently resorted to by Norman commanders (pages 222-226).

We know little of Richard's style of leadership when on active campaign, but it is safe to assume that it was compelling. The cavalry charge he led at Civitate in 1053 (pages 154-155) must have been very well timed to have produced the results it did, and Richard, in charge of the right flank of the Norman army, must have initiated the action as a result of his view of the poorly ordered Italian infantry in front of him. It was one of his finest moments.

Richard assisted in or directly commanded a number of sieges. In 1059 he was alongside Pope Nicholas II conducting a siege at Galeria in order to capture the Pope's rival Benedict X. Richard's approach to siege warfare – at least in the case of his capture of Capua – is also revealing. His first siege of the city in 1057–58 had been achieved by setting up fortified towers outside the city, which denied the citizens access to the produce of the surrounding district. The subsequent hunger drove the inhabitants into submission. Although Richard demanded nothing less than the title of the prince of Capua, he was prepared to leave the city's citadel and gates in the hands of the townsmen. It was not until 1062 that Richard took the whole city, having completed a second siege of the place which was technically already his. The taking of the citadel was usually a sign of an intent to subjugate. Until 1062 it may well have been the case that Richard had not felt this measure to be necessary. Richard, then was clearly a competent siege commander. After reconciling himself with Robert Guiscard, the two agreed on a joint approach to the problems presented by Salerno and Naples. Guiscard sought Richard's aid in the siege of Salerno and in turn supported Richard's siege of Naples in 1077.

There is not enough evidence to suggest that Richard I of Capua was anything other than an able all-round commander, with experience in battle, campaign and siege warfare. His character, however, may well have been given over to overt self-aggrandisement, but in this he was surely not alone in the Norman world.

Chapter 6

Roger I, Count of Sicily
(d. 1101)

Timeline of Roger I, Count of Sicily

1057	Arrives in southern Italy. Joins Robert Guiscard on a campaign of Conquest in Calabria. Failed siege of Reggio as Roger plunders around Gerace
1058	Falls out with his brother Robert Guiscard and allies with another brother William. Sets up base at Scalea Castle. Full reconciliation with Robert and half share of Calabria. Sets up new base at Mileto
1059	Defeats the governor of Gerace and the bishop of Cassano
1060	Siege of Reggio. Small sortie sent out to Messina in Sicily
1061	Milazzo and Rometta campaigns in Sicily. Roger's forces trapped on the shore and scramble for ships. Messina falls. Battle of Enna. Reconnaissance-in-force to Agrigento
1062	Marriage to Judith of Evreux. Sets up bases at Troina and Petralia. Falls out and reconciles with Robert Guiscard at Gerace
1063	Besieged at Troina. Victory in June at the Battle of Cerami
1064	First attempt to take Palermo thwarted by spiders around Monte Tarantino
1066	Refortification of Petralia
1068	Victory at the Battle of Misilmeri
1071	Joins with Robert Guiscard in the latter stages of the siege of Bari. Naval success
1071-72	Siege of Palermo and assumption of the title of Great Count of Sicily
1075	Defeat at the hands of the Emir of Syracuse
1077	Siege of Trapani and the fall of Erice in Sicily
1079	Fall of Taormina
1083	Revolt of Roger's son Jordan in Sicily
1085	Naval battle at Syracuse and fall of the Emir
1086	Siege and capture of Agrigento. Supports his nephew Roger Borsa duke of Apulia against nephew Bohemond
1087	Capitulation of Enna

1091	Fall of Noto, the last bastion of Muslim independence in Sicily. Expedition to and surrender of Malta
1098	Siege of Capua in support of Roger Borsa and the exiled Prince Richard II of Capua
1101	Dies at Mileto

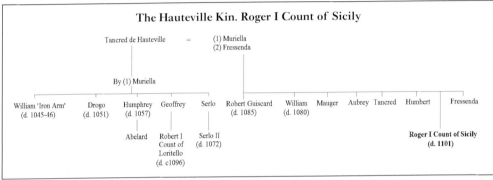

The Hauteville Kin. Roger I Count of Sicily

Fig. 6

His [Robert Guiscard's] younger brother Roger, who had up to now been kept at home because of his youth and the affection felt for him by his family, now followed him and came to Apulia. Guiscard was extremely pleased by his arrival, and received him with the honour which was his due. For he was a most handsome young man, tall and well-made, a most fluent speaker, shrewd in counsel, far-sighted in the planning of things to be done, cheerful and pleasant to everyone, strong and valiant, fierce in battle: through these qualities, in a short time he achieved general admiration. Since he was ambitious for both power and praise, as is usual in one of his age, he attracted other ambitious young men to follow him, and whatever he could obtain was freely and generously shared with them. *Malaterra (I.19)*

Character and Career

Of all the de Hauteville brothers to descend into Italy, the eighth son of Tancred de Hauteville is perhaps the most complete character of them all. Arriving in 1057 at the age of twenty-six, Roger de Hauteville immediately gravitated towards the new Norman fortress of Melfi. Soon, however, he was serving within the *familia* of his newly invested brother Robert Guiscard, the duke of Apulia. He campaigned around Calabria alongside him, reaping much plunder and showing himself to be a reliable member of his brother's household. But he would soon fall out with his brother and their relationship would wax and wane.

In 1058 Roger turned to another brother, William de Hauteville, count of the Principate, whose seat was in the lands to the south of Salerno. Here, at a dramatic hilltop castle known as Scalea, Roger made his base and drew great profit from the countryside at the expense of his own brother. However, Duke Robert, in the wake of a disastrous Calabrian famine and subsequent uprising in the region, turned once again to Roger, offering him half of all Calabria (including that part south of Squillace to Reggio, which had yet to be taken). Roger's new base would be at Mileto, ideally situated for a southern thrust into the toe of Italy. Roger duly responded with his growing army and fell in once again with Robert Guiscard.

William de Hauteville, Count of the Principate

William arrived in Italy alongside his brothers Geoffrey and Mauger in around 1053. He quickly distinguished himself, fighting in the Battle of Civitate that year. Two years later he established himself after taking the fortification at San Nicandro near Eboli. This formed the centre of his Principate, with which Humphrey de Hauteville invested him in 1056. Due to a marriage to the daughter of Duke Guy of Sorrento he inherited lands in the principality of Salerno and began a long war against Prince Gisulf II of Salerno, slowly eroding what little land Gisulf had left. He also inherited the Capitanate from Mauger when he died in the late 1050s, but gave it to another brother, Geoffrey. He sometimes fought against his brother Robert Guiscard and sometimes alongside him.

Sicily seems to have had a particular attraction for Roger. Although Robert Guiscard had been invested by the Pope with the future conquest of Sicily in mind, his younger brother would make the project his own in the years to come. But in 1059 Calabria still needed to be subdued before any such mission could be undertaken. Gerace was overcome and the stubborn Reggio, which had held out against the combined efforts of Roger and Robert in 1057, would soon capitulate.

The brothers' early campaigns in Sicily had mixed fortunes, but ultimately success came with the capture and fortification of Messina in 1061. Roger subsequently devoted himself to Sicilian campaigning and the fortification of key outposts, including Troina, where he spent his first Christmas on the island. His first step was to marry Judith of Évreux. He had known her since his youth. Judith was not only beautiful, she was also very well connected in Normandy. Her father was the first cousin of William the Conqueror and her brother and guardian Robert de Grantmesnil, abbot of Saint Evroul-sur-Ouche, had fled from Normandy after a serious falling out with the duke. Judith, along with eleven monks, came first to Rome and then was warmly welcomed by Duke Robert Guiscard. Roger wasted no time. He hurried back to Calabria and married her more or less where he found her. So quick was the union at San Martino that there was no time to celebrate. The celebrations came later, in great pomp at Mileto amid a crowd of musicians. The honeymoon was cut short as Roger returned to business in Sicily. Despite his wife's tears at his early departure, he took his small army across the straits again and set about establishing a garrison at Petralia and strengthening that at Troina. Soon, though, Roger would be back at Mileto and reunited with his wife, who later returned with him to Sicily.

Roger's conflict with his brother Robert Guiscard came to the fore again in 1062. It was an extraordinary falling out. Roger needed to enfeoff his new wife with a quarter of his wealth according to law of morgengab. Yet despite all his military successes, he had very little to give. He had been promised half of Calabria, but all he had was his castle at Mileto. So Roger issued an ultimatum to Robert at Melfi. If forty days were to pass without any good result, Roger would take what he needed by force. A furious Robert Guiscard came to besiege his brother at Mileto and there seems to have been some genuine fighting between their men, with Roger's knights able to frustrate the duke's men by preventing them from setting up camp. Judith's brother Arnold was killed during these struggles.

There followed a bizarre drama at Gerace. Roger stole away there during the siege of Mileto and was followed by Robert, raging with indignation. Robert slipped into Gerace under cover seeking his brother, but narrowly escaped death at the hands of an angry mob after he was spotted by a house servant who raised the alarm. Malaterra tells of angry scenes in the town. But the brothers publicly made it up with one another, almost at once. After skirmishes in the Calabrian countryside, Robert finally agreed to Roger's requests and Roger was able to enfeoff his wife. A delicately balanced power-sharing system was put into place around Calabria as a result. Roger de Hauteville embodied all the qualities of tenacity and determination his other brothers possessed and certainly seems to have been able to take on Guiscard and get what he wanted. It is a feature of their relationship, however, that he could not stay at loggerheads with Robert for long.

Roger returned to Sicily with Judith and looked to improve things at Troina. The town's first Norman garrison had fled after the assassination of Roger's Saracen ally Ibn at-Timnah. The local Greek population, supported by the Saracens, rose up against the new Norman garrison after Roger had left his wife at the citadel within it. Malaterra gives us another tale of the strength of the love between Roger and Judith. Returning hurriedly to protect her, Roger found the town split into two sections with the Greeks having barricaded themselves for protection. Worse still, the Normans were clustered around the citadel and Roger and his men had no choice but to join them as the other parts of the town were hostile. The Greeks were being supplied by numerous Saracens from the surrounding countryside while the Normans were beginning to starve in the citadel. Winter took hold and four long months of intermittent fighting passed. One cold winter night, Malaterra reports, the Normans observed the Saracens asleep at their posts, drowsy with wine they had drunk to keep out the cold and supplement the lack of food. The Normans quietly approached the enemy barricades, climbed over them and slew many defenders where they slept. One of the chief conspirators was hanged as an example to the others. The victory must have been a huge psychological blow. Judith was even able to establish herself once again whilst her husband went back to Calabria for reinforcements and supplies.

A series of campaigns followed which saw Roger ultimately prevail against the Saracens at the Battle of Cerami in 1063 (pages 157-160). But Sicily did not yield to the Norman lance quickly. In 1064 Roger and Robert Guiscard teamed up once more and, in a change of strategy, focusing now on the great capital city, they headed for Palermo. They were thwarted not by men, but by nature. They had chosen a camp site at Monte Tarantino, outside the great city, which was infested with tarantula spiders. Spider bites afflicted a great many of the Normans, forcing them to give up the campaign. Guiscard returned to Italy. For four years Roger bided his time in Sicily, moving his base forward to Petralia and refortifying it.

The stalemate was broken when Roger had his opportunity to finally defeat the Muslims at the Battle of Misilmeri in 1068 (pages 161-162). After this, his star was in the ascendancy. He waited for his brother to put down insurrections in Apulia before eventually joining with him in 1071 in the latter stages of the siege of Bari; their bond still very strong. The following year their cooperation saw the fall of Palermo, which was perhaps their most glorious combined achievement. Robert returned in triumph to Italy to concentrate on affairs on the mainland, leaving Roger to consolidate his rule of the island. Much of Sicily was now his, although Robert retained direct ownership of much of the Val Demone in the northeast, half of Palermo and half of Messina.

Roger's political and cultural sensitivity towards the peoples of the island was a marked feature of his government in later years. There were Greeks, Saracens and now Normans in the political mix, with the Islamic faith and two forms of the Christian faith to preside over. Robert Guiscard may already have been given the anticipated overlordship of Sicily by the Pope, but it was Roger de Hauteville, the Great Count of Sicily (a title bestowed on him by his brother), whose name was permanently linked with the success of this great Norman adventure. Roger ensured that the law of Islam was still adhered to in local courts, and

Coin of Roger I of Sicily showing Norman warrior with kite-shaped shield and lance with gonfanon.

Arabic was declared an equal language to Latin, Greek and Norman French. Some of the mosques which had been converted from churches were reconsecrated, and there was a move towards the Latinization of the Christian element of religious life, but Roger's general approach to governing the people of Sicily was tolerant and enlightened.

Roger continued to support his brother when he could spare the men. In 1083 he sailed to the Italian mainland and helped Guiscard put down a revolt. After the duke's death in 1085 Roger took Robert's daughter Helena under his wing. She had been more or less imprisoned in a Byzantine convent for years. Helena came to his Sicilian court after her release and her accommodation by Roger showed compassion. Roger also became involved in the aftermath of his brother's death in Apulia and Calabria. From 1085 he supported Robert's son and heir Roger Borsa in the new duke's struggles against Bohemond and Jordan of Capua. Roger was even present at the siege of Capua in 1098, alongside his nephew. It was his reputation among the Muslims, however, which marked him out as a thoughtful ruler. Roger had refused to join a Pisan and Genoese expedition against Temim, the North African Zirid Sultan of Mahdia. He was clearly aware of the importance of trust between himself and other Muslim leaders and was not prepared to break these bonds.

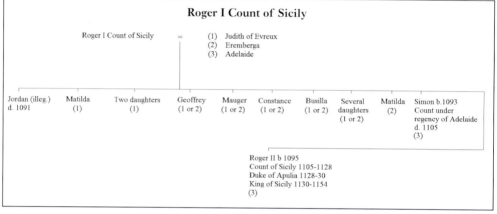

Fig. 7

Like many of the de Hautevilles, Roger had numerous children. Jordan, his illegitimate son, had briefly rebelled against his father in 1083. Judith, his first love, had died in 1076 leaving him numerous daughters and one or more sons. The next year he took Eremburga of Mortain as his wife and she gave him further daughters and one son, Mauger count of Troina. But she too died, leaving Roger to marry once again. He took Adelaide del Vasto as his third and final wife and she bore a daughter and two sons, Simon and Roger. Simon would inherit his father's patrimony in 1101, but was very young at the time. He had no time to show any promise and he died barely into his teens. His brother Roger II, however, showed greater promise and rose to become one of the greatest medieval kings in western history, uniting Sicily, Apulia and Calabria into one kingdom.

On 22 June 1101, Count Roger I of Sicily died. He had come from relative obscurity to astonishing wealth and power and had embodied many of the positive aspects of his extraordinary family's character. Above all else, he was politically astute in his dealings with the papacy and his multicultural subjects and allies. But as head of a military household, this great man was also a commander, and we will examine his military capabilities below.

The Commander

Roger de Hauteville is one of the few commanders in whom we can discern an evolution in his approach. His early years in Calabria are characterised by a panache and ambition not dissimilar to that of his brother Robert. His key concern in these years was to establish himself as a leader who could attract a following. At Scalea castle in Calabria in 1058 the opportunity to do this presented itself, as Malaterra reports:

> ...a man called Bervenis, coming from Melfi, announced that some Amalfitan merchants, laden with precious commodities, would be travelling from Melfi to Amalfi and would pass not far from the castrum. Hearing this he [Roger] was very happy, sprang on his horse and, accompanied by thirteen knights, he encountered the merchants between Gesualdo and Carbonara. He captured them and brought them to Scalea, deprived them of everything which they had with them, and even made them ransom themselves. Aided by this money, which he handed out generously, he bound one hundred knights to him, and with them he harried Apulia with frequent and wide-ranging raids, and put Guiscard to such trouble that, forgetting about the conquest of Calabria, he came near to losing what he had already acquired.

We do not know the details of Roger's early victories in Calabria after his reconciliation with Robert, but we do know from Malaterra (I.32) that he built upon a growing reputation for his military decisiveness. He also employed the element of surprise, using a forced march against the governor of Gerace:

> One day in the year 1059, when he was attacking the castrum of Oppido, the Bishop of Cassano and the praesopus (we would call him the provost) of Gerace raised a very large army and set out to attack the castrum of San Martino in the valley of Saline. When this was announced to Roger, he abandoned the siege and force marched to the place where he had heard that they were. He attacked and brought them to battle, trapped almost all of them and scarcely one escaped.

Having already experienced an inconclusive visit to Reggio with his brother Robert, Roger took time to prepare properly for a siege in 1060. It was the first time since the Normans had arrived in southern Italy that they had prepared and used siege engines of their own without relying on Lombard allies. On seeing the preparation of Roger's siege engines, the townsfolk lost their nerve and surrendered the city, the garrison fleeing to the rock of Scilla and eventually on to Constantinople.

However, Roger was still young when he crossed the Straits to take on Messina in 1060. These campaigns revealed a brave but perhaps impetuous style of command from which Roger would draw important lessons for the future. Towards the end of 1060 he took a force of just sixty knights over to Sicily. His small force was chased by the Messinan garrison and Roger drew them out with a feigned flight. In the following year Roger took a force of 160 knights over to Sicily, landing at Clibano. This was more of a reconnaissance-in-force than the earlier expedition and was a response to the appeal of the Sicilian emir Ibn at-Timnah in late February, a man whose struggles with his Saracen peers provided the perfect excuse for the Norman Sicilian adventure.

Particularly important in this early campaign was the peninsula around Milazzo, which juts out into the Tyrrhenian Sea forming a useful bridgehead for an invading force. Leaving their ships at Cape Farò the Norman army marched along the coast road towards the peninsula, raiding as they went. Milazzo soon fell to them and then Rometta. The force took much plunder, most of it on the hoof. Malaterra waxes lyrical about Roger's prowess on this expedition and recalls how he killed a man with a single blow of his sword. The problem for Roger was getting his spoils to Italy without being caught on the beach at Messina by a large Muslim cavalry force while he was loading his ships. Hampered by contrary winds, Roger was only saved by the actions of a man upon whom he would soon come to rely. As the Messinan force closed in on the Normans a certain Serlo II, son of Serlo de Hauteville, sprang into action. This young warrior was Roger's nephew. He was sent against the enemy on what appears, from Malaterra's wording, to have been a well-timed flank attack on a force in retreat:

> ...he [Roger] sent out ahead his nephew Serlo... with instructions that if they wished to flee, as indeed they did, they should be allowed to do so. He himself pursued them at great speed while they attempted to flee, and intercepted them to such effect that scarcely one among the whole multitude escaped.

Roger set up camp and attempted a night attack on the city, which appears to have been repulsed in some confusion. At daybreak, Amatus tells of a desperate Norman breakout through fear of being surrounded – a perilous situation in which the Normans had to disperse to find narrow defiles to descend to the shore. Because of rough seas, three more nervous days were spent stranded on the beach. When the fleet finally got away, it was pursued by a Saracen fleet and only just got into the harbour at Reggio, sustaining losses en route.

This episode was a harsh lesson for Roger. He had been impulsive in these early campaigns and had lacked foresight in terms of logistical planning. The campaign in May of that year, however, was better planned. It is not clear how significant the guidance of Duke Robert was on this occasion. The brothers, while their fleet was blockaded at Santa Maria Del Faro, north of Reggio, by the emir of Palermo's ships, undertook their own reconnaissance in two nimble galleys. Roger came

Cape Milazzo, northern Sicily, an important early bridgehead for the Norman invading forces from Calabria under Roger de Hauteville, who became Great Count of Sicily.

down to Reggio with around 270 knights in thirteen ships. He then crossed the straits under cover of darkness and landed about five miles south of Messina. He sent his ships back to the mainland and was fortunate to come across a large Saracen mule train accompanied by an important financial official, which he ambushed. Soon 170 fresh horsemen were sent to him from Calabria by his brother and, as dawn broke, the Messinans began to fear the worst as their garrison was out on patrol. Roger subsequently took the town and set about refortifying it with assistance from Robert Guiscard.

Descriptions of Roger in battle mainly come from Malaterra. For example, the Sicilian campaign moved on to Enna where Malaterra says that Robert Guiscard and Roger divided their forces into two divisions, with Roger leading the attack against the emir Ibn al-Hawas's three divisions, which were predominantly made up of cavalry. This opening clash led to the retreat of the Saracens and the death of many of them in the rout as they fled back to Enna. Later, at the battles at Cerami (1063) and Misilmeri (1068) Malaterra's narrative is infected with the fantastical element. We can only surmise that Roger was capable of understanding the impact of psychological warfare at the second battle (page 161). As to Roger's temperament when on campaign, however, we are given a small clue. After the victory at Cerami, Roger campaigned southwards around Agrigento collecting plunder. He split his men into three groups, with the main plundering division protected by a front and rear covering force, but in a carefully planned ambush the plunder was recovered by the Saracens. Roger flew into a rage at his men for their cowardice and told them to pull themselves together, berating them for lacking the courage of their ancestors. Failure was not an option, if the partisan Malaterra is to be believed.

Roger's participation in the great sieges of Bari (1069-71) and Palermo (1072) show the full extent of his military cooperation with his brother Robert. However, it is important to recognise that Roger, as the count of Sicily was able to call upon the human resources of Sicily to assist in other large-scale sieges, such as the one recorded by the English monk Eadmer at Capua in 1098. Eadmer, who was present at the siege, recalls the many thousands of Roger's Saracen troops gathered beneath the walls. He also recalls how loyal the Saracens seemed to their Norman count. That is not to say that he did not undertake the conquest of Saracen strongholds. In 1091 Roger successfully besieged and exacted tribute from Mdina on the island of Malta, much to the relief of its Christian community, who still pray for the count to this day.

Roger was clearly a consummate military commander. It is fair to say that in Sicily he was not hampered by other Norman families whose southern heritage was already a generation or more in the making. In this way, he had more freedom than his brother to build trust within his own patrimony. His energy was no less than that of the illustrious Guiscard, but there were differences in character and style. His propensity to freely share his riches with his men is in contrast to the character of Robert Guiscard. His offensive campaigns show him to have been decisive in the field and he certainly seems to have learned from any failures in preparation or reconnaissance. His military leadership skills and personal influence over his *familia* are clear. Above all, Roger was a thoughtful and considered man, both as a commander and a ruler. Despite the defeats at Messina (1061) and a later reversal at Syracuse (1075), he achieved outstanding long-term success, providing the platform for Roger II to build a remarkable kingdom.

Chapter 7

William II Rufus, King of England (1087–1100)

Timeline of William II Rufus

1087	Becomes king of the English after the death of the Conqueror
1088	Anglo–Norman barons' rebellion. Sieges of Pevensey, Tonbridge and Rochester. Subsequent siege of Durham Castle and trial of William, bishop of Durham
1089	Death of Archbishop Lanfranc
1089-91	Norman campaigns against brothers Duke Robert II Curthose and Henry
1092	Invasion of Scotland
1093-94	Appointment of Anselm as archbishop of Canterbury. Further campaigns in Normandy against brother Duke Robert. Welsh campaigns and further uprisings whilst away in Normandy
1095	Second baronial uprising - campaigns against Robert de Mowbray across the north of England and Wales and the siege of Bamburgh
1096	Acquires regency over Normandy whilst Duke Robert II Curthose goes on crusade
1097	Welsh campaigns. Exile of Archbishop Anselm. More campaigns in Scotland
1098	Campaigns in the Vexin and re-conquest of Maine
1099	Further campaigns in Maine
1100	Rufus is killed in a hunting accident in the New Forest. Brother Duke Robert II Curthose returns from crusade and resumes role as Norman duke. Brother Henry becomes King Henry I of England

Character and Career

We have a reasonable, if slightly posthumous, description of William II Rufus. Orderic Vitalis almost always called him 'Rufus' and may have borrowed this description from oral tradition. William of Malmesbury in Book IV of his *Gesta Regum* mentions that the king 'had a rufous complexion and yellow hair'. He also mentions different-coloured eyes, short stature and great muscular strength, along

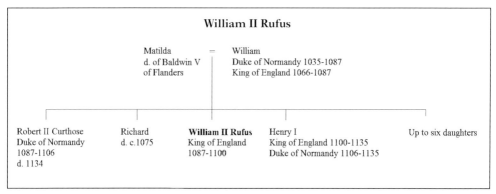

William II Rufus

Matilda   =   William
d. of Baldwin V   Duke of Normandy 1035-1087
of Flanders   King of England 1066-1087

Robert II Curthose	Richard	**William II Rufus**	Henry I	Up to six daughters
Duke of Normandy	d. c.1075	King of England	King of England 1100-1135	
1087-1106		1087-1100	Duke of Normandy 1106-1135	
d. 1134				

Fig. 8

with a protruding belly. Malmesbury says the king wore his blond hair long, parted in the middle, exposing his forehead. This is in marked contrast to the brutally short Danish-style haircuts of his Norman forebears. There was also a lack of eloquence in public and when the king got angry he stuttered and was difficult to understand. Despite a tendency to a quick temper, he was apparently quickly calmed. He was wise enough to handsomely reward people, mainly with riches that did not necessarily impinge on the royal demesne, and yet at the same time was ridiculed for his vanity and poor understanding of the financial value of things.

Later twelfth-century writers repeat the theme of the king's ruddy countenance. For Wace, he was simply William the Red. This third son of William the Conqueror is another Norman against whom the contemporary and later historians have waged a war of propaganda. Whether it was for his suspected homosexuality, the lax morals of his court, his frequent attacks upon the church, his vain and extravagant fashion sense or his fiery temper, we cannot be sure. But in Rufus we have, perhaps unfairly, a character with a lot of ground to make up.

On the Conqueror's death in 1087 Rufus's brother Duke Robert II Curthose succeeded to Normandy. As eldest son, Robert acquired the ancestral land of his father. However, the kingdom of England was a huge prize won by conquest. Orderic tells us that the kingdom of England was entrusted to God himself and that William II Rufus should have it if the Almighty saw fit. Henry, Rufus's younger brother, received a sum of 5,000 pounds. Given the difficult relations between the Conqueror and his son Robert, it is thought likely that the dying king may even have intended Rufus to have the whole package until he was persuaded to reconcile himself with his eldest son at the eleventh hour.

The division of the Conqueror's empire exacerbated the strained relations between the brothers, an antagonism present from an early age. However, it was William II Rufus who returned to England with the future chancellor and bishop of Lincoln Robert Bloet, clutching a sealed letter from the Conqueror to Archbishop Lanfranc and very possibly the royal regalia as well. Significantly,

Rufus was also given control of the English hostage Wulfnoth Godwinson, King Harold's brother. In addition, he took control of another hostage, the former English earl of Northumbria, Morcar.

At Westminster Abbey on Sunday 26 September 1087 Archbishop Lanfranc crowned William II Rufus. His seal would bear the inscription 'William by the Grace of God, king of the English' and he would take as confidants William of Saint Calais, bishop of Durham and Roger Bigot, both of whom had been prominent during his father's reign. And yet William was to be directly challenged. At the heart of this first rebellion was Odo, bishop of Bayeux. The fact that the new king came out on top certainly shows much for his tenacity amid a situation which could well have descended into civil war. By July 1088 it was clear to the barons of England that William would remain as the king of the English. Later in the year one of the key conspirators and the former friend of the king, Bishop William of Saint Calais, was tried for treason. His castle at Durham was besieged. The bishop grudgingly surrendered Durham to the king, who had famously uttered his favourite expression (taken by some to be a profanity) at the bishop's trial:

As you won't accept the judgement of my court, you must now surrender your castle... by the face of Lucca, you'll never escape my hands before I have the castle.

The bishop of Durham sailed from Southampton to join with Robert II Curthose in Normandy. Rufus had flexed his muscles and shown some determination. William of Saint Calais would not be restored to Durham until the autumn of 1091. Some of the rebels were treated with leniency, such as Roger Bigot, but others were less favourably dealt with. The Mowbray family, for example, continued to struggle against the king. Similarly the Clares of Tonbridge were regarded by the king with suspicion. Rufus built a new generation of nobles around him, rewarding them handsomely and playing some clever politics with their appointments. For example, Robert FitzHaimo, the son of the sheriff of Kent, was given Queen Matilda's lands (much to the consternation of the future Henry I) and the honour of Gloucester.

There was a period of peace following the crushing of the rebellion. That same year Lanfranc the Archbishop of Canterbury died. His death marked the beginning of a new era for the king, whose tutor and former patron was now gone. William was much criticised for keeping Canterbury vacant and profiting from its income. Not until 1093 (at a time when the king thought he was terminally ill) was the new archbishop Anselm appointed. The years to come would be marked by disputes with Anselm, who was vocal about the morality of the king's court and a keen ecclesiastical reformer. His opposition to the king would see him exiled in 1097, and his war of words with Rufus damaged the king's reputation.

Another churchman rose to high office under Rufus. His name was Ranulf Flambard. He eventually became bishop of Durham and more or less ran the kingdom while the king was away in Normandy, and he was renowned for his role in extraordinary money-making schemes for the king. With a flair for administration (he had been a key figure in the compilation of the Domesday Book), Flambard was keeper of the king's seal and an energetic builder. He was behind the expansion of the White Tower at London and the building of the city's first stone medieval bridge.

William II Rufus's reign, apart from the constant friction with Anselm, was characterised by energetic military campaigning and the suppression of another revolt in 1095, that of Robert de Mowbray in the north of England. His acquisition of the duchy of Normandy after his brother Robert pawned it to him for 10,000 marks in 1096 was a remarkable moment in his career, plunging him into a set of problems similar to those faced by his father.

There is one moment, of course, which attracts more literature than any other aspect of the king's life, and that is the manner of his death. Hunting accidents in the New Forest were not new. In 1099 Richard, the bastard son of Duke Robert II Curthose, had died in what people called an 'accident' while riding with royal knights hunting deer. One of his own men had shot him with an arrow by accident. There are few discernible undertones of foul play in this report, but the following year the same thing happened to King William II Rufus and still the controversy about what happened rages.

On 2 August 1100, probably near Brockenhurst, the king went hunting. He had delayed his usual dawn start until after his midday meal. Some said he had a hangover from the night before, others that he had a premonition. Within the hunting entourage were Robert FitzHaimo, the king's brother Henry, William of Breteuil and one Walter Tirel (whose affiliations lay with the Clare family of Tonbridge). There were many others too, some with plausible motives for being involved in a plot against Rufus.

William of Malmesbury relates that the hunting party dispersed in its usual way and Walter Tirel and King William were alone together. The sun was low in the sky when William shot at a stag in front of him, which he wounded. Walter shot at a second stag, but hit the king in the chest with an arrow. William broke the arrow off and fell to the ground. Tirel rode up, saw the stricken king and rode away quickly. William of Malmesbury is the first writer to name Tirel as the king's slayer. Some later writers try to suggest that he was not there at all. Orderic Vitalis tells a tale of a blacksmith arriving in the morning with six arrows, two of which the king gave to Tirel, remarking that the deadliest shot should get the sharpest arrows. A monk then arrived from Gloucester bearing a letter to the king from Abbot Serlo, stating that a monk's vision had revealed it was God's intention to punish the king with death for his mistreatment of the church, all of which the king laughed off as superstition. Just a generation after the event, there are

A fanciful depiction of the death of William II Rufus, showing a sheepish Walter Tirel fleeing in the background. By Alphonse de Neuville, 1895.

conflicting accounts of what really happened. Orderic has the hunting party taking their individual stands after scattering in the woods. Walter Tirel, after the king stepped back, unleashed an arrow which grazed the hide of an animal and flew straight into the king, killing him instantly. Henry immediately rode to Winchester (to seize the royal treasury) and Tirel rode away to the coast and fled to France. A few peasants took the body – still copiously bleeding – to Winchester where it was buried in the Old Minster under the tower the next day. Several great magnates were present, but many fled to protect their estates from likely unrest.

Subsequent reports of dire premonitions of churchmen are no surprise, since the king's lifestyle was scorned by them. Nor is it a surprise to learn of the phenomenon of a bleeding well in Berkshire, or the appearance of the Devil himself in woods and other dark places. But history still asks the question – was Walter Tirel the assassin, and if so, did he have criminal intent? Was his connection to the rebel family of the Clares close enough for him to harbour a grudge against the king, or was he simply his friend? We may never know the true answer. The speed with which Henry made his way to Winchester may be a case of understandable opportunism, but there remains the stench of foul play. A king with no direct heir had died in his prime at the age of forty in a hunting incident. That is about as close as we will ever get.

The Commander

It is a striking feature of William II Rufus's military career that he seems not to have fought any major pitched battles. Whether his premature death is the reason for this oddity, or whether this is simply symptomatic of the Norman approach to warfare, is debatable. When dealing with rebellions, Rufus was a competent commander. However, he did not have the devastating resolve of his father when on an offensive campaign. In fact, Rufus's campaigns were often cautious and ponderous affairs resulting in negotiated settlements. But William could not brook any insurrection or threats to his patrimony and he was usually effective at dealing with them.

With this in mind, we should expect the evidence to show the king as a good strategist and this is precisely the case in the first rebellion of 1088. Alongside Odo of Bayeux, there was Odo's rebel brother Robert of Mortain; Earl Roger of Montgomery (whose role is ambiguous); Bishop Geoffrey of Coutances; his nephew Robert de Mowbray (whom only Orderic places alongside the rebels); William the new bishop of Durham; Robert de Bellême and Eustace III of Boulogne. Many others joined in the rebellion and they represented no small part of the landowners of Norman England at the time. The thrust of the rebellion seems to have come from these Norman magnates and not necessarily directly from the duke of Normandy for whom they were agitating. The diocese of Worcester was invaded by Osbern, son of Richard Scrop, and others including the men of Earl Roger, whilst in the East Midlands and East Anglia Hugh of

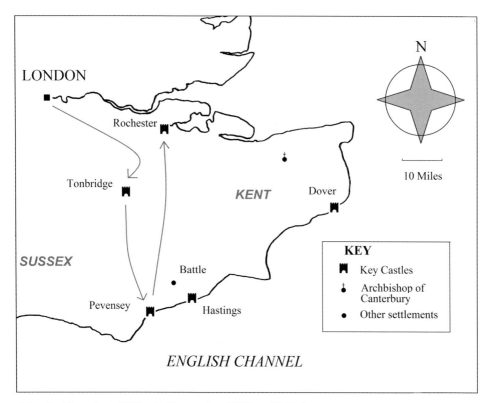

Map 5: Map of the 1088 rebellion against William II Rufus

Grandmesnil (the sheriff of Leicester) and Roger Bigot organised their resistance to the king. But the rebellion was centred on the southeast of England.

Many of the rebels failed to attend the king's Easter court of 1088. This was an obvious sign of things to come. Bishop Geoffrey attacked Bristol and Bath, whilst Count William of Eu attacked the royal estate at Berkeley in Gloucestershire. While Worcester, under Bishop Wulfstan, resisted, Norwich fell under the sword of Roger Bigot. The king raised a force in response. What is important is the order in which the new king took the rebels on. The castles at Rochester, Tonbridge and Pevensey were the key rebel bases. William chose to take out the middle one of these first and conducted a two-day siege against Gilbert FitzRichard at Tonbridge, bringing about its quick surrender. This had a two-fold advantage. The king would not have an enemy directly to his rear when he chose to take on Rochester. Moreover, he had severed the land-based communications between Robert of Mortain's Pevensey garrison and Odo's at Rochester. It was the king's intention to turn from Tonbridge to Rochester after securing the fall of Gilbert FitzRichard. He changed his mind on hearing that Odo had gone to Pevensey. He besieged Pevensey by both land and sea for six weeks. By June the garrison was starved out. Duke Robert II Curthose's relieving naval force had also been defeated and the Rochester siege began in earnest. As the loyal earls gathered with the king and tightened their grip on the castle at Rochester, pestilence gripped the garrison, said by Orderic to be up to 500 men strong under Odo. Without their lord from overseas, and with conditions rapidly declining, the negotiations began.

The closing-out of a siege (when the relieving force fails to appear) was usually a carefully orchestrated matter, with honour at stake for the besieged. It was clear that the rebels would face banishment from England and confiscation of their lands. Odo demanded an additional concession. The trumpets should not sound as he rode out to offer himself, he said. This traditional symbol of surrender was too much for Odo. It also implied that there would never be a second chance to rise against the king. Rufus refused Odo's bizarre request. It was to be a deserved humiliation.

In 1090 the duchy of Normandy was in turmoil. Rufus decided to launch a campaign to punish his brother Robert and to answer an appeal from the Norman church. This campaign shows the king on the offensive and his approach was different to that taken with the Rochester rebellion. William secured garrisons in numerous castles in Upper Normandy with mercenaries, at his own expense, and bought the allegiance of many scattered barons. The campaign came to a head within the walls of Rouen, where an insurrection against Duke Robert was defeated by Rufus and his younger brother Henry, whom he had only recently imprisoned. Later, the differences between the two brothers William and Robert were addressed by a treaty at Rouen in which Robert was to grant William the county of Eu, Fécamp and Cherbourg, while William retained the barons he had

The vestiges of Bishop Gundulf's work at Rochester Castle, in Kent, England, built after the baronial rebellion against William II Rufus in 1088.

Pevensey Castle, Sussex, England. Showing later medieval castle and western entrance. The earlier Norman castle featured in the rebellion against William II Rufus of 1088. To the right of the wooden bridge would have been the sea front, long since receded.

The early Norman Motte at Tonbridge Castle, in Kent, England, from within the bailey (top) and from outside the thirteenth century gatehouse (bottom). Besieged and taken by William II Rufus in 1088.

bought. William was to help the duke recover all their father's lands and give Robert lands in England, restoring the losses of Robert's supporters in the 1088 rebellion. Each brother would become the other's heir if one of them died. There were two losers in the arrangement. The Englishman Edgar the Ætheling lost his Norman lands and subsequently fled to Scotland, while the young Henry became the target of his two elder brothers in a siege at Mont-Saint-Michel in 1091. That siege eventually ended in honourable agreements, which was characteristic of Rufus's campaigns in Normandy.

During the siege at Mont-Saint-Michel, Henry and his men ran short of water. He sent out envoys to Duke Robert decrying his wickedness at allowing his own sibling to suffer. Robert then sent water into the fortification, to the fury of his brother King William. The king's comment to his brother the duke, as recorded by William of Malmesbury, perhaps outlines which of the two elder brothers was the more ruthless: 'A fine sort of general you are, sending water to the enemy! How can we possibly conquer them if we provide them with food and drink?'

The brothers William and Duke Robert returned to England in 1091 in order to confront a Scottish invasion of the north of England by Malcolm III, king of the Scots, which was launched in May, striking terror into the inhabitants. Suspecting Welsh intrigue, William also campaigned in Wales, where he lost many men and horses and was said by William of Malmesbury never to have quite grasped the difficulties of the terrain and poor weather. Warfare in this country was characterised by chance encounters, ambushes and trickery and cost many a leader, both Norman and Welsh, his life. However, it was the work of his Marcher barons rather than William himself which saw consolidation and gains in the years 1092–93.

William's subsequent invasion of Scotland came after a successful attack against the Scots by the Norman nobleman Nigel d'Aubigny. Rufus's campaign saw no set-piece battles, but succeeded in bringing Malcolm to an agreement whereby the Scot became the English king's man in much the same way as he had been under the Conqueror. What is more to the point is that the expedition – by both land and sea – had echoes of the past in it. The great Anglo-Saxon king Athelstan (924–939) had journeyed into Scotland in 934, supported by a naval force and achieved great successes with the aim of subjugating the ruler of the Scots. William's expedition, although fraught with setbacks, was designed to do the same thing. The fifty ships which sailed up the coast in late September were laden with corn from Wessex to support the land troops who had marched up the Great North Road. The ships, however, were wrecked upon the shores of Coquet Island to the north of Tynemouth, but it is a measure of the king's determination that William pushed on with his land force and still managed to bring Malcolm to an agreement.

William came to Cumbria the next year with a large army and drove out an obscure leader called Dolfin – a subordinate of the Scottish king – and established an English settlement at Carlisle, where he built a castle, thus restoring what had been the frontier of England and Scotland to its pre-eleventh century lines. As for Malcolm, he would meet his end in an ambush on his fifth and final raid against England, organised by Earl Robert de Mowbray on 13 November 1093.

With Wales subdued, Carlisle firmly fortified and Scotland at least managed, William turned his attention to Normandy after a falling out with Duke Robert over certain failures in fulfilling the treaty of Rouen. Inconclusive campaigning followed in Normandy with only one success reported for William – the capture of Helias of Saint Saëns's castle at Bures-en-Bray and the taking of Duke Robert's garrison there. These prisoners were sent back to England. Eadmer accuses William of spending a huge amount of money for no real purpose in this campaign and, despite the bias of Eadmer (who was Saint Anselm's biographer), this is true of William's approach to foreign offensive wars as a whole.

William faced a new baronial plot in 1095 spearheaded by Robert de Mowbray, earl of Northumbria. It was in some way linked via its members to the revolt of 1088. Apart from the earl himself the principal rebels were Hugh and Philip, the sons of Roger of Montgomery, William of Eu, Gilbert FitzRichard (who soon went over to the king and became an informer) and Stephen of Aumale who, after the failure of this second rebellion wisely chose to go on crusade.

The triggers for the uprising were said to have been the king's heavy taxation of his subjects to pay for his wars and also an extraordinary incident in which Robert de Mowbray and his nephew Morel plundered four recently arrived Norwegian merchant ships for which the king had to indemnify the complainants. Rufus summoned the earl to his court, but refused to grant him safe conduct. Robert did not come. And so the king headed north.

Robert de Mowbray steeled himself. He sent his (unnamed) brother to hold the line along the River Tyne while he held back further north. The first obstacle for William was the newly built fortress at Newcastle (built in 1080 by Duke Robert II Curthose and now in the hands of Mowbray). The king, always energetic when dealing with rebels, chose to cross the Tyne much further to the west, probably at Corbridge. He attacked the small castle at Morpeth on the River Wensbeck, which fell quickly, and this capitulation caused the more southerly castle at Newcastle to be isolated. After two months it fell. Robert de Mowbray retreated to Bamburgh followed by the king. The king's strategy bears similarities to the Kent campaign of 1088 inasmuch as he had taken out the middle castle. He then advanced on Bamburgh. During his approach to the famous northern citadel Gilbert FitzRichard warned Rufus of a plot to ambush him and admitted he had been one of the conspirators himself. Consequently, knowing that he could not directly assault the fortress due to its formidable disposition, William set up a counter castle (for the roles of which, see pages 196-199 below) named 'Malveisin' or 'bad neighbour' and settled for a siege. Whilst at Malveisin, William heard that the Welsh had taken Montgomery and were once again in revolt. He was comfortable enough with the effectiveness of the fort at Malveisin that he was able to release part of his army to attend to a new Welsh campaign.

Robert de Mowbray planned to escape from the castle. Under cover of darkness, he slipped out of Bamburgh with thirty of his men and headed to Newcastle. But the garrison of Malveisin spotted him. He fled instead to the monastery of Saint Oswin at Tynemouth. Here he was besieged by the forces of the king and in the fighting he lost many men and was wounded himself. Robert was dragged from his sanctuary and conveyed to Bamburgh, where the king threatened to put his eyes out before the walls of the castle unless it surrendered. The citadel duly fell and William subsequently took Northumbria into his control and threw Robert de Mowbray into jail at Windsor. Robert languished in prison until his death some two or more decades later. As for William of Eu, one of the leading rebels whose defection had upset the king greatly, his fate at the hands of his castrator was perhaps worse than that of Robert. He did not recover from his wounds.

After the king had obtained control over Normandy from Duke Robert, who went on crusade in 1096, his concerns were once again with the borders of his kingdom: his Marcher barons were on the offensive in Wales. There were two royal expeditions in 1097. On his return from one of them William was incensed by the quality of some of the knights Anselm had sent him, complaining that their training was not fit for purpose. It is an interesting comment. Earl Harold Godwinson, on his successful campaigns in Wales in the early 1060s, had deliberately ordered his usually heavily armoured housecarls to wear lighter body armour in a bid to adapt to the difficult terrain. Perhaps the Norman king expected a similar degree of flexibility.

Scotland also beckoned in 1097. But this was not guerrilla warfare in mountainous terrain like it had been in Wales. Rufus sent Edgar the Ætheling to confront the new Scottish king Donald Bane and he managed to defeat him in open battle with an army which he was allowed to recruit from England. The eventual result of this victory was the placement upon the Scottish throne of a more agreeable candidate (another Edgar, son of Malcolm).

William II Rufus soon prepared to leave for Normandy. According to the *Anglo-Saxon Chronicle*, while waiting for favourable conditions to depart, his army at Southampton did more damage in the area than a raiding army. This behaviour was an aspect of Rufus's military approach which contemporaries viewed with consternation. Discipline when on campaign was very important to the Norman commanders and here, in his own country, the king can perhaps be found wanting.

With Normandy now in his care, and his brother Robert far away en route to the Holy Land, the English king saw an opportunity to lay claim to the Vexin. This region, with its principal towns on the French side at Chaumont, Mantes and Pontoise, had been the focus of his father's final campaigns in the late 1080s. Between 1097 and 1099 the Vexin wars against the forces of the French king Philip I

(1059–1108) proved to be expensive (for William recruited a great many French mercenaries) and were poorly recorded by the English sources. Robert de Bellême seems to have been the English king's Magister Militum, or commander in the field. Others who accompanied William on these campaigns included his younger brother Henry, Walter Giffard, William of Evreux and Hugh of Chester. It was during these campaigns that the king laid the foundations for the impressive frontier castle at Gisors, with the assistance of Robert de Bellême, before going off with the latter to campaign in Maine.

Gisors castle in the Vexin, France. Begun by English King William II Rufus (1087-1100) and improved with walls and towers by Henry I (1100-1135), the castle stood on the frontier between Normandy and lands controlled by the French king.

The main feature of the fighting in the Vexin was the capture of prisoners on both sides. The English king demanded high ransoms for his prisoners, which he knew the French could ill afford to pay, and so he held on to them, making them swear allegiance to him and fight on his side. Conversely, when one of Rufus's own men was captured, he paid up promptly to the French king who then ploughed the revenue back into the war effort.

In Maine, the campaigns were more aggressive. They were driven by Robert de Bellême's struggle against the northward expansion of Helias of Maine. Robert already had a total of nine castles in the region, but it was Helias's establishment of a castle at Dangeul, just a day's march from Bellême, which represented a threat to Robert and William alike. Soon Helias was to fall foul of Robert's ambush tactics – he was captured in a wood while raiding from Ballon along with seven of his men. He was handed over to the English king who incarcerated him in Bayeux.

There was, however, an Angevin reaction to this aggression: Fulk of Anjou occupied Le Mans. William held a council at Rouen and summoned his vassals. The barons decided that operations in Maine would take precedence over those in the Vexin. In June the army set off, passing Alençon and heading for Le Mans. Ballon was captured and garrisoned and an unsuccessful siege of Le Mans followed, which was thwarted by a lack of supplies for William's horses. William therefore turned back for Normandy, intent on returning after the harvest, giving Fulk's men an opportunity to take the initiative. One morning when the Angevins were camped in their tents around Ballon eating breakfast, their ill-preparedness was observed by some local beggars who alerted the garrison. The garrison rode out and captured four castellans and 140 knights.

At the end of July King William came again to Ballon with his army. Here, we learn of William the soldier king observing the knightly code, to the surprise and admiration of those around him. The Angevin prisoners cried to the king of the English for their freedom when he entered the town. William ordered their release on parole and asked for them to be fed a good meal alongside his own men, placing trust in them because they were knights. Fulk, however, had re-entered Le Mans. This prompted the imprisoned Helias to call for the leading citizens of Le Mans to come to him and agree to surrender the town to William, which they did. Fulk apparently acquiesced. A treaty was arranged, after which Robert of Montfort, William's commander, took 700 knights into Le Mans to take over from the Angevin garrison and William himself entered the town in great pomp and splendour amid scenes reminiscent of those his father had enjoyed in 1063. As for Helias, he was eventually released – after a heated argument with the English king over the nature of his future possessions – and went back to Maine, where he gathered his strength once again, closely watched by Robert de Bellême.

Robert de Bellême

The eldest son of Roger of Montgomery, Robert de Bellême was heir to important estates on the southern marches of Normandy, which straddled Norman and French territories. His career was an example of how Norman noblemen could easily shift their allegiance from one lord to another. He supported Duke Robert II Curthose before switching allegiance to William II Rufus in 1094, returning to Curthose after the latter's death. He had a long period of struggles with Henry I, which eventually saw him imprisoned for life in 1112. He had been acquisitive and was particularly strong after 1098, when he added the rape of Arundel and the earldom of Shrewsbury to an impressive list. But Robert de Bellême was also a consummate commander. He led the king's *familia* into Maine and was widely known for his mastery of siege warfare. Robert also had a reputation for extreme cruelty, even by the standards of the day. He often tortured his enemies after capturing them.

Further campaigns in the Vexin followed for the English king, including a significant setback at Chaumont (see page 201). He returned to England in 1099 with the Vexin wars unconcluded. We can never know how he would have approached a resumption of the campaigns, or whether he would have broken through the screen of castles protecting the French king and gone on to Paris itself.

In 1099, when the king was back in England, he received news that Helias had entered Le Mans and the Norman garrison was under severe pressure. Once again Rufus showed himself to be energetic in responding to a challenge to his authority. The sources write of him jumping on his horse and heading for the English coast, not even pausing to issue a summons for warriors to follow him. He was sure, they said, that his men would rally to him. He persuaded a ship's captain to navigate the choppy Channel and when he arrived in Normandy he made for Bonneville, where he sent orders for an army to assemble.

With Robert of Montfort as his commander, the king's army was gathered and quickly marched on Le Mans. Helias wisely withdrew to the south. The city had been virtually burnt out. William rode through it and camped with his army on the other side of the River Huisne. He did his best to prevent his army from wrecking Le Mans and it was Helias, not William who burned towns in his wake as he withdrew. Finally, Helias made a stand at Mayet. The king came to him here, settling for a siege after observing a truce for a few days in which both sides made preparations for the fighting that would follow. At the launch of the direct assault on Mayet, the garrison poured cauldrons of burning charcoal into the ditches below them, which William had filled to make the ground level. As the flames leapt up a knight standing next to the king was struck by a stone and killed, much to the delight of the defenders. William realised that a direct assault was not possible and instead settled for a wide-scale ravaging of the countryside. Content with this strategic action and the retaking of Le Mans, William returned to that city and paid off his army. He then returned to England at Easter 1099.

Before his unexpected death William had every right to feel enthusiastic about the future. He was even entertaining thoughts about a move into Aquitaine. His Whitsun court at Westminster in London was a spectacle to behold. There was great feasting in the new Westminster Hall, a building he commissioned that still stands today. He also had a surrounding wall built around the White Tower in London, a project masterminded by Gundulf, bishop of Rochester and begun by the Conqueror in 1078.

While many medieval commentators saw faults in the king's character, as a military commander he had fewer detractors. William II Rufus was a hard-hitting soldier king, born into the military way of life with scarcely a moment spent away from it. He took strong control of his subordinates and generally appointed good and loyal sub-commanders. As a strategist he was masterful, as the campaigns of 1088 and 1095 in England show. Yet his swiftness in dealing with rebellions was not matched by the way in which he tackled more general campaigns. These were attritional, usually costing him dearly in money and equipment. His courage was second to none, and like many courageous commanders he rode his luck well. Writing later in the twelfth century John of Salisbury wrote favourably of the Maine campaigns and dared to compare Rufus with the other great commanders of the age, even promoting him in honour above his own father.

If there was a negative side to the military man, it might be his lack of regard for the populations his army passed through. This was a legacy perhaps born out of life-long soldiering, or simply contempt for the common folk. This notwithstanding, he displayed – like his father before him – the same mixture of cruelty and magnanimity which so characterised the Norman leaders. Were it not for a single arrow, shot either by design or accident, we should have known so much more.

Chapter 8

Robert II Curthose, Duke of Normandy (1087–1106)

Timeline of Robert II Curthose, Duke of Normandy

1062	Betrothal to Margaret the count of Maine's sister who later dies
1077-78	Rebellion against father William the Conqueror
1079	Battle of Gerberoi, in which Robert unhorses and nearly kills his father
1080	Robert reconciled with William. Invasion of Scotland
1083	Further rifts with William
1087	Death of William I. Robert inherits Normandy and William II Rufus inherits the kingdom of England
1088-91	Brothers Duke Robert and King William II Rufus in conflict. Robert fails to attend an English rebellion against his brother. Campaigns in Maine
1091	Reconciliation and the drawing up of the Constitutiones et Justice on the rights of the Duke of Normandy
1096	Goes on the First Crusade and mortgages Normandy to William II Rufus for 10,000 marks
1097	Fall of Nicaea and the Battle of Dorylaeum
1097-98	Siege of Antioch
1099	The fall of Jerusalem and the subsequent Battle of Ascalon
1100	Return from the crusade, death of William II Rufus in a hunting incident
1101	Lands in Portsmouth in England. Treaty of Alton whereby Robert relinquishes his claim to the throne of England
1103	Suffers defeat to Robert de Bellême at Exmes
1105	King Henry I of England lands at Barfleur with a strong Anglo-Norman force
1106	Battle of Tinchebrai. Defeat and capture. The Anglo-Norman realm is reformed. William Clito, son of Robert Curthose is given refuge by the king of France

1106-1134 Incarceration at Devizes castle and Cardiff castle for the rest of his life

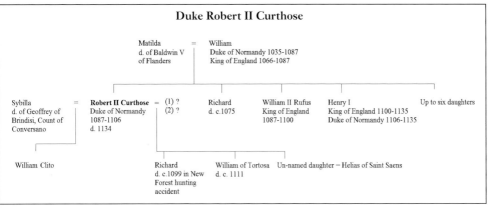

Duke Robert II Curthose

Matilda = William
d. of Baldwin V   Duke of Normandy 1035-1087
of Flanders   King of England 1066-1087

Sybilla = Robert II Curthose = (1) ?   Richard   William II Rufus   Henry I   Up to six daughters
d. of Geoffrey of   Duke of Normandy   (2) ?   d. c.1075   King of England   King of England 1100-1135
Brindisi, Count of   1087-1106   1087-1100   Duke of Normandy 1106-1135
Conversano   d. 1134

William Clito   Richard   William of Tortosa   Un-named daughter = Helias of Saint Saens
                                       d. c.1099 in New   d. c. 1111
                                       Forest hunting
                                       accident

Fig. 9

Character and Career

History has not been kind to Duke Robert II Curthose, the eldest son of William the Conqueror. Those who wrote about him in the twelfth century, such as Orderic Vitalis and William of Malmesbury, did so with the knowledge of Robert's disastrous loss of Normandy in 1106 and subsequent lengthy incarceration. Robert did not die until 1134, having been held captive at Devizes Castle and later at Cardiff Castle. He died at the age of eighty-three with his reputation in tatters; a reputation which remains stubbornly negative, despite many attempts to restore it.

Robert's own father coined the phrase 'curtaocrea', or 'short boots' to describe his son, and it was hardly meant as a term of endearment. The main accusations against Robert were of his inattentiveness, idleness (failing even to attend the rebellion in England in 1088, which might have put him on the throne), a love of the finer things in life and the oft-repeated assertion that Robert II Curthose was simply too magnanimous with his enemies and other wrongdoers. Orderic Vitalis leads the charge against Robert in this respect, adding to his list of Robert's failings that the duke's loss of his Norman duchy after the Battle of Tinchebrai in 1106 was down to the judgement of God.

But there were two sides to Duke Robert. For all the allegations that he was extravagant and lavish and wanted to please others, he was also a pious crusading knight whose bravery was much commented upon. He was an adventurous man in these accounts and he was also an eloquent communicator – even Orderic tells us this much. Perhaps Robert's character was shaped by family dynamics. His mother Matilda seems to have favoured him on at least one occasion (even funding him during his rebellion against her own husband, William the Conqueror), but it was his relationship with his brothers William II Rufus and Henry I, and with his father, which seem to have dictated his actions throughout his political life. Robert probably felt he deserved so much more after the split of England and Normandy in 1087, but he was indecisive. The duke acknowledged his own failure to assist the 1088 rebellion in England. On 7 July that year he issued a charter in which he added the phrase 'when I should have crossed to England'. Robert did, however, try to prosecute a claim to the English throne in 1101, but his quick-thinking brother Henry outmanoeuvred him and had already had himself crowned, despite the fact that Rufus and Robert had agreed to be each other's heir. After landing at Portsmouth Robert found his support was weak and at the subsequent treaty of Alton he was forced to renounce his claim to the throne in return for a generous stipend.

Robert's brothers out-foxed him on a number of occasions. Sibling rivalry was never far from the surface, with two of them joining forces against the third. However, one incident probably outlines Duke Robert II's character the best, if we choose to believe it. In 1078 Robert demanded from his father the control of Normandy and Maine. In fact, later in his ducal reign there are hints that Robert considered his rule to have started from this time and not ten years later on the death of his father. However, in one (perhaps fictitious) incident recounted by Orderic Vitalis, things came to a head at a bizarre incident at L'Aigle when the young brothers Henry and William tipped a full chamberpot over Robert's head. Spurred on by the encouragement of others and angered that William the Conqueror had not chastised his sons, Robert not only flew into a rage, but also went off and started a full-blown rebellion.

Robert was able to call upon the support of important nobles in Normandy, indicating that his reputation was not always poor. He was particularly attractive to the sons of some of these nobles when he was at loggerheads with his father. William of Breteuil (the son of William FitzOsbern), Yves and Aubrey, the sons of Hugh of Grandmesnil and Roger, the son of Richard FitzGilbert, all sought to follow Robert at one stage or other.

A picture emerges of a man caught up in family frictions who had a difficult relationship with his father – a man also prone to favour the negotiated settlement, and to indulgence and lechery. The year before his final disaster at Tinchebrai Robert is to be found one Easter morning with an almighty hangover after a night of carousing and womanising. His 'friends' stole his clothes, forcing Robert to stay in bed all day long. As a consequence he missed the Bishop of Sées's Easter sermon. But it is on a note of piety that the story turns for Duke Robert, the much-maligned duke of Normandy. His religious fervour led him to answer the infamous call of Pope Urban II, issued at the Council of Clermont in 1095, and he set off on the First Crusade (1096-1099). His reputation as a Christian warrior far outshone his general reputation as a ruler. But what, if anything, can we glean about his style of warfare?

Gloucester Cathedral, England. Tomb of Duke Robert II Curthose, Duke of Normandy (1087-1106) who died in prison in 1134.

The Commander

Those who seek to defame Duke Robert II Curthose suggest that his crusading zeal was a reaction to the fact that he could not bear the pressures of rule in Normandy. Orderic Vitalis even says that everyone had abandoned him and that Normandy was in turmoil in 1095. This may have been the case, but the duke probably did feel he was answering a genuine spiritual call. Moreover, he was one of the more experienced commanders on the First Crusade and his influence appears to have been great. There were of course, many other Western nobles who answered the call of Pope Urban II, such as Stephen Count of Blois, Robert II Count of Flanders, Raymond of Toulouse, Bohemond (pages 100-114), Tancred de Hauteville, Baldwin of Boulogne, Godfrey of Bouillon and Hugh of Vermondois. Robert's own military experience, however, was greater than many of them.

From what we know of Robert's style of warfare in his native Normandy, it would seem that it was no different than that of his father William the Conqueror and many before and after him. Sieges predominated. When Robert was besieged by the Conqueror at Gerberoi on the Vexin frontier in 1079, he sallied out from the castle and wounded and unhorsed his father. According to the chronicler John of Worcester, on recognising his father's voice Robert gave him his own horse to escape on. When Robert took over the duchy after his father's death in 1087 he was faced with a patchwork of differing loyalties and many of the nobles in the region were hostile to him. Recovering castles at Alençon, Evreux and Conches therefore took up much campaigning time.

Robert is sometimes accused of lacking the ability to instil discipline in his armies. This is borne out by the example of the siege at Vignats in 1102. Orderic describes it thus:

> ...but because the duke was indolent and soft, and lacked the firmness proper to a prince, Robert of Montfort and other fellow conspirators, who were divided among themselves, deliberately set fire to their own tents, created turmoil in the army, and fled the scene without anyone pursuing them. In this way they forced others with ill will toward the hateful Robert to join them in their shameful flight. The garrison saw the disgrace of the Norman army and howled derisively after them.

In the run-of-the-mill campaigning and small-scale siege warfare that characterised his military affairs in Normandy Robert was sometimes ineffective, but during the first crusade he seems to have been more successful. Robert had certainly proved capable of keeping discipline in the ranks when on crusade. The behaviour of his contingent on its landing at Dyrrhachium en route to Constantinople is an example. Previous crusading groups had clashed with Byzantine forces whilst out foraging, but this was not the case with Robert's forces. Reaching Constantinople in April 1097, Robert and Stephen of Blois met with the emperor and swore oaths to him. On reaching Nicaea, he joined with Raymond of Toulouse and Robert of Flanders, committing himself to the southern section of the siege. The city fell on 19 June 1097, but it was the Byzantines who organised and implemented its takeover, much to the crusader's chagrin.

The crusaders headed for Jerusalem, shadowed by a Turkish force under Kilij Arslan. The resulting Battle of Dorylaeum, fought on 1 July 1097, was a huge and complex affair in which Robert's contribution earned him respect for keeping a tight and disciplined formation, exhibiting personal bravery and for having the leadership skills so seldom attributed to him.

Robert's contribution to the continuing fight en route to Jerusalem is next evidenced at the bridge over the River Orontes in October 1097. His army was now in the vanguard of the crusader forces and succeeded in defeating a defending force here. Antioch was the next target. But Robert withdrew from the subsequent siege of Antioch, retiring to Latakia on the Syrian coast. This port was crucial to Antioch, so Robert's arrival there and the fact that it had been taken by the Englishmen in the service of the Byzantine emperor probably had more to do with the logistical operation at Antioch than it had to do with Robert preferring an easier life away from the siege. Robert, however, turning a suspiciously deaf ear to pleas for his return, finally came back in February 1098, although he took no part in the crusader's defeat of a Turkish relieving force under Ridwan of Aleppo on 9

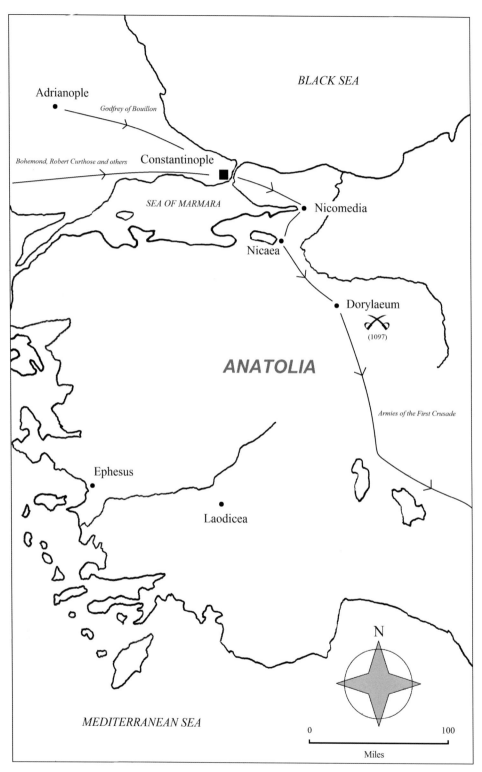

BLACK SEA

Adrianople

Godfrey of Bouillon

Bohemond, Robert Curthose and others

Constantinople

SEA OF MARMARA

Nicomedia

Nicaea

Dorylaeum

(1097)

ANATOLIA

Armies of the First Crusade

Ephesus

Laodicea

N

MEDITERRANEAN SEA

0   100

Miles

Map 6: The First Crusade in Anatolia

February. Antioch fell to the crusaders in June 1098. There were high-profile desertions among the crusaders and many hardships. However, Robert was among those who remained (along with Bohemond and Raymond of Toulouse), all three of them swearing oaths not to leave. There followed arguments between Bohemond and Raymond as to who would control Antioch (the crusaders were in no mood to hand it to the Byzantines). Here, Robert gained a reputation for diplomacy lacking in some of his contemporaries.

Finally, after further dissent and infighting, on 7 June 1099 the crusaders wept as they approached the city of Jerusalem. Robert was among them. Quite what impact the resulting massacre in the streets of the city had on Robert is difficult to tell. The fall of Jerusalem remains controversial, and in Robert's case we have only snippets of material to give his view of it all. He actively contributed to the assault on the city. However, William of Malmesbury asserts that he refused to become the king of Jerusalem, later being punished for it by God by the loss of his beloved Normandy in 1106. Had it not been for that loss of his duchy, one wonders what Robert's reputation as a military man might have been. His finest hour was in August 1099 when the Fatimid Egyptian ruler sent an army under Vizier al-Afdal to Jerusalem. There was a major battle at Ascalon to the south-west of the city where Robert, Godfrey of Bouillon, Robert of Flanders and Tancred occupied the vital centre of the crusader line. Robert charged directly at the enemy standard-bearer's tent and captured the standard itself, for which he was highly praised.

And yet Robert, the spirited and devout crusading knight, still lacks something as a commander. Strategically, he appears to have lacked the decisiveness of his father or the resourcefulness of his two brothers. Tactically, a direct charge at an enemy standard-bearer may have produced results, but the exact circumstances are unclear. It is also true that Robert's brothers were more wily and perhaps more cut-throat in their approach to military matters. That is not to say that Robert could not exercise some measured cruelty of his own when on campaign. In 1088, to inspire terror in Maine, he had the castellan of St-Céneri blinded and others mutilated, although once again his campaign appears to have petered out.

Robert suffered a humiliation in 1103, after he had ceded many rights to the turbulent Robert de Bellême. The duke had gone to Exmes in order to subdue de Bellême, who had taken many castles. Orderic Vitalis tells us that the duke's forces were drawn out by the rebellious count and repeatedly attacked. Although the two opposing commanders would soon ally together against King Henry I of England, this vaguely recorded encounter at Exmes resulted in a defeat for the post-crusade Duke Robert and a disastrous downturn in his reputation as a commander. He even suffered the ignominy of the capture of William of Conversano, his wife's brother and close advisor.

The defeat to his brother Henry I at the Battle of Tinchebrai in 1106 (pages 133–137) spelt the end for Robert's military career. His subsequent life as a political prisoner in England seems a very long way from the parched battlefields of the Holy Land. Later writers thought Robert had escaped his brother's prison and tried to raise an army against him. By the time Matthew Paris and Roger of Wendover were writing in the early thirteenth century, the story had developed to the point where it was said that Henry I imprisoned his brother on an even stricter basis after his recapture. There is also the suggestion that he may have been blinded, although this seems unlikely. Perhaps the old man's eyesight simply failed. We may never know if Robert had the courage and guile to escape, but if there is a kernel of truth in the story, Robert's reputation may yet be rescued. What is more certain is that he died in captivity in February 1134 in Cardiff and was subsequently buried in Saint Peter's Abbey, Gloucester. Today, Duke Robert's reputation is being re-evaluated by modern historians, but the power of medieval propaganda may be too strong for opinion about him to change.

Chapter 9

Henry I, King of England (1100–1135), Duke of Normandy (1106–1135)

Timeline of Henry I, King of England (1100-1135)

1100	Becomes king of England after William II Rufus dies in the New Forest
1101	Treaty of Alton
1102	Campaign against Robert of Bellême in England. Siege of Bridgnorth
1103	Self-imposed exile of Archbishop Anslem
1105-06	Campaigns in Normandy. Battle of Tinchebrai, 1106. Capture and imprisonment of Robert
1109-14	Death of Archbishop Anselm. Defensive campaigns in newly acquired Normandy
1109-11	Campaigns against King Louis VI of France around the disputed Vexin region
1111-13	Campaigns in Maine against the count of Anjou
1116-19	More campaigns in defence of the Norman duchy
1118	Defeated at the Battle of Alençon
1119	Victory over the French king at Battle of Brémule
1120	White Ship disaster: Henry's heir William Adelin is drowned off the coast of Barfleur
1121	Campaigns in Wales. Wounded by an arrow in Powys during ambush
1123	Campaigns against rebels in Normandy and invasion from Anjou and France
1124	Henry's *Familia Regis* performs outstandingly at the Battle of Bourgthéroulde
1135	Henry dies on 1 December and his body is brought from Normandy and buried in Reading Abbey

Character and Career

Henry was perhaps the most colourful of the Conqueror's brood. Born somewhere in England after the coronations of his parents in around 1068, Henry was thus born 'in the purple'. He would not forget that he was a Norman at heart. His tireless campaigns in Normandy after 1106 were fought to retain his father's

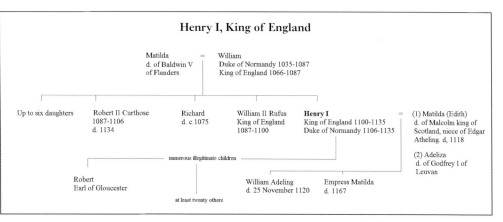

Henry I, King of England

Matilda d. of Baldwin V of Flanders	= William Duke of Normandy 1035-1087 King of England 1066-1087

Up to six daughters

Robert II Curthose
1087-1106
d. 1134

Richard
d. c.1075

William II Rufus
King of England
1087-1100

Henry I
King of England 1100-1135
Duke of Normandy 1106-1135

(1) Matilda (Edith)
d. of Malcolm king of
Scotland, niece of Edgar
Atheling. d, 1118

(2) Adeliza
d. of Godfrey I of
Leuvan

numerous illegitimate children

Robert
Earl of Gloucester

William Adeling
d. 25 November 1120

Empress Matilda
d. 1167

at least twenty others

Fig. 10

patrimony and he spent a good deal of time away from England. Nonetheless, there is a school of thought which presents him as something of an anglophile, who paid close attention to the need for continuity in the royal succession from the time of the Anglo-Saxon kings, and even encouraged intermarriage between his Norman nobles and the indigenous English. This is perhaps to overstate the king's fondness for the English (for which he was ridiculed by some), but it does show a considerable degree of political acumen. Henry did not, however, promote Englishmen to positions of rank.

Educated probably by Bishop Osmund of Salisbury, and later mentored by Bishop Roger of Salisbury, who more or less ran his government for him, Henry's intellect displayed itself on the campaign trial, in political alliances and on the battlefield itself. Knighted by his father in 1086, the eighteen-year-old Henry knew that he lived in the shadow of his two older brothers. As the youngest son, he would have felt that his entitlement to the lands of his mother Matilda should have been automatic (as was traditional), but this did not occur when his father died. Henry had to endure a long wait for a fief from which to draw an income and build a future.

On the death of the Conqueror in 1087 Henry received his cash payment from his father in English coinage. He wept at this inheritance – his older brothers had received so much more in landed wealth. The dying king had said to his son that he would one day inherit the whole patrimony. It would be a long time coming. Often accused in later years of loving wealth and riches, Henry sped away from his father's deathbed and had his inheritance weighed. His fastidious approach to his finances would earn him the sobriquet 'clerc' and 'beauclerc' in the thirteenth and fourteenth centuries. But his love of money did him no harm when he was king of England. He was able to gather around him a well-paid and supplied military household. He also acquired some exotic creatures, including a porcupine, which he kept at Woodstock, and many relics which he collected and gave to his beloved Reading Abbey later in life.

Henry was the only one of the three brothers to attend his father's funeral, after which he embarked upon thirteen years of wanderings, moving between the courts of his brothers William and Robert. While he made little political progress in these early years, he began his career as a womaniser. His first acknowledged mistress was Ansfrida, whom he met at Abingdon, but there were many others including a Welsh princess, one or more Englishwomen and even ladies of noble rank within the Norman and Anglo-Norman community. The illegitimate children, some of whom would play significant roles in his reign and thereafter, numbered over twenty.

Henry used his inheritance to buy a grant of rights over the Cotentin in Normandy from his brother Duke Robert. From now on, he would have lordship over the lands of Earl Hugh of Chester and those of the community at Mont-Saint-Michel. But in 1088 suspicion about Henry's loyalties grew when he returned from an unsuccessful trip to see King William II Rufus, where he had made a plea for his mother's lands which was eventually rejected. Along with Robert de Bellême Henry was imprisoned by Duke Robert. He is unlikely to have forgotten the six months he spent incarcerated by his brother. On his eventual release he turned to Rufus and was rebuffed. He then retreated to his castles in the west, narrowly escaping imprisonment again.

Accusations of cruelty are sometimes thrown at Henry. In 1090 he came to the aid of his brother Duke Robert during a rebellion in Rouen. Both he and Gilbert de l'Aigle defended the town from an uprising inspired by Conan, son of Pilatus (who had probably been a local burgess). Between them Henry and Gilbert crushed the revolt and Henry turned on Conan, marching him to the top of the tower, mockingly showing him the land he might have taken from his duke, and then, to the growing horror of Conan, who guessed what was coming, he threw him off the tower to his death. Henry's was a starkly contrasting character to that of Duke Robert. In one cruel stroke (although it should be borne in mind that Conan was not a nobleman) he had demonstrated the authority his brother lacked. But soon Henry was to find himself on the wrong side of both his brothers and under siege from them at Mont-Saint-Michel. A treaty William and Robert had made at Rouen had left Henry sidelined.

After the siege at Mont-Saint-Michel Henry wandered once again, variously reported in the Vexin or at the French court. Then the garrison at the border castle at Domfront appealed to him after his brothers' falling-out. It was a turning point for Henry. By 1094 he was spending Christmas in England with William II Rufus. When Duke Robert went on crusade Henry was recognised by William, not just in the Cotentin, but also in Bessin and therefore in Bayeux and Caen. The sources are silent for the next four years. Henry accompanied William on his Vexin campaigns and must have fought alongside Robert de Bellême (long since released), and may even have gone to Maine with the king. What we do know, however, is that Henry was in the New Forest on the day William was killed.

On 5 August 1100, with the Treasury at Winchester secure, Henry was crowned king of England. Only three days had passed since William's death. At the coronation promises were made about the abolition of unjust taxes and freedom for the church and, as an example, Ranulf Flambard, one of Rufus's most valued bishops, was arrested and imprisoned in the Tower of London, from which he would later escape. The exiled Archbishop Anselm was asked to return to England as well. Henry quickly realised his claim to the throne would carry more weight in the country if he took a bride of royal standing. He chose Matilda (formerly Edith), the daughter of Malcolm, king of the Scots. She was the niece of Edgar the Ætheling and a direct descendant of the ancient royal house of Wessex. It was a monumental moment in English history. The male offspring of such a union would bring the hope of uniting England and Normandy through the ancient bloodline. In 1103 a boy was born who was named William Adelin (or 'Atheling'). Although the couple already had a daughter, Matilda, William Adelin carried the title given to Anglo-Saxon princes and on his shoulders rested a great burden of tradition.

Statues of Henry I (left) and his wife Matilda (right), Rochester Cathedral, England. Matilda, or more appropriately 'Edith' was descended from the Anglo-Saxon royal line. Here, her statue is entirely defaced. Opponents of Henry mockingly referred to them both as 'Godric and Godiva.'

The early years of the century were occupied by campaigning in England against Robert de Bellême and further campaigns in Normandy, where Henry was becoming increasingly dissatisfied with the ineffective rule of his brother, who had now returned from crusade and teamed up with Robert de Bellême. After the Battle of Tinchebrai and the wresting of control over Normandy, Henry promoted some of his key supporters. Nigel d'Aubigny was given lands in the region of Argentan at Château-Goutier and also handsomely rewarded in Yorkshire, and the veteran Count Robert of Meulan was made earl of Leicester, to name but a few. But these years of Henry's reign were overshadowed by the spectre of the claim to the duchy of Normandy from William Clito, Duke Robert's son. Clito was an influential man and for some time had the support of the French king Louis VI (1081–1137). Henry – a master of the political alliance – tried tirelessly to strategically weaken the threat. His daughter Matilda went to the German court of Henry V, and there was also a renewal of an earlier Anglo-Flemish treaty in 1110. Helias of Saint Saens (Clito's guardian) was chased out of his castle and eventually Clito fetched up in Flanders, from where he would prosper, being taken in by Baldwin VII, the new count.

With the entrapment of Robert de Bellême in 1112, Henry showed his political skills once more. The old enemy was asked to attend court at Bonneville-sur-Touques and turned up believing he was under the French king's safe conduct because he was his envoy. He was going to demand Duke Robert's release from custody. However, when he got there he found himself arraigned on numerous charges, including previously failing to appear and variously acting against the king's interests. Robert was imprisoned at Cherbourg and then again in Wareham in England. He would spend the rest of his life in prison, but his son William Talvas became a new thorn in the English king's side. Protracted warfare ensued. A marriage alliance joining Henry's son William Adelin to the daughter of Count Fulk of Anjou was promulgated. Its goal was to detach the Angevin count from King Louis VI. In the negotiations which followed Louis was forced to recognise a *fait accompli* and also ceded Bellême to Henry (usually held from the French king), although Henry would have to fight for it first.

Flemish support for William Clito resulted in the collapse of the Anglo-Flemish relationship as Baldwin and Louis launched a series of attacks against Henry's supporters. By the end of 1118 things looked particularly dark for Henry in Normandy. His wife Matilda had died in December and he had already lost a battle at Alençon (pages 137-138). In 1119 came an episode in which Henry's cruelty might seem to have over-stepped the mark from a measured approach to downright barbarism. Breteuil had been held by Henry's daughter Judith and her husband Eustace. Eustace was incited by Amaury de Montfort to move against the ducal castle of Ivry. Henry, wishing to prevent this, arranged to give Eustace a hostage – the son of the castellan of Ivry, Ralph Harenc. In return, Henry would hold Eustace's daughters – his own granddaughters. But Eustace put out the eyes of Ralph's son, and the father went to the king to complain. Henry gave Ralph the two girls, whom Ralph blinded and cut off the tips of their noses. In the subsequent investment of Breteuil by the king, an understandably furious Judith took a shot at Henry with a crossbow from the keep of the castle, narrowly missing her father. She then unceremoniously escaped by jumping into the moat. There are few contemporary comments on this episode. Orderic Vitalis writes about it but remains silent in his judgement. Henry's situation was desperate in 1119, and the increasingly paranoid king slept with a sword in his bed. His harsh actions may have been perceived by many as a step too far, but they might also have been seen as simply fulfilling an agreement, however barbaric.

The situation was eased slightly by the marriage, in June 1119, of William Adelin and Fulk's daughter Matilda. Baldwin VII of Flanders died in the same month. There was further fighting in which the king defeated Louis VI at the Battle of Brémule (pages 138-142). But, with Louis's formal restoration of Normandy to William Adelin in October 1120, things must have looked good for Henry's son and grim for Clito. But events were soon to unfold which would affect Henry for the rest of his life.

The Phare de Gatteville at the tip of Barfleur, Normandy. Off this rocky shore on 25 November 1120 the White Ship *foundered, probably on the submerged Quillebœuf Rocks. With Henry I's heir William Adelin drowned, English history and Henry's outlook on the world took a dramatic turn.*

The king was said never to have smiled again after the news was broken to him. On 25 November 1120 a man called Thomas, son of Stephen the Steersman, had come to Henry. He had begged for his father's fief. His father had transported the Conqueror to England in 1066. Thomas had the fine *White Ship* at Barfleur harbour, ready to assist the royal party and again transport his lord across the waves to England. Henry agreed to Thomas's request, but told him he had already chosen a vessel for himself. He was happy for his sons, William Adelin and Richard, plus numerous valued members of his household, to board the *White Ship*.

About 300 people crowded onto the vessel and the crew asked William for drink, which he liberally supplied. The ship set sail and fifty oarsmen got to work, but there was drunken revelry and tomfoolery on board. The king's fleet had already put out to sea and the inebriated passengers compelled Thomas to make haste after them. Amid the treacherous and swirling waters off the coast of Barfleur, the greatest tragedy to strike the English monarchy thus far came to pass as the vessel veered off course and foundered on the submerged rocks at Quillebœuf Rock (or perhaps at Catteraz, a little further out). It was when the sailors tried to push the vessel off the rocks that it capsized. Nearly all of those on board were lost to the sea. William Adelin, who turned his small boat around to rescue his sister, the countess of Perche, perished beneath the waves when crew members swamped his vessel in desperation. Somewhere in the distance the king of England could hear the cries from afar, but he was not told what his own crewmen feared was the truth. His only legitimate son and heir was drowned.

The *White Ship* disaster forced Henry to think again about how he could secure the succession. His thoughts turned to his daughter Matilda, wife of Emperor Henry V. The English king remarried in 1121, taking Adelize of Louvain as his new bride, but as the years went by there was no issue from the union. In 1122 he hoped to meet up with Matilda, but she was prevented from travelling with safe passage through Flanders by the pro-Clito Count Charles. Of course, the Clito camp found new heart in the wake of Henry's tragedy. At its head was Waleran de Beaumont, whose struggle against the king ended in defeat at Bourgthéroulde in 1124 (pages 142-144). Worse for Henry was the move to marry William Clito to another of Fulk of Anjou's daughters, Sybil. Henry, ever the politician, began to campaign for the annulment of this marriage and his efforts finally bore fruit in June 1124 when Cardinal John of Crema recognised it as falling within the prohibited degrees of consanguinity. Henry invoked the help of his son-in-law, the German emperor, who with his army headed west with the intention of attacking Rheims. As it transpired, the emperor turned back at Metz but his advance was enough of a distraction for Louis VI to allow time for Henry to plan further gains, although his scheme to devastate the Vexin was not successful.

Henry's daughter came back to her father after the death of her husband in Germany. The king's thoughts turned to the old Angevin alliance which had previously promised so much. A great oath-taking was arranged on 1 January 1127 in favour of Matilda's English succession, although there are differing interpretations of it. She was to be the lady, or 'Domina', which does not quite place the crown upon her head. By 22 May, however, she was betrothed to Fulk's son Geoffrey and the marriage took place on 17 June 1128 at Le Mans. Here began a tale which would throw the English succession crisis into the next generation. It was not an altogether happy marriage, but the couple would bring the future King Henry II (1154–1189) into the world. The years which followed 1135 would witness England fall into anarchy as Matilda's camp slugged it out with that of King Stephen. But what was more troubling even than the succession problem was the situation presented after the murder of Count Charles of Flanders in March 1127. William Clito was chosen to replace him. This could have spelt disaster for Henry, as the new count of Flanders was also established with the French king's support in the Vexin.

William Clito ravaged the countryside around Boulogne and once again the situation looked ominous for the English king. But English money sent to Clito's enemies, and the emergence of Thierry of Alsace as Clito's rival, reduced the pressure on Henry. Then Louis VI was distracted by a palace revolution, and this gave Henry the chance to thrust south beyond Paris, as far as Epernon where he stayed for eight days. However, the final blow for Clito came when he was wounded at the siege of Aalst on 28 July 1128. He had seized a lance with the fleshy part of his hand and the subsequent infection killed him.

Henry I had survived a tremendous series of wars, during which his political guile had been a key to his overall strategic success. Clito, knowing he was dying, wrote to the king. He asked him for forgiveness and for the release of his followers. Eventually Waleran and Hugh FitzGerald were indeed released. But these later years for Henry were coloured by a falling out with Matilda over ownership of the royal castles and his general mistrust of Geoffrey of Anjou. There was also trouble in Wales.

And so, whilst on campaign in Normandy, once again strengthening the southern border, Henry ate supper at Lyons-la-Forêt where, against his physician's advice, he consumed too many lampreys. He fell ill and died a few days later. In a novel move for an English king, his viscera, brains and eyes were removed and interred in his favourite church at Notre-Dame-du-Pré. Henry's body was conveyed with honour to Caen and eventually shipped to England, where it was met by the man who had stolen a march on the Empress Matilda. Stephen of Blois, who had reacted swiftly to the news of the king's death on hearing of it in Boulogne, had crossed the Channel and seized England's treasury. He had been crowned king of England on 22 December 1135. We are told that he had loved his uncle Henry. It was Stephen, the new king, who accompanied the body to its final resting place at Reading Abbey.

Henry I had been a lustful and avaricious man, and he never enjoyed being the butt of satire. A certain Luc de la Barre, who had been allowed to exit a siege at Pont-Audemer on the understanding that he would not turn to the king's enemies, knew the king's wrath well. He joined the rebels and was sentenced to have his eyes put out. He had also composed satirical songs about the king and had them sung in public. De la Barre chose to avoid his fate and committed suicide by beating his brains out against his cell wall.

There is something about Henry's character that inspired a perfect mixture of fear and respect in his subjects. His cruelty – bar one incident – was measured, like that of many other Norman leaders. Even the hanging and castration of forty-four thieves in 1124, and the castration of fraudulent moneyers later in his reign may perhaps be seen in the context of their time. But it was his political acumen that made him one of history's greats. Henry of Huntingdon placed the following words into the mouth of Robert Bloet, the king's staunch supporter and bishop of Lincoln. It could have served as a warning to all Henry's enemies. When told he had been praised in his absence he replied 'the king only praises one of his men whom he has decided to destroy utterly'.

The Commander

With such a long reign to consider, there should be many examples of Henry's command capability and the sources do not disappoint. It is thought he received his training from a Robert Archard, whose origins are mysterious but who may have been linked to the men of Domfront, who later came to Henry for aid during his wandering years. We have seen how Henry's political alliances often won him strategic mastery, but what is also clear is that his personal influence over men governed his leadership success. When he took the royal treasury in 1100 he drew his sword in an argument with William of Breteuil in a show of determination which left no one in doubt as to his intentions. But it takes more than such a demonstration to win people over. It was relatively early in his reign that he legislated against the depravities of the court and army when on campaign. This installation of a new courtly discipline instilled trust from both within his *familia* and also among the long-suffering outside community.

Henry's return to the Flemish money-fief policy (see pages 180–181) in March 1101 was similar to the arrangements his father and brother had made. It demonstrates an obvious strategic awareness. That same year, the treaty of Alton dissolved what could have been a dangerous situation, with Robert II Curthose in arms and at the doorstep of Winchester. The terms of the treaty favoured Henry and he retained the strategically important Domfront as a result. Henry's war against Robert de Bellême tested the Alton treaty to the full and, because each brother had to deal with the enemy of the other, Duke Robert found himself failing to overcome Robert de Bellême's men at Vignats in Normandy. Henry's subsequent expulsion of de Bellême from England led to continued trouble in Normandy for Henry's men until the duke reconciled himself with the troublesome lord.

Henry's campaigns of 1105–06 in Normandy were typical of the commander at his peak. He was infuriated by the capture of Robert FitzHaimon in 1105 and gathered an allied army of Normans, Englishmen, Bretons and Angevins. An intimidating sacking of Bayeux and the surrender of Caen followed. Caen was taken more by guile than by bloodshed after the capture of some of its townsmen, even though the duke himself was present. But the dénouement the next year was Tinchebrai. Here, Henry's tactical-level mastery in a pitched battle situation was faultless (pages 133-137). It is clear from Tinchebrai that Henry had a profound knowledge of the capabilities of a combined-arms army in a battle situation. He used archery, cavalry and infantrymen each to great effect, and it was the dismounting of his knights which was often noted by his enemies as providing a resolute battlefield position. Henry was clearly well-versed in how to organise a flanking attack and how to use mounted troops to surround an enemy. In 1101 he had demonstrated to Englishmen how to stand firm in the face of a Norman cavalry charge, surely a most valuable lesson. There is a distinctive move towards the acknowledgement of the infantryman's role in battle situations under King Henry I which stays with medieval military history in England for generations.

Although Henry could clearly decide to force an issue on the battlefield itself, it was not always the case that he sought it. After Tinchebrai, Henry took Gisors castle. He and Louis VI met at Planches-de-Neaufles in March 1109 where Louis demanded that Gisors be handed over, saying that unless this were done it must either be destroyed or won in battle. There was even an argument about whose army was to cross the river and where to fight, Henry insisting that he would only do so when in a position to properly defend himself. Both forces rushed to the riverbank but were unable to cross and so retired for the night. The French awoke first but Henry retreated to the castle the next morning in the face of the enemy. He was accused of cowardice, but it was clear that holding Gisors was far better than losing it. Once again, the impression we get is of a commander who knew when and when not to fight a battle.

As a siege commander, Henry was widely experienced but probably no more or less successful than his contemporaries. In 1102 he reduced Robert de Bellême's men systematically at Arundel, Bridgnorth and Shrewsbury. He also took a leading role in directing operations. On one occasion, when besieging Bellême from 1 May 1113 against a local faction who held it against him, Henry prevented his knights from fighting on the Feast of the Invention of the Holy Cross, which fell on 3 May. However, Theobald of Blois and Rotrou of Perche's knights challenged those of the garrison to come out and fight and general carnage ensued at the gates of the castle, which were left wide open. Eventually the king's army was able to get in over the bodies of the dead, but this quick result was a lucky one and not the norm.

Another example of Henry's battle-avoidance approach was the show of strength he made in Wales in 1114 when the Marcher lordships of England had been under sustained attack. Richard of Chester had been attacked by the forces of Gruffud ap Cynan of Gwynedd in the north and in the centre Owain ap Cadwgan had been threatening to upset the balance of power. Henry organised a huge alliance which included forces from Alexander, king of the Scots, Earl Richard, Gilbert FitzRichard, lord of Ceredigion (with Cornish and south Welsh troops) and the king himself. Henry went as far as Tomen-y-Mur in Merionethshire. He bought off Owain by offering to grant him his land free of tribute, and when Gruffud heard of this he too sued for peace, but had to pay a large tribute. The show of strength in the heart of Welsh territory had been enough. There was no repeat of the painful and costly encounters of Rufus's reign. Henry then set about installing his own trusted men in the political structure of the Marcher areas, thus bolstering his interests in the region.

Ralph the Red of Pont-Echanfray

Ralph the Red was a leading member of King Henry I's *familia* during his wars of 1118–19. In his younger years Ralph had followed Robert Guiscard's son Bohemond to the Holy Land and had gone on to both Constantinople and Jerusalem. He was a key figure in the defence of the English king's Norman duchy in the centre and the south and was the personal rescuer of Richard, one of King Henry's bastard sons. Ralph himself was also captured by the troops of King Louis VI of France but then ransomed.

Probably because the fief of Pont-Echanfray depended upon the honour of Breteuil we find Ralph energetically rushing to its defence against an attack by the French king. He was also a commander at sieges, notably at Evreux against Amaury de Montfort. Ralph may have served in expectation of great reward. Although he did receive a small grant out of the revenues of Glos, Ralph would not survive to reap the full promise of the king's purse. He perished in the *White Ship* disaster on 25 November 1120.

Henry knew he could not win the cyclic wars in the Vexin using the same strategy as he had in Powys. Although the king's presence was always advantageous in this frontier region, men of the calibre of Ralph the Red of Pont-Echanfray were vital. These were wars in which events unfolded quickly, allegiances changed overnight and a quick victory or the seizure of a castle could change the game unless it was countered. Ralph was sorely missed by Henry after he died in the *White Ship* disaster, and it is easy to see why. When Richard of La Ferté-Fresnel teamed up with his lord Eustace of Breteuil, they plundered and ravaged around Verneuces. Orderic Vitalis, whose community of Saint-Evroult was close by, says that when Ralph the Red saw the smoke from the fired houses at Verneuces he gathered Henry's knights from Le Sap and Orbec and took on a much larger force than his own at Charentonne, capturing supplies and taking prisoners. Ralph was then able to advise the king that the castle at La Ferté was not in a position to defend itself and so, when Henry approached it, it surrendered. After the success at Brémule, Ralph continued to distinguish himself in this landscape of conflicting loyalties.

There are hints that Henry's military decisions to inflict suffering were not taken as lightly as one might think. In 1119 Evreux castle was still held by the rebel Count Amaury. Henry's army was unable to take the castle, but the obvious next step was to deny the garrison the resources of the town by destroying the town entirely. Henry seems genuinely to have been concerned. He turned to Bishop Audoin, the refugee bishop of Evreux, and told him of his plans, saying that churches and innocents would be burnt. He asked the bishop for his advice. The bishop consented to the devastation only when Henry offered to restore the churches to better than their former glory. The promise was later kept. There were other lucrative concessions to the bishop, including proceeds from the fair at Nonancourt, Verneuil and the port of Vernon, a grant of a manor in England and a house in Rouen. So, in the heat of summer, Ralph de Gael lit the first fire to the north of the town, which was dry and hot. Evreux and the bishop's cathedral church of Saint Mary were razed to the ground.

Henry's military ability was a match for any of his enemies. He succeeded in outsmarting and outfighting the French king in a series of dangerous and closely-fought wars in which the future of his duchy was balanced on a knife edge. He was non-committal when he needed to preserve his forces and decisive when he needed to bring on a battle. Strategically masterful in both the political alliances he made and in the management of the military landscape, Henry deserves a reputation near the top of all the Norman commanders.

In 1106, when Henry was back in England, a military man arrived in France from the east. He was a renowned Norman warrior. His name was Bohemond, prince of Antioch. He was on a recruiting campaign. Bohemond sent messages to Henry asking his permission to cross to England. Henry, with admirable political insight, advised this illustrious warrior that a winter crossing would not be safe, and said that he would himself be coming to Normandy soon before Easter, where the two could meet up. Bohemond therefore continued to recruit across northern France, taking with him many fine fighters. Ralph the Red of Pont-Echanfray had been persuaded and so too Robert of Montfort, among others. But who was this fine and charismatic soldier Henry had expertly rebuffed, and what exactly was the nature of his appeal to Norman fighting men?

Chapter 10

Bohemond, Prince of Antioch (d. 1111)

Timeline of Bohemond, Prince of Antioch

1079	Early defeat against Abelard
1081	Fights alongside father Robert Guiscard at Dyrrhachium
1082	Illyrian campaigns. Siege and victory in battle at Ioannina. Further victory against Byzantines at Arta
1083	Siege of Larissa
1084–1085	Failure of Illyrian expedition and return to Italy. Death of Robert Guiscard
1085-1095	Consolidation and gains in Italy. Wars with brother Roger Borsa
1096	Becomes key leader of First Crusade
1097	Siege of Nicaea and battle with Turks. Battle of Doryleum
1097-1098	Siege of Antioch. Battle near Harem in February 1098. Fall of Lower Antioch and defeat of Kerbogha
1100	Bohemond captured at Battle of Melitene
1103	Bohemond released after Baldwin of Edessa pays ransom
1104	Defeat at Battle of Harran. Return to Italy
1106–1107	New Illyrian campaign against Alexius Comnenus ends in army starvation outside Dyrrhachium
1107	Treaty of Devol. Antioch becomes Byzantine vassal state
1111	Death and burial in mausoleum at Canosa

The appearance of this man was, to put it briefly, unlike that of any other man whether Greek or Barbarian seen in those days on Roman soil. The sight of him inspired admiration. The mention of his name terror… His stature was such that he towered almost a full cubit over the tallest men. He was slender of waist and flanks. With broad shoulders and chest, strong in the arms; overall he was neither too slender, nor too heavily built and fleshy, but perfectly proportioned – one might say that he conformed to the ideal of Polyklitos [a classical sculptor]. His hands were large, he had a good firm

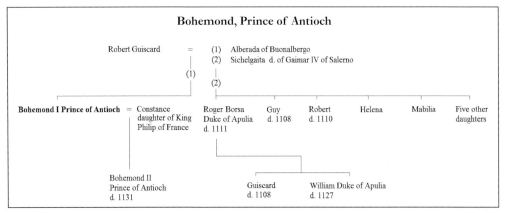

Bohemond, Prince of Antioch

Robert Guiscard = (1) Alberada of Buonalbergo
(2) Sichelgaita d. of Gaimar IV of Salerno

(1)

(2)

Bohemond I Prince of Antioch = Constance   Roger Borsa   Guy   Robert   Helena   Mabilia   Five other
daughter of King   Duke of Apulia   d. 1108   d. 1110   daughters
Philip of France   d. 1111

Bohemond II   Guiscard   William Duke of Apulia
Prince of Antioch   d. 1108   d. 1127
d. 1131

Fig. 11

stance, and his neck and back were compact. If to the astute and meticulous observer he appeared to stoop slightly, that was not caused by any weakness of the vertebrae of the lower spine, but presumably there was some malformation there from birth. The skin all over his body was very pale, except for his face which was pale but with some colour to it too. His hair was light-coloured and did not go down to his shoulders as it does with other barbarians; in fact, the man had no great predilection for long hair, but cut his short, to the ears. Whether his beard was red or of any other colour I cannot say, for the razor had passed over it closely, leaving his chin smoother than any marble. However, it seemed that it would have been red. His eyes were light-blue and gave some hint of the man's spirit and dignity. He breathed freely through nostrils that were broad, worthy of his chest and a fine outlet for the breath that came in gusts from his lungs. *Anna Comnena*, The Alexiad XIII. 10

Character and Career
Here again is thinly veiled admiration from Anna Comnena for another Norman warrior. The sexual charge in her writing is perhaps understandable, as she was just a teenager when she met him. She said Bohemond was second only to her father in fortune, eloquence and other natural gifts. He was every bit Robert Guiscard's son. Anna styles Bohemond as a born conqueror, one who went east not for the sake of piety, but for conquest. His conversations were carefully worded and his answers were guarded. Here was a man who was a politician and a general rolled into one. On the face of it, it might seem that Bohemond's ambition out-paced his command capability, but this would be to severely underestimate the size of the tasks he set himself, some of which he achieved.

Bohemond's career falls into some reasonably well-defined phases. His early years are relatively obscure, however. He acquired the nickname 'Bohemond' after his father had heard tales of a legendary giant of that name, which gradually

Mausoleum of Bohemond, prince of Antioch. Canosa Cathedral, Puglia, Italy.

replaced his baptismal name of Marc. He appears to have been well educated during his formative years in Italy, learning Latin and possibly other languages. He seems to have had a variable relationship with his younger half-brother Roger Borsa as the years went by. Bohemond's earliest defeat was at Troia in 1079 when he was beaten by his cousin Abelard, but it was with his father's campaigns against the Byzantine Empire between 1081 and 1085 that Bohemond grew in ambition and ability as he stepped onto a truly international stage. The Empire, weakened by the disastrous Battle of Manzikert in 1071, which saw the whole of Anatolia crumble to the Turks, was softened up by the politicking of Guiscard, who sought to implant a predatory family interest in Constantinople itself. By 1085, after the death of his father, Bohemond returned to Italy and embroiled himself in the Apulian succession crisis that followed his father's death.

In 1096, Bohemond was caught by the same crusading 'fervour' that had attracted Duke Robert II Curthose. But that is where the comparison between the two ends. Bohemond's adventure eventually saw him establish a Norman principality at Antioch, which outlasted the Norman kingdoms of both England and Sicily. He was its prince between 1099 and 1104 and he briefly came back to the West, during which period he married Constance, the daughter of the king of France. But the end for Bohemond came not long after he threw his resources once again at the emperor Alexius, a move which ended in a failure at Dyrrhachium and later a climb-down for the prince of Antioch at the Treaty of Devol in 1108, in which he agreed to become the vassal of the emperor. On his death in 1111, Bohemond was buried in a fine mausoleum at Canosa, which still stands today.

Bohemond was energetic and ambitious and the methods he employed to achieve his goals were almost on a par with those of his father. He could mesmerise his men, and his reputation among his enemies was deeply impressive. He was perhaps the most overtly 'Norman' of all of the Norman commanders, embodying the vaulting ambition that seems to have inspired so many of them. But Bohemond lost battles and campaigns as well as winning them. His story is dominated by warfare. He was the most warlike of them all, and he had some stiff competition. What sort of a commander was he?

The Commander

Bohemond's military fortunes changed when his father was called back to the Italian mainland in the wake of their 1081 victory at Dyrrhachium (pages 162-170). Robert had to deal with more Byzantine-inspired insurrection and a threat to Rome. With the departure of the duke in May 1082 and the dramatic campaigns across Illyria which followed for Bohemond, change was afoot.

Robert Guiscard had left his son to face Alexius Comnenus, a general of roughly Bohemond's age who had only recently been blooded against him at Dyrrhachium. Just before his departure, the duke and his son had captured Kastoria, a lakeside citadel to the south of the Via Egnatia in which 300 Varangians (Anglo-Saxon and Viking mercenaries) had been posted. The southern flank of the ancient Roman road to Constantinople would occupy Bohemond's mind. Much of the campaigning took place in the south, as Bohemond decided to divert

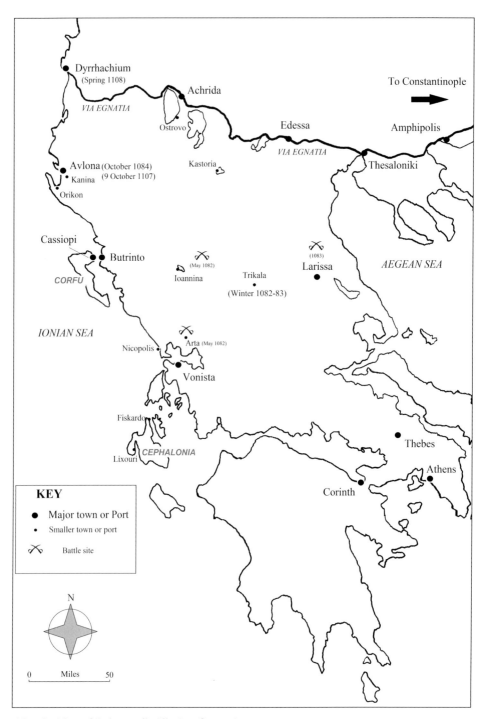

Map 7: Map of Bohemond's Illyrian Campaigns

to Ioannina and delay any attack on Thessaloniki, an obvious target. It may have been on his father's advice that the son was now seeking to secure strongholds in regions where the Vlach populations were strong. These groups of Latinised Greek-speakers were historically antipathetic towards the Byzantine government. Moreover, Bohemond had picked up some defecting Byzantine officers on his march to the south. Ioannina subsequently fell to the Normans, who set about upgrading its fortifications. The emperor Alexius, after his defeat at Dyrrhachium, was once again stung into action.

Anna Comnena's account of the battle that took place at Ioannina contains revelations about both commanders, Alexius and Bohemond. She specifically states that the emperor was afraid of the first charge of the Norman cavalry. The emperor wanted to learn of Bohemond's disposition and capability, so he employed skirmishing and scouting tactics after he arrived with his small force. Then, in fear of the expected onslaught of Bohemond's cavalry, Alexius employed light chariots or wagons with four spears attached to them. These were to be pushed forward by hidden infantrymen when the charge came. The idea, Anna says, was to break up the continuous line of the charge. It may have been the dissident Byzantine elements in Bohemond's ranks who gave him prior knowledge of the tactic, but at Ioannina in May 1082, Bohemond's generalship was decisive. He split his cavalry units into two flanking divisions and nullified the enemy's tactics. As his men crashed into the Byzantine flanks, the enemy casualties began to mount. Alexius was once more defeated. He fled back to Achrida to reorganise. The Byzantine emperor was getting used to the idea that this was no ordinary enemy.

Another battle took place several weeks later at Arta further to the southwest. Alexius had to get some mercenaries ready and march again to face Bohemond. Once again, fear of the Norman cavalry dominated his thinking. Iron caltrops, usually used in camp defences, were carefully laid out on the plain where the Norman cavalry were expected to charge. Byzantine lancers were to step out and meet the enemy at carefully arranged points, while the emperor's archers would shoot in from the sides. But Bohemond got wind of this plan. Once again, his cavalry evaded the obstacles and crashed into the Byzantine wings at either end of the line, who soon melted away in fear as their morale collapsed.

The victorious Bohemond now expanded his operations. He moved on to Skopje and Achrida accompanied by commanders Peter of Aulps and Raoul, Count of Pontoise (who later defected), while the Emperor cooled his heels in Thessaloniki. More towns were invested along the southern flank of the Via Egnatia, with varying degrees of success including settlements on the outskirts of Thessaloniki itself. Bohemond stayed here for three months until he was ready to move on to Kastoria. But as winter approached, he decided to head further south and over-winter at Trikala in a warmer area. His forces took the town of Tziviskos before he turned his attention to Larissa on St George's Day. A six-month siege followed, during which the Byzantines sponsored insurrections among the Norman leaders and also sent for help from the Turkish leader Sulleyman I, who provided 7,000 men under a commander named Kamyres.

The emperor once again headed out to meet the Normans, but this time he was concerned not to meet them in open battle, but to defeat Bohemond by strategy. He marched around Larissa and headed out to Trikala where he arrived in early April 1083. He asked the locals to tell him about the topography of Larissa so he could lay ambushes for the Normans. When it came to the battle near Larissa, Alexius planned to employ repeated feigned flights followed by ambushes. He ordered his commanders to draw up in the same way they had in the previous defeats, only this time they were to withdraw from the frontal engagement 'in disorder' to a place called Lykostomion (the 'wolf's mouth'), where Alexius would lie in wait near to the Norman camp with his cavalry. The Byzantines sent out a distraction unit to engage the Normans while Alexius took his position. The next morning Bohemond and his sub-commander, the count of Brienne, led the expected charge. They saw a place in the line where they thought the emperor was positioned. The Byzantines retreated, but Alexius had ordered his own archers to pursue the Normans and shoot only at their mounts. Anna Comnena says '…all Kelts [Franks, or Normans] when on horseback are unbeatable in a charge and make a magnificent show, but whenever they dismount, partly because of their huge shields, partly too because of the spurs on their boots and their ungainly walk, they become very easy prey…' Meanwhile, Alexius was able to enter the Norman camp and slaughter its inhabitants. The men of the count of Brienne were caught in a whirlwind of dark dust and arrows as they fell from their horses. Somehow the Norman count was able to get word to Bohemond about the disaster. There he was, on a small island in the River Salabrias apparently eating grapes and bragging that he had 'thrown Alexius to the wolf's mouth'. Anna's account is confusing at this point and has Bohemond reacting in anger to the news of the defeat and sending more cavalry into a successful charge. Then the story shifts to the next day and the scene is a narrow marshy area ending in a defile on the outskirts of Larissa. The emperor ordered Turkish and Sarmatian horse archers to fire into the Normans, but Bohemond responded 'with superb knowledge of military tactics' by dismounting and forming a time-honoured infantry shield-wall. With this formation he was able to repulse his attackers. However, in the rout one of the mercenary leaders was able to spear Bohemond's standard-bearer and seize the standard from him, waving it around and then pointing it to the ground as if to signal a defeat. This appears to have signalled a general retreat to Trikala and heralded Alexius's first real victory over the Normans.

The campaign began to falter for Bohemond. The counts in his army, inspired by the Byzantines, demanded two years of back-pay, which Bohemond knew he could not honour. He fell back to Kastoria and by August 1083 he had retreated to Avlona. By October Kastoria had fallen to the Byzantines. As Bohemond sailed back to Italy in 1084 even Avlona fell. Then, after the death of his father on the second campaign in 1085, Dyrrhachium was recaptured by the Greeks. But it had not all been a total disaster. Bohemond the commander had shown his skill in victory after victory and had even shown tactical decision-making capability under pressure at the close of the Larissa episode. This had been a critical campaign, in which Bohemond demonstrated to the wider world the strengths and weaknesses of the Norman war machine.

Bohemond spent ten years in Italy dealing with internal matters. These years are characterised by his ongoing struggles against his brother Roger Borsa, the new duke of Apulia. There is nothing like the detail of the Illyrian campaign to allow us to assess any command capabilities. However, Bohemond can be seen receiving control of Oria, Taranto (after which he was posthumously named as 'prince'), Otranto and Gallipoli as he vied for a fiefdom with his half-brother. Soon the lands of Geoffrey of Conversano would fall to him and his power on the mainland would reach great heights. After a short period of peace in 1086, Bohemond launched another offensive against Roger Borsa, which included a defeat to him at Fargnito. But the war dragged on to 1089. There were reconciliations, however, and the two fought together beneath the walls of Rossano and Castrovillari, along with their uncle Count Roger of Sicily, in a successful bid to bring William of Grandmesnil to heel.

The crusading Bohemond gives us a fuller picture of the commander in action. It was inevitable that Bohemond would gain experience fighting the Turks and others in Asia Minor and Syria when on crusade. It is suggested that he only had around 500 knights when he set out. There were probably about five times as many infantry. Alongside him marched many important Apulian Normans, including Richard of the Principate and Humphrey of Montescaglioso. We find Bohemond in Constantinople on 17 April 1097, swearing oaths to the emperor alongside his fellow crusaders. Then they headed for the city of Nicaea. Knowing that the army needed supplies to assist in its siege of Nicaea, Bohemond successfully arranged materials to be brought up to Nicomedia. The subsequent siege of Nicaea was interrupted by the arrival of Kilij Arslan I and several thousand Seljuk Turks, but they were unable to surround Bohemond and the crusaders because of the constriction of the ground and thus chose to retreat. Soon Nicaea fell; not to the crusaders, but to the Imperial detachment that had come with them.

As the crusading army neared Dorylaeum, Bohemond was in its van. The Seljuks this time were more successful in surrounding them. The encircling tactics nearly cost Bohemond dear, and would have done so had it not been for the timely arrival on the flank of Godfrey of Bouillon, whose men charged the Turks and routed them. Bohemond had asked his infantry to guard the baggage, while his cavalry were put in the difficult position of having to hold the line, dismounted. Bohemond had now seen the massed horse-archer tactics of the Turks. He learned that his cavalry charges, designed to relieve the pressure, came

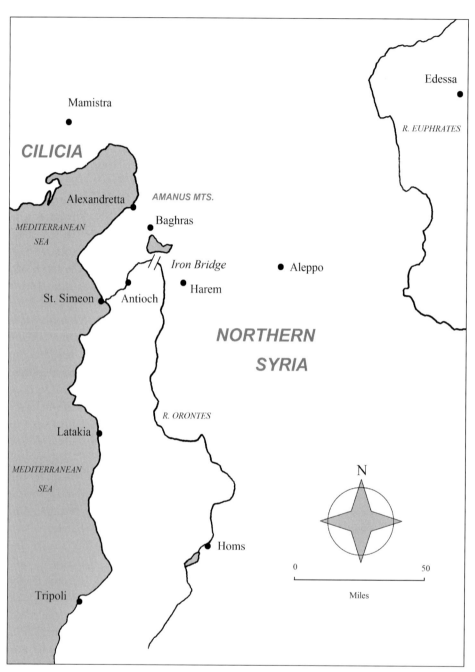

Map 8: The Region of Antioch, Northern Syria

to nothing as the enemy simply parted before them. He had to simply take the punishment.

During the subsequent siege of Antioch, Bohemond once again assumed the position of head of logistics and supply. In fact, although the crusaders had chosen Stephen of Blois as their nominal leader, the reality on the ground was that Bohemond was the commander. He fought numerous small-scale battles to protect crusading foragers. One source of constant harassment from the enemy operated out of Harem Castle, three hours to the east of Antioch. By using a feigned flight, Bohemond drew the Turks into an ambush in which many were captured and then brought to the walls of Antioch and beheaded as the defenders watched. But the enemy was now different. The besieged Yagi Siyan had sent out for help to surrounding emirs. The forces the crusaders faced in the winter and spring of 1097–98 in the region of Antioch consisted of a mixture of Arabs, Seljuks, Iranians and even Bedouins. They encountered them at first on their necessary foraging expeditions, but on one occasion both Bohemond and Robert of Flanders were able to counter-charge them.

The news that Ridwan of Aleppo had amassed a huge force of over 12,000 men to march on the besiegers of Antioch probably prompted the defection of the Byzantine commander Tatikios (a veteran of Dyrrhachium), although Anna Comnena blamed his departure on Bohemond's ambitions to have Antioch for himself. This controversy notwithstanding, it was Bohemond who took the initiative. The crusaders had already experienced a victory over a smaller relieving force sent by Duqaq of Damascus, but now, with an almost entirely mounted army, Bohemond took 700–1,000 men and camped between the Orontes and Lake Bangras on the night of 8 February 1098. The Battle of Harem that followed was a large-scale ambush set by Bohemond, who kept his own unit in reserve while deploying five others in front of him. As the enemy came into the narrow defile, they attacked Bohemond's forces, who gave ground and led them into the area where Bohemond's men were able to charge at them and put them to flight. Bohemond had used the geography of a location to prevent the enemy horse-archers from practising their encircling tactic. Thus they were prey to the Frankish cavalry charge.

The lower part of the city of Antioch finally fell to Bohemond, by treachery and not starvation, on 3 June 1098. The traitor was a guardsman of the walls, one Firuz, of Turkish or possibly Armenian origin. It cost the inhabitants the inevitable consequences of a sacking and Yagi Siyan was murdered during his flight by some Armenian peasants. The citadel held out and soon enough Bohemond, far from secure within the walls, would face another battle outside the city. This time, it was the governor of Mosul, Kerbogha, who had brought his force to Antioch and placed it under siege. History might have us believe that it was Peter the Hermit's famous discovery of the Holy Lance that turned the tide for the beleaguered crusaders, but it was Bohemond who formulated a battle plan

Walls of Antioch, from an 1894 engraving by T.A. Archer.

to face the new danger and once again he used the landscape to his advantage. The crusaders sallied out of the western Bridge Gate of Antioch on 28 June 1098.

Bohemond's army was in four main divisions. Their enemy was on the north bank of the Orontes. Hugh of Vermondois, Robert of Flanders and Duke Robert II Curthose of Normandy would form Bohemond's right wing, its flank pinned to the River Orontes. Godfrey of Bouillon formed the centre and the men of Provence and Aquitaine would be on the left under Bishop Adhemar, with their flank pinned to the rising ground and mountains of the west. Bohemond was concerned to avoid the encircling tactics of the enemy once again. Tancred de Hauteville and his kinsman Bohemond would hold themselves in reserve. The crusader left wing under Bishop Adhemar was the last to cross the bridge over the Orontes on exiting the city and therefore was the last to form up on the battlefield. It may have been this that Kerbogha or one of his subordinates had seen. Thousands of Turks galloped around the crusader left flank and consequently divorced themselves from the main body of their army. They fought closely with crusaders but were repelled by a screen of infantry who were learning to cope with their tactics. Hugh and Godfrey were also doing well to the front. The details of the fighting are obscure, allowing room for a number of theories. Kerbogha's forces do seem to have been more spread out than the crusaders. However, it is clear that the combined use of an infantry screen and a cavalry unit held in reserve was enough to win the battle for Bohemond.

On observing the fate of Kerbogha's army, the men who held the citadel in Antioch finally capitulated to Bohemond. But Bohemond would not participate in the crusaders' sack of Jerusalem. The crusaders sent out to tell Alexius that Antioch had fallen, but he had already withdrawn. A complex series of relationships between the Byzantine Emperor and individual crusaders ensued, and between Bohemond and his deeply suspicious ally Raymond of Toulouse. Bohemond, as the new prince of Antioch, busied himself trying to secure the Byzantine port of Latakia, with mixed results. As he became involved in the politics of the region, it seems that Bohemond the commander forgot his basic military skills on one important occasion, unless history is concealing circumstances beyond his control.

The town of Malatia in Anatolia was in Armenian hands in 1100. However, it was under threat from the north-east from the Danishmend emir Malik Ghazi. Bohemond responded to the call of the Armenians by sending out a force of around 500 knights. He seems to have neglected vital reconnaissance en route. The result was the disastrous Battle of Melitene, at which the Turks were able to completely surround Bohemond's forces. Bohemond was captured along with Richard of the Principate. It was a humiliation. The prince of Antioch was not released until Baldwin of Edessa stepped in and ransomed him in 1103. The reasons for Bohemond's lack of foresight in this battle are not clear.

There would be another more substantial disaster than Melitene. Bohemond and Baldwin of Edessa set out to attack the town of Harran, some twenty-four miles to the east of Edessa. They began by besieging it. A relief force of around 10,000 Seljuks soon arrived. On 7 May 1104 the Battle of Harran took place, most likely on the plain around ar-Raqqah, some two days' march from Harran. The deployment of the crusaders was initially the same as it had been before, with a frontal screen of infantry. There were also three divisions of cavalry. The Turks performed their usual encircling tricks, but also instigated a feigned flight which – surprisingly – the crusaders fell for. They pursued them to the eastern hills of Harran where they pitched camp for the night. During that night they were set upon by the Turks and do not appear to have had any prior warning from either scouts or guards. Baldwin of Edessa and Joscelin of Courtenay were captured and their forces routed. Bohemond escaped to Edessa, but it was clear that his principality was now in danger not just from the Turks, but from the Byzantines as well. It was too much to face with the resources he currently had. He left his nephew Tancred as the ruler of both Antioch and Edessa and in late 1104 or early 1105 he sailed to Italy. On his mind was the struggle he would now face with his old enemy Alexius Comnenus. Whether his new plans amount to a 'crusade' against Byzantium is a moot point. Also, Anna Comnena has a vibrant and improbable account of Bohemond sailing off in a coffin, faking his own death, but managing to get a menacing message to Alexius via the governor of Corfu telling him exactly what he could expect next.

Bohemond prepared his fleet from August 1106 to the late summer of the following year. From Bari his army marched to Brindisi to board the ships. On 9 October 1107 the fleet arrived once again at Avlona. All the various sources give wildly differing numbers, but Bohemond's fleet once again comprised several thousand cavalry and almost a greater number of infantry. They had been drawn from France, Italy, Germany and Spain, and Anna Comnena says there were even men from Britain who would ordinarily have been in the service of the Byzantines. She may have been speaking of Anglo-Saxons, but it is not unlikely that Bohemond's recruitment campaigns had attracted some Anglo-Norman mercenaries after all. By late October Bohemond was preparing his siege engines outside the walls of Dyrrhachium once more. Then disease struck the army and significantly delayed matters. By the next spring the army was sufficiently recovered for Bohemond to take the measure used by his father many years before and burn many of his vessels. And so another great Norman siege of Dyrrhachium was renewed.

Alexius had managed to gather an army of many thousands consisting of Greeks, Seljuks, Alans, Turcopoles, Pechenegs and Cumans (steppe horse-archers). But this time there were no Varangians. Alexius had learned from 1081 and 1082. He did not launch into an offensive against Bohemond. He chose to tighten the blockade and summoned three Norman defectors, some of whom had experience of the 1081 campaign. He sent them to Bohemond's officers carrying letters, the contents of which were designed to spread confusion and rebelliousness within the ranks. Bohemond was not fooled by the ruse, but one of the men summoned by Alexius was Peter of Aulps, who had left Antioch for the imperial army in 1098. He must have given the emperor valuable tactical information. Later sources even accused Bohemond's brother Guy of intriguing with the emperor, but Anna, who might have jumped at the notion, does not. Furthermore, Alexius sent for four of his most trusted commanders and also blocked the roads beyond Dyrrhachium with felled timber.

Bohemond was feeling the pinch at his camp around the city. The noose was tightening and conditions were deteriorating. Hunger and illness spread. He did, however, launch attacks against the Byzantines. On 5 April 1108 he sent out Guy and two other commanders, one called Saracenus and another called Pagan – a probable indication that he was deliberately employing men who might know the tactics of the Imperial mercenaries better than his own men. They succeeded in surrounding from both sides and destroying the division of one of the newly sent imperial commanders, Eustathios Kamytzes. Another Byzantine commander Alyates was also caught in the open by Bohemond's men. Alexius then sent Cantacuzenos to Glabinitza to take on Guy's forces, which had recently defeated Michael Cecaumenos. From here, Cantacuzenos fought against the Normans in a pitched battle and sent them back towards the castle at Mylos, charging at their centre and, in a rare reversal of tactics, completely breaking the Norman formation. Cantacuzenos had further successes against forces sent out by Bohemond, including a classic strategic victory at the river crossing of the Bouses.

Bohemond was in a dire situation. Behind him off the shores of the Adriatic lay the ships of the Byzantine navy, preventing the once plentiful reinforcements arriving from Apulia. Beyond him in the hinterland were countless ambushes, guardsmen and army detachments waiting to pounce on foragers and armed reconnaissance units. Moreover, when the Normans sortied, the target of the Byzantines was to be their horses, without which the emperor knew they were at a disadvantage. The city had also withstood several ingenious attempts to break its walls, much to the delight of the citizens (page 205).

By September 1108 Bohemond, a proud and courageous man, knew he had to come to terms with Alexius. He had been outdone by the emperor's vital strategy of not offering him a pitched battle. The climb-down of the Norman, as ratified by the Treaty of Devol, granted him many concessions and has been the subject of some controversy, but he must have been profoundly disappointed by it. In a nutshell, the prince of Antioch would become the vassal of the Byzantine Emperor, and he would be given the title of Sebastos. He would retain some regional townships, but lose others to the empire. His territory would now be a buffer-state for the empire. Bohemond left the Illyrian coast, not for Antioch where Tancred stubbornly held out against Byzantine interests, but for Apulia, where in 1111 he died, a proud but deflated man.

Bohemond the commander was a man who had displayed a rare characteristic in the warfare of the period. Unlike Alexius and many of his Norman contemporaries, he was a battle-seeker, a warrior who had inspired fear in the Byzantine court and elsewhere by the very mention of his name. Each of the commanders we have observed either went out of his way to avoid battle, or carefully considered when to bring it. Bohemond stands out as different. His battle count is higher than the others, probably because of the ambitious goals he set himself. Now we must take some choice examples of the battles and campaigns of the Norman era and assess how our Norman commanders performed.

Part 3

Battles and Campaigns

Chapter 11

Introduction

Our observations about Bohemond notwithstanding, pitched battles were not usually the preferred method of warfare except for where a decisive victory was the only possible means to an end. The reason for this is simple: it was a very risky business. When battles did take place they were usually carefully executed by the Norman commanders to produce the desired results with fewest casualties. Only on rare occasions was the struggle so important that a commander would throw all his forces at the enemy. To avoid battle was certainly practical, since the Normans – particularly in southern Italy and Sicily – were frequently heavily outnumbered by their Saracen, Papal or Byzantine enemies.

Sieges and attritional campaigns of reduction were far more common than pitched battles, but there were more than a few of the latter. In fact, the battles of Civitate (1053) and Hastings (1066) both represented a huge punctuation mark in the histories of the countries they occurred in. These, plus the battles of Val-ès-Dunes (1047), Tinchebrai (1106), Cerami (1063), and Dyrrhachium (1081) were recorded to such an extent by contemporaries as to permit us to draw some conclusions about specific aspects such as deployment, terrain, troop types and formations, numbers, troop abilities and the wisdom or otherwise of commanders' tactical decisions made in the field.

The Normans certainly lost some battles. Whether the Norman mercenaries who fought at Cannae in 1018 were wholly responsible for the defeat is not possible to know. But there were other setbacks, such as the debacle on the beach at Messina in 1061 and Bohemond's defeats in Illyria. On the whole, our Norman commanders performed as well as their biographers would have us believe. But there is a word of warning. Most of the battles set out below were part of a wider historical picture, and few of them were the result of chance encounters.

Chapter 12

In the North

Val-ès-Dunes 1047

Introduction
By 1046 William, the seven-year-old bastard son of Duke Robert I of Normandy, was facing open hostility from a number of factions. He would soon turn to his feudal overlord Henry I, the king of France. The challenge to the duke's authority emanated from the Lower Normandy region and the goal of the rebel movement was to overthrow William in favour of one of their own.

The Armies
The armies that fought in the battle at Val-ès-Dunes in 1047 were based around the comital *familia* of each leader. That is to say, they were mounted household troops, or knights. Chief among the opponents of Duke William was his cousin, Guy of Burgundy, who had long seen himself as a successor to William. Guy held the castles at Vernon on the Seine and Brionne on the Risle. His army, however, would be drawn from rebels further west. Nigel I, vicomte of the Cotentin and Rannulf I, vicomte of the Bessin took the command of the combined force. They would be joined by other lords from Lower Normandy drawn from the region of the Cinglais between Caen and Falaise. Ralph Tesson, Lord of Thury, Grimoald of Plessis and Haimo Dentatus, lord of Creully, were among their number.

As an example of the desperate situation Duke William found himself in, there is a tale told by Wace (who had been a cleric at Caen) in the *Roman de Rou*. Grimoald attempted to seize and murder William while he was at Valognes on the Cotentin. William was warned of the plot and quickly rode across the Vire estuary in the dark and then on to Ryes, from where he rode to Poissy to appeal to the French King Henry I. The conspirators, who had hatched their plot at Bayeux, were now committed to war. It is not known what sort of a state Duke William was in when he threw himself at the mercy of the king, but his overlord duly obliged with his full support. And so early in 1047, a royal army crossed into Normandy.

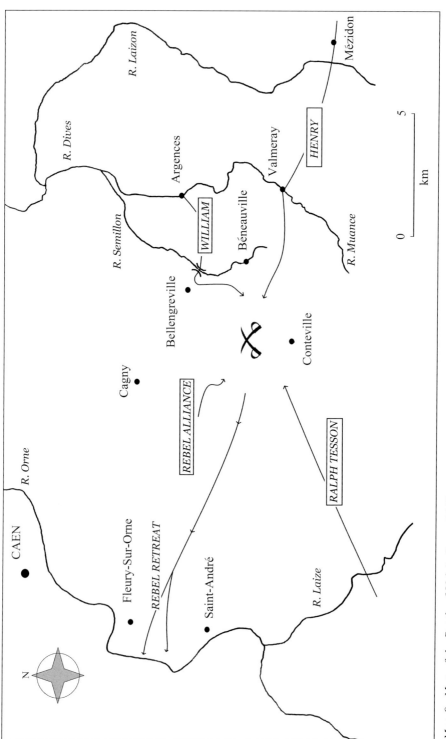

Map 9: Map of the Battle of Val-ès-Dunes 1047

The Castle at Melfi, Italy
The Normans and their Lombard leader Ardouin were given Melfi in 1042. Later, the Normans would make this fortress their base for the conquests of southern Italy. Here, twelve Norman commanders were awarded twelve counties, although some of these had yet to be conquered. In 1059 the Pope would invest Robert Guiscard 'by the Grace of God and Saint Peter Duke of Apulia and Calabria, and in future, with the help of both, of Sicily'.

The Sanctuary of Monte Sant' Angelo, Gargano, Italy
The famous shrine in the cave beneath this beautiful building is where the archangel Michael, the Normans' favourite warrior-saint made his earthly appearance in 490AD. It was also where the Lombard rebel Melus made his appeal for help to Norman pilgrims in around 1016.

The Abbey at Monte Cassino, Italy
Without Amatus of Monte Cassino our knowledge of the Norman conquest of southern Italy would be shrouded in mystery and contradiction. This famous and iconic monastery played a key role in both the politics and the recording of the eleventh century Lombard struggle against the Byzantines, which ultimately paved the way for Norman expansion.

The Natural Defences at Enna, Sicily
An impressive fortress in the centre of Sicily, Enna, usually known as Castrogiovanni, was the focus of many attacks, most of them thwarted by the town's natural defences. In the early 1060s Ibn al-Hawas was defeated outside the city but successfully withstood a Norman siege. Later, Serlo de Hauteville teased some of the garrison out of the town with a feigned flight but suffered greatly before he could bring them to a place where a Norman ambush had been set.

Gerace, Calabria, Italy
During a dispute between Roger de Hauteville and his brother Robert Guiscard, this hilltop town in Calabria became the focus of a curious struggle in which Robert Guiscard slipped into the settlement under disguise only to be spotted by a house servant who raised the alarm. Robert's own powerful oratory saved him from an angry mob of Roger's supporters, although the wife of the man whose house he had been found in was brutally murdered.

Paternò Castle in Catania, Sicily
Following the capture of Palermo, Great Count Roger of Sicily built a number of castles, of which this one at Paternò is a beautiful example, dating originally to 1073. Later modified and now heavily restored, it still stands in its picturesque setting, placed to protect the Simeto valley from Islamic raids.

Hastings Castle, East Sussex, England

This is the probable site of the earliest motte and bailey fortification erected after the Norman landings in England in 1066. Other such constructions are known from Edward the Confessor's (1042–1066) time in the marcher areas of England, manned by Norman castellans. However, this was the first constructed to deliberately dominate an important coastal town. The white stone placed in the wall in the foreground comes from Falaise castle.

Mont-Saint-Michel, France

Standing impressively at the mouth of the Couesnon, this monastery was reclaimed from the Bretons in 933 by William Longsword, the second ruler of Normandy. It was also the scene of a siege where in 1091 the two brothers Robert II Curthose and William II Rufus besieged their younger brother the future Henry I of England. William was dismayed to hear that Robert had offered their brother water during the siege.

Fiskardo Bay, Cephalonia

Sailing to meet his son Roger Borsa, Robert Guiscard was taken ill on board ship. This great Norman warrior, now nearly seventy years old, sailed around Cape Ather in Cephalonia. His concerned seamen put in either here at one of the tranquil bays which still bears his name, Fiskardo, or at the beach of Atheras further south on the island. On 17 July 1085, with his wife Sichelgaita at his side, the great man died. Later, he was taken back to Venosa and buried alongside his kinsmen.

Abbey of Santissima Trinatà at Venosa, Italy
After the Council of Melfi in 1059 the cathedral church was transformed into an abbey. It was a favourite with the de Hauteville family. The remains of five of the great Norman family are buried in the Old Church. The bones of William Iron Arm, Drogo, Humphrey, Robert Guiscard and his brother William of the Principate lie here in one tomb and in a separate structure Alberada the mother of Bohemond, prince of Antioch, is commemorated.

Church of San Giovanni Dei Lebbrosi, Palermo, Sicily
Whilst waiting for the sea support from his brother Robert Guiscard, Roger de Hauteville, on approaching the suburbs of Palermo, headed for the castle of Yahya, at the mouth of the Oreto. Of the Muslim garrison of forty-five men, fifteen were killed and thirty taken prisoner. It marked the beginning of a bloody siege lasting from 1071 into 1072. The castle of Yahya was converted into a stronghold by the Normans and then later into a church. In 1150 it became a leper hospital. The inner walls of this church comprise masonry from the original fortress.

Ruined Donjon of Domfront Castle, Normandy
Situated in the strategically vital border area of Lower Normandy and Maine, Domfront looks over the Varenne valley. First built by William de Bellême in 1010, it was taken by William the Conqueror from Geoffrey Martel (count of Anjou) in 1055. The Donjon is attributable to Henry I. It has a first floor doorway in common with many contemporary Norman structures.

Chepstow Castle, Monmouthshire, Wales
Built in stone, from the very outset the Norman keep or Donjon at Chepstow demonstrates the formidable power of the Normans in the marcher areas between England and Wales. Established by one of the chief architects of the Norman Conquest, this seat was held by William FitzOsbern, a close companion of the conqueror. Entry was via the doorway on the first floor.

Bayeux Tapestry, Norman supply cart

Supplies and weapons were distributed by packhorse, shipping and cartage. Here, in 1066 the Normans pull a cart of spears and armour, which also includes a large quantity of wine. The mail hauberks are carried by men who have threaded a wooden pole through the arms of the garment to make it easier to bear the load. Supplies for archers and crossbowmen were also carried in carts drawn by oxen. William II Rufus warned his adversary Helias of Maine in 1097 that he would face 'carts laden with bolts and arrows'.

Miscellany on the Life of St. Edmund

In a manuscript of around 1130 depicting the English Saint Edmund routing the Danes, the 'couched lance' style of mounted fighting can be seen. Inaccurately thought to have evolved between *c*.1066 and the mid-twelfth century, it is often cited as the secret of the Norman 'shock' impact on the battlefield. Far more important in that respect – as this picture shows – is the tightness of the formation of the horsemen. Anna Comnena, the Byzantine biographer of her father Alexius's life and reign, wrote 'A mounted Kelt is irresistible; he would bore his way through the walls of Babylon'.

Roger II is crowned king of Sicily in 1130, Santa Maria dell' Ammiraglio, Palermo, Sicily
This magnificent achievement sparked a cultural and political revolution when the son of Great Count Roger was crowned king in Sicily. The hand placing the crown on the head is that of Christ himself. However, Roger II, despite some military successes, did not have the same firebrand energy as his father and uncle. It was the tenacity and military skill of Robert Guiscard and Great Count Roger whose campaigns paved the way for one of the greatest medieval kingdoms in history.

Bamburgh Castle, Northumbria, England
An ancient and renowned fortress, Bamburgh was besieged by King William II Rufus in 1095 during the rebellion of Earl Robert of Mowbray. The king chose not to assault the castle, but built a counter castle to the north, preventing Robert getting help from northern allies. The structure the king built, to the jeers of the defenders, was called Malveisin (or in English 'Bad Neighbour').

The traditional battlefield site of Hastings at Battle Abbey, East Sussex, England
Some suggest the battle took place at Caldbec Hill, near to King Harold's forming-up point and camp. Whilst it is not unlikely there was fighting there, the traditional steep ridge further south is still the most likely place for the initial confrontation. Here, the later medieval abbey's dormitory range is heavily buttressed to support it on the steep slope rising to the north. William of Poitiers begins the battle account with 'The duke and his men, in no way frightened by the difficulty of the place, began slowly to climb the steep slope'.

Rochester Castle, Kent, England
Strategically important, Rochester Castle commands the River Medway. The earlier Norman castle was located on Boley Hill, erected as the Normans moved towards London in 1066. It became Bishop Odo's base for a rebellion in 1088 against King William II Rufus. When the king besieged it he erected siege castles around the site and forced the capitulation of Odo's supporters. The existing fine Norman tower dates to 1127 and was built by William de Corbeil, Archbishop of Canterbury.

Exchequer Hall at Caen Castle, Normandy, France
The fortifications at Caen were attended to by William the Conqueror in the years after the Battle of Val-ès-Dunes in 1047. This twelfth-century secular hall was built by King Henry I of England and was a particular favourite of his, probably providing the seat of the Norman Exchequer. The kitchens were on the lower level and the main hall on the first floor.

Deployment and Terrain

The countryside to the south-east of Caen is mainly flat, with a gentle slope towards the east. It is 'without hill or valley' according to Wace, and is ideal terrain for a pitched battle. The French army advanced towards Caen via Mézidon where some of William's troops joined from Upper Normandy. The duke had summonsed them from the areas around Evreux. Through Valmeray the joint force marched and here the king heard mass. Here also the royal troops were arrayed in battle order. Then the army came to the plain of Val-ès-Dunes where it was joined by William's main force arriving from its camp at Argences. From the west came the rebels, having crossed the River Orne in search of their prey.

William deployed to the right of the French king, with both divisions facing to the west. Against him in the distance stood 126 of Ralph Tesson's knights. Ralph's men reminded Ralph of his feudal obligations. He then rode directly to William and sought him out. It was clear that Ralph considered that his bonds to William were more important than his promises to the rebels. He remained with William for the battle to come.

The Battle

Wace gives us a detailed account of what followed in his *Roman de Rou*. It was a battle which raged across a wide landscape. He says William advanced towards the rebels and some of his men pointed out the enemy leaders. The battle appears to have been mainly a cavalry battle, although we cannot be certain of this. Wace recounts that there was a 'great stir' over the battlefield and horses were 'curvetting' (leaping with hind legs leaving the ground just before the forelegs touch the ground). The French war cry '*montjoie*' was heard, along with the Norman '*Dex Aie*'. Some knights retired, while others came up to the fray. Each side charged at the other with levelled lances. And then a man from the Cotentin struck the king of France himself.

The French king was apparently removed from his horse by a charging Norman rebel, who was trampled for his pains. The king's armour held firm and he was soon remounted. Haimo Dentatus fell next. A Frenchman struck him after he too had attacked King Henry. Haimo fell upon his shield and was carried away upon it, dead. The fighting became thicker at this point. Ralph Tesson became embroiled, and then the young Duke William thrust a lance into the throat of one of the enemy. The rebels wavered and there began a disordered retreat, much to the dismay of Nigel I. Rannulf I had already fled. The rout would turn to disaster. All of the rebels fled in confusion 'by fives, sixes and threes', says Wace. They sought out the safety of the Bessin as riderless horses scattered in all directions. The rout accounted for many of the dead. The rebels were chased to the River Orne and the bodies of those who perished in the river were said to have stopped-up the nearby mills.

The victory was greater than anyone could imagine. The anarchy of recent years would now be put right. The instigator of the rebellion, Guy of Burgundy, took refuge in Brionne before eventually returning to Burgundy. Grimoald was thrown into jail and Rannulf I was later pardoned. Haimo's estates were confiscated, but were ultimately returned to his son, Robert FitzHaimon. As for the duke himself, history would tell the rest of the tale. William the Conqueror had emerged from his minority with all the fighting spirit of a future king. He had won a typical cavalry engagement on an open plain.

Hastings, 14 October 1066

Introduction

The Battle of Hastings acts on the collective English mind as a momentous event in the country's history. We have much contemporary and near contemporary material upon which to base theories about Norman army formation, tactical capabilities, weapons, strategic awareness and numbers and so forth. One might think that with all this material the controversies would subside, but they have not. Recently, even the location of the battle site itself has been challenged.

The key texts which allow us to get a fairly reliable picture of events during the tumultuous autumn of 1066 vary in their content and usefulness. These are William of Poitiers' *Gesta Willelmi*, William of Jumièges's *Gesta Normannorum Ducum*, the *Anglo-Saxon Chronicle*, John of Worcester's *Chronicle*, the *Carmen de Hastingae Proelio* and of course the famous Bayeux Tapestry, the threads of which bring an epic tale to pictorial life.

It is what these sources can tell us about the way in which the battle came about, how it was fought and why it was won, which is important. Hastings was a prolonged set-piece battle which Duke William of Normandy simply had to win. The longer he remained in hostile territory with his army unrewarded, the worse things would get. Unlike the situation in Italy where battling principalities provided the opportunity for slow Norman mercenary infiltration before they finally took over, the situation in the sophisticated and centrally organised Anglo-Saxon kingdom of England meant that the kingdom could only be taken in one way, by eliminating the man who had taken the English crown from under Duke William's nose.

The political build-up to the Battle of Hastings is a tale which covers nearly a century of English and Norman history. Key moments along the way include the marriage of the English King Ethelred II Unræd (979–1016) to Emma of Normandy in 1002 and the subsequent raising of their half-Norman children Edward (soon to become 'the Confessor', king of England from 1042–1066) and Alfred. The exile of these two young men was followed by the murder in 1035 of the returning Atheling Alfred in cold blood near to Guildford in Surrey. It was an act for which the Normans squarely blamed Earl Godwin of Wessex, whose house had risen during the years of the Danish kings of England (1016–1042). Then, of course, there was the so-called 'promise' sworn in around 1064 on holy relics at Bonneville by Earl Harold of Wessex, son of Godwin. Tradition has it that Harold swore to promote Duke William's claim to the throne of England. Edward the Confessor died in January 1066 and in his place Earl Harold was elected, not – much to his dismay – Duke William. It took the duke many months to prepare for an invasion of England and in late September King Harold had defeated another pretender to the throne, the Norwegian King Harald Siggurdson at the Battle of Stamford Bridge.

William's invasion fleet was said by Wace to have been 700 ships strong. On 28 September 1066 it sailed from Saint Valéry-sur-Somme, having finally caught the eagerly anticipated south-westerly winds. However, its earlier starting point had been at Dives-sur-Mer further west. When it set out from here, the fleet was nearly wrecked upon the lee shores of north-east France before putting in at Saint Valéry.

William of Malmesbury tells us that the duke had told Harold 'he would claim what was his by force of arms and come to a place where Harold supposed his footing secure'. To the west of Pevensey lay the rich Sussex estates of Harold's family, as well as the Steyning estate, seized by Harold from the monks of Fécamp Abbey. The Dives Estuary is directly opposite these English areas on the other side of the Channel. However, on the morning of 29 September 1066 it was at the old Roman fort of Pevensey where William set up his first temporary fortification on the western side of a salt marsh. His appearance on the south coast of England went largely unchallenged, save for the crews of a few errant vessels that strayed onto the defended shore line at Romney.

In the north of England King Harold, who had already dismissed his Isle of Wight fleet, heard news of the landing. Then came word that the Norman fleet had moved up the coast to Hastings and was ravaging around it. Within two weeks Harold was back in London, where he would not wait long before he moved against William. In London Harold's brother Earl Gyrth, according to Orderic Vitalis, is said to have offered to lead the army into Sussex for the king so Harold could keep a force in reserve. The two English earls, Edwin and Morcar, were also present in London, along with Archbishop Aldred. They too may have been told to keep forces in reserve. Harold had just achieved a complete victory at Stamford Bridge using the element of surprise against King Harald of Norway, and it is possible that he was anxious to repeat the performance against William. It is possible too that the English fleet was being prepared in London for a blockading action in the English Channel, to prevent the Norman fleet from turning back.

Harold was no fool of a general. He does, however, seem to have been hung up on the 'surprise' strategy in the Hastings campaign. It is mentioned by William of Jumièges. If this was his thinking, Harold need not have waited for huge reinforcements. Jumièges says that William had already told his men to prepare for it. William of Poitiers says that Harold's plan was for a night surprise, supported by a fleet of 700 ships to finish off the retreaters. The Carmen mentions the surprise attack too. With such weighty evidence for Harold's plan for a surprise attack on William's position at Hastings, in light of the eventual outcome we might conclude that something went wrong. It was William, and not Harold, who achieved surprise at Hastings. John of Worcester tells us more:

> Thereat the king at once, and in great haste, marched his army towards London; and although he well knew that some of the bravest Englishmen had fallen in his two [former] battles, and that one half of his army had not yet arrived, he did not hesitate to advance with all speed into South Saxony [Sussex] against his enemies; and on Saturday the 11th of the kalends of September [a mistake by John], before a third of his army was in order for fighting, he joined battle with them nine [sic] miles from Hastings, where they had fortified a castle. But inasmuch as the English were drawn up in a narrow place, many retired from the ranks and very few remained true to him.

So, with 'half' an army Harold had marched into Sussex. Before even a third of these troops had deployed, battle commenced. On the morning of 14 October 1066, at Senlac in the modern town of Battle in East Sussex, two medieval armies faced each other. The Anglo-Saxon force found itself blocking the road to London against William's army, which had stolen a march on it and arrived where it had not been expected – far too close to the forming-up place chosen by Harold for his own army to gather additional regional forces and then march onto Hastings. The tables had been turned. The element of surprise was all William's.

The Armies
It has been said that the armies that faced each other at Hastings were technologically and organisationally different, and the impression we get from commentators over the centuries is that on the one side you had the 'modern' feudal army (the Normans), with all the sophistication in combined arms that brings, and on the other you had an archaic, obsolete infantry force in the Anglo-Saxons. This is a grotesquely over-simplified view. If any of us had seen Harold's men riding south from London and William's army riding north from Hastings, we would have been hard pressed to tell them apart. At the elite end of the spectrum, the English housecarls and senior thegns were equipped in the same way as the Norman milites, or knights. Each had a mail hauberk or 'byrnie', each had a shield, sword, spear and side-arm. We might observe subtle differences in the design of the mailcoat. Judging by the Bayeux Tapestry the Normans had a curious square patch on the front of their chests, which has been interpreted as a mailed veil of some sort, which they could pull up under their conical helmets, whereas the English do not appear to have these. Perhaps the most distinctive feature we would have recognised in the senior warriors of Harold's army would have been the great

Dane-Axes of the housecarls. And yet the Norman baggage train in the Bayeux Tapestry is equipped with such weaponry. However, the solid infantry phalanxes of later Anglo-Saxon England, brave and impressive though they were, lacked a tactical capability when compared to the force which William brought. Manoeuvrability was the issue. The English – by all accounts – dismounted to fight. The Norman army had its own complement of infantry (strangely absent from the Bayeux Tapestry), but of course there were cavalry and archers too.

The size of the respective armies has been a matter of heated debate for centuries. From the Ship List of William the Conqueror and other educated guesswork it is likely that the Norman army at Hastings totalled in the region of 7,000 men, including 1,500 archers, 2,000 mounted knights and the remainder heavy infantry. The Ship List is a document written between 1130 and 1160, probably copied from an original list compiled at Fécamp shortly after the Conquest. It details the probable results of agreements made between William and fourteen of his vassals as to who was to provide the necessary ships and also indicates in a few instances how many knights they were to supply. These vassals all held harbour rights in Normandy, either on the sea coast or along the major rivers. In its first section the document mentions a total of 776 ships, but in its

Duke William's flagship, the Mora, *from the Bayeux Tapestry, which is also described in a twelfth-century document known as the 'Ship List'. Note the golden infant figure on the prow blowing a horn and pointing to England.*

second increases this to 1,000 plus sundry others. This discrepancy may be due to the document not mentioning the duke's own ship contribution. There is a third part to the document which describes how William's wife Matilda provided the ship called the *Mora* for the duke. She made a golden infant figure for the prow, with its right finger pointing to England and with its left hand pressing an ivory horn to his lips. The very same vessel can be seen on the Bayeux Tapestry, sailing for Pevensey.

Harold's army is supposed to have been larger, but we have already observed that not only did he have fewer men with him than desired, but also that he was caught out before his army had fully come together. We will never know the accurate numbers. But of names, we have more evidence. In fact, the list of participants known to have fought at Hastings in Table 1 below (more comprehensive, of course, for the Normans), gives a small and yet treacherous clue to possible numbers. If we bravely assume that each of the names on the Norman list represents someone important enough to command his own *conroi*, or squadron of knights, and then guess at the average size of a *conroi* being roughly twenty-five men, then the total of mounted knights suggested by these names alone would be in the region of 900 to 1,000. What is more, of the fourteen names on the Ship List only four owe a specific number of knights (280 in all), which averages out at seventy knights for each of those on the list, if we can assume that those listed without knight quotas did in fact owe some. Strangely, this gives a total of around 1,000 knights from the Ship List alone. This we might assume to be the lowest possible number of knights for the expedition, taking into account those not mentioned in the sources. It is all speculation, however, and clearly fraught with difficulty. What is clear, is that the Hastings expedition and the subsequent battle on Senlac Ridge were in no way small-scale events.

TABLE 1

Probable combatants at Hastings (fatalities indicated by 'k'. Ship numbers from the Ship List indicated by figure in bold):

The Norman Army	The English Army
William, Duke of Normandy	Harold II Godwinson, king of England (k)
Odo, Bishop of Bayeux (**100**)	Gyrth (Harold's brother), Earl of East Anglia (k)
Robert Count of Mortain (**120**)	Leofwine (Harold's brother), Earl of Kent (k)
Eustace, Count of Boulogne	Hakon (Harold's nephew) (k)
Geoffrey, Bishop of Coutances	Ælfwig (Harold's uncle), Abbot of Winchester (k)
Alan the Red of Brittany	Leofric, Abbot of Peterborough

Robert, count of Eu (**60**)
William FitzOsbern (**60**)

Aimeri, Vicomte of Thouars

Turstin, son of Rollo, standard bearer

Hugh (Ivo) of Ponthieu
Walter Giffard I (**30**)
Walter Giffard II
Roger de Beaumont (**60**)
Roger de Montgomery (**60**)
William, son of count of Evreux
Geoffrey, son of count of Mortagne
Humphrey of Tilleul
Ralf de Tosny
Robert de Beaumont
Fulk d'Aunou (**40**)
William count of Evreux [or possibly
  his father Richard] (**80**)
Hugh of Montfort (**50**)
Hugh of Grandmesnil
Hugh of Avranches (**60**)
Nicholas abbot of Saint-Ouen (**15**)
William de Warenne
William Malet
Gulbert of Auffay
Robert of Vitot (k)
Engenulf of Laigle (k)
Remegius monk of Fecamp (**1**)
Rodulf (Ralf) de Tancarville
Gerelmus of Panileuse
Robert FitzErneis (k)
Roger, son of Turold (k)
Taillefer (k)
Erchembald
Vital
Wadard
Pons
Hugh of Ivry
Richard FitzGilbert
Gerold the steward (**40**)

Ælfwold, abbot
Ansgar the Staller, sheriff of
  Middlesex
Godric, sheriff of Fyfield, Berkshire
  (k)
Thurkill, thegn of Kingston Bagpuize,
  Berks (k)
Eadric the Deacon of East Anglia
Ælfric, thegn of Huntingdonshire
Skalpi, housecarl
Alwi of Thetford
Ringolf of Oby
Breme, freeman (k)
'Son of Helloc' (k)

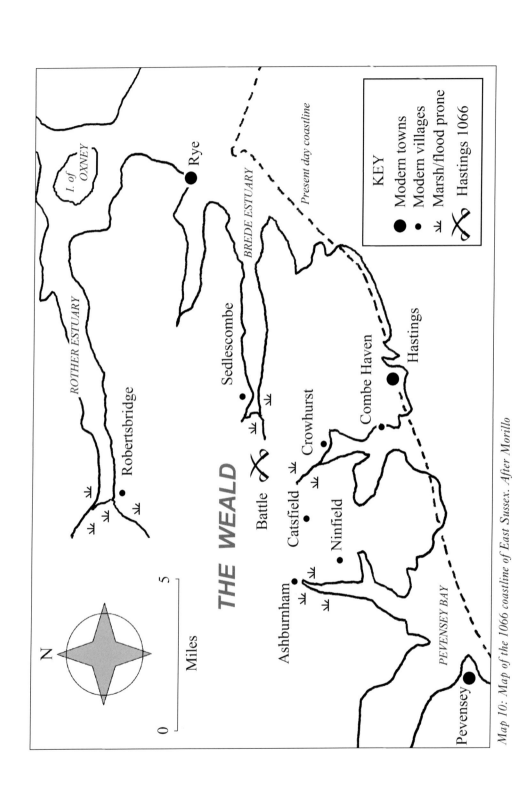

Map 10: Map of the 1066 coastline of East Sussex. After Morillo.

Deployment and Terrain

The Sussex coast has changed since 1066. When William landed at Pevensey a whole area to the east of the fort was salt marsh and untraversable. Tidal inlets prevented an army going through it. For William's force to march to the settlement at Hastings he would have to take a circuitous route. Leaving behind a garrison at the fort they would have to march through Standard Hill at Ninfield, and down the seven mile ridgeway road to Hastings. Far better to take the sea route. As is evidenced by The *Carmen*, the Bayeux Tapestry and William of Poitiers, the Normans sailed to Hastings ('as soon as they were fit' says the *Anglo-Saxon Chronicle*). Two hours after setting off at high tide they would have arrived at Combe Haven near to Hastings. William had brought with him a pre-fabricated wooden fortification, which the Normans constructed on the site of the present castle on top of a newly constructed motte. A long road to London from Hastings stretched along the ridgeway to the north and penetrated the thickly wooded weald of Sussex. William then commenced the systematic reduction of the Hastings area. To the west of him was Combe Haven and to the east the landscape curved around to the north from the Fairlight cliffs. To the north the Brede Estuary stretched as far inland as Sedlescome. William was in effect, at the wrong end of a peninsula. There was only one way out of this place and that was directly to the north.

But where did the battle take place? Harold had marched his way through the thickly wooded weald to the place of the 'hoary apple tree', a meeting point at the junction of three separate hundreds. His purpose was surely to meet with the forces he had summoned to help him. Here, on the high ground at Caldbec Hill, Harold was a short march from the Norman camp at Hastings some seven miles away. But this is where the tables were turned on Harold. One of King Edward the Confessor's Breton ministers had visited the duke in his camp at Hastings to tell him of the expected numbers of English who might swallow him up in the countryside if he ventured out. William must have known by now that the longer he waited, the more likely he was to be overwhelmed. He headed out of the Hastings peninsula before he was trapped within it.

William of Poitiers says that before the battle an exchange of embassies took place. Harold had sent a trusted monk to William at Hastings telling him to leave the kingdom. The duke, who responded in person by pretending to be his own seneschal, sent the monk back to Harold with his own embassy, Hugh Margot, the next day. Much dialogue ensued over the broken promise, but the English king was told the duke was not going home. Harold then put it to God to decide. By now, Harold's position was known to the Normans and it probably came as a surprise to William to learn just how close he was. Tradition has it that William's army camped at Telham Hill and chose to deploy at the foot of a slope across the London to Hastings trackway. At the top of the slope was a lateral ridge only 900 yards wide with steep drops and forested valleys on either side. To the north was

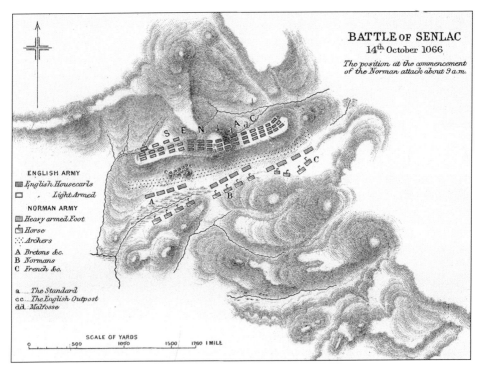

Victorian historian E.A. Freeman's map of the Battle of Hastings showing topographical detail, a defensive English palisade (after Wace) and neat units. The map itself may still have much to recommend it, although Freeman was later the victim of J.H. Round's wide-ranging invective over countless topics in 1895.

Harold, now aware of the arrival of an army he had not expected. Somewhere behind him in the weald and beyond to the north, reinforcements were making their way towards him. But the battle would take place over a constricted front with Harold's men fighting many ranks deep, and some of them at the rear unable to bring their weapons to bear. For William, the gamble would be to have to fight the most costly of all types of battle – a frontal assault.

Wace, in his *Roman de Rou*, is very specific on William's deployment. He says William's Breton contingent was on the left flank in company with the men of Poitou (sometimes called Aquitanians in other sources). With them were also the men of Maine. In the centre section were the Normans of Duke William with some of his men spilled over to the right under the command of Roger of Montgomery (who is thought by some not to have arrived in England until the following year) and William FitzOsbern. On this flank too were the men of Poux in Picardy, the men of Boulogne and some Flemish mercenaries.

As for the English, there is a suggestion by William of Malmesbury that Harold placed his standards at the highest part of the slope. Wace has a defensive palisade constructed by the English. It has been suggested in recent years that not only did Harold line the ridge, but he also pinned a flank on a small hill on his right. His line, instead of being bent round the contour of the hill, would have been flatter and skewed at right angles to the road to Hastings. It is argued that the lightly armed men seen in the Bayeux Tapestry desperately defending a small hillock are in fact trying to hold this flank.

Recent efforts have been made to shift the focus of the whole battle to Caldbec Hill (the place of the English camp) and it makes sense to argue that some of fighting took place here. It is certainly the case that many thousands of people (the combined size of the forces) would have covered a wide area of the landscape and we should be looking at a bigger picture, away from the confines of the ridge itself. It is conceivable that the first stage of fighting took place on the slopes where the medieval abbey stands and then, after the English were chased up the ridge towards their baggage at Caldbec Hill, a second phase developed. To localise the battle entirely around Caldbec Hill, however, is something of a leap of faith. This notwithstanding, we know that the terrain was difficult for both sides and that it was one of the hardest fought frontal assaults in medieval history. Apart from the usage of the Norman feigned flight there was little room for the tactical freedom usually expected for the Norman knights. This was a battle in which bravery on both sides would play the largest part.

The Battle
The battle began with the approach towards the English army of Taillefer, a Norman juggler. Henry of Huntington has him juggling his sword in front of the enemy and heading straight for the English standard, where he slew two men before meeting a predictable fate. The sound of horns then heralded the real beginning of the battle. It was the Norman infantry, according to Poitiers, who advanced first, probably the bowmen, who provoked the English lines with their 'missiles'. But they got too close and were met with a missile riposte.

The Norman cavalry rode to rescue the infantry, who had got into difficulties. An exchange of ranks is suggested by Poitiers – a very complex evolution – and it resulted in the Norman horsemen being able to hack their way towards the English lines as the bowmen retreated. But the response was emphatic. Soon, the duke had to rethink. Both Poitiers and the *Carmen* remark upon the difficulty of the place, the latter going as far as saying that the English dead could not even fall down to the ground, but remained rooted shoulder-to-shoulder with their comrades. Poitiers hints that the assistance given to the infantry by the Norman cavalry at this stage came from William's central command and included the duke himself. But here we enter the mists of tradition again, with the insistence by Poitiers that the Normans instigated the tactic of the feigned flight (pages 222-223). He has it done once by accident at this early stage of the battle and twice more deliberately.

The Bretons yielded first. They fell back with the infantry on the left flank and caused almost the whole army to break. The duke then rode in to personally rally the troops and, as the rumours of his own untimely demise were spread, the duke lifted his helmet to reveal he was still alive. Harold might have ordered his whole army to advance at this stage and capitalise on the enemy disarray, but the English still stood largely rooted to the spot, except for a number of Harold's men who ran from the hill and were cut off and annihilated. Perhaps this missed opportunity reveals a difficulty in communication between Harold and his front line.

Harold's brother Gyrth, according to the *Carmen* is then set against the duke himself. Duke William then mistakes Gyrth for his brother Harold. It is probably here that Gyrth fell in battle, having been at his brother's side until this point. The war of attrition was now edging in favour of the Normans. The English were unable to tactically manoeuvre and had to stand and take the repeated onslaught.

Harold moved his standards to the eastern flank of his army away from the summit. Here, it is said by the *Brevis Relatio* (written by a monk from Battle Abbey), that the High Altar of the Abbey Church was set in remembrance of where Harold fell. There must have been some trouble on this flank. It was the shallower of the two flanking slopes of the English lines and it is probable that the Franco-Flemish wing had been gradually carving its way up the English flank. The king came forward to his lines to reinforce a desperate situation and it seems this was where the famous last stand took place. Historians have struggled to reconcile this interpretation with William of Jumièges's statement that Harold fell in the first wave of attacks. Jumièges's words are that Harold fell '*in primo militum congressu*' meaning 'in the first military encounter'. For Harold, the move to the eastern flank and the stepping into the front line to shore up a problem would indeed have been *his* first military encounter in the battle, if we accept William of Malmesbury's notion that the king had set his standards way up at the top of the hill. Therefore, this might have been the first (and the last) of Harold's actions on the battlefield.

The Norman archers were busy at this crucial stage. Infantrymen were sent towards the English standards. Robert FitzErneis raced forward to grab the English standard, but was cut down by blades, his mangled body discovered later at the foot of the fallen English standard. But the pressure on Harold's household troops was too much. He was slaughtered there on Senlac Ridge, wounded in the chest, decapitated and maimed in the leg. The Normans had removed the head of the English government in one single titanic struggle.

The English army began to retreat. Back along what was to become Battle High Street they stumbled, towards the camp at Caldbec Hill which they had left earlier that day. Those of any rank who were left must have held on to thoughts of making it back to London, or linking up with the northern earls Edwin and Morcar, but for the most part the English army's morale was destroyed.

Darkness began to creep over the Sussex hills. Five sources tell of some Norman horsemen chasing the defeated English to the north. These knights

The site of the High Altar at Battle Abbey, the traditional site of the death of King Harold of England.

suffered a catastrophe at a huge ditch they knew nothing about. William of Poitiers says the Normans rode after the English until the enemy found an excellent position on a steep bank with numerous ditches. William of Jumièges says that some long grass had hidden from the Normans an 'ancient causeway', into which they fell with their horses. William of Malmesbury says the English had taken possession of an 'eminence' and drove the Normans down as they strove to gain the higher ground. The English had arrived by a short passage known to them. They trod underfoot so many Normans as to make the ditch level with the ground. The name given to this ditch is provided by the twelfth-century *Chronicle of Battle Abbey*. 'Between the two armies lay a dreadful chasm' it says – the *'malfosse'* ('evil ditch'). It was a natural cleft or something which had been 'hollowed out by storms'.

Orderic Vitalis explains that there was an ancient rampart concealed by long grasses. The Norman horsemen fell into it at a gallop. The English then saw that they could be sheltered by the 'broken rampart and labyrinth of ditches', and so re-formed their ranks and made a stand against the Normans, killing 15,000 [sic] of them, a surely exaggerated number. The location of the 'malfosse' has been much debated. E.A. Freeman, the eminent Victorian scholar, thought it was a ditch behind Battle Church, whereas Francis Baring in 1906 had it on the western side of the battlefield at a place called Manser's Shaw. Far more likely is that the Normans chased the English to their camp at Caldbec Hill and carried on chasing them to the north as they continued their retreat. Six hundred yards to the north of Caldbec Hill, just beyond Virgin's Lane, is a colossal chasm in the ground known to locals as Oakwood Gill. The ground falls away sharply into a wooded glade. It is so remarkably huge that it is easy to miss. It is probably here that the famous incident took place.

Oakwood Gill, to the north of Caldbec Hill, near to Virgin's Lane. Battle, Sussex. This deep chasm in the ground is possibly the site of the famous 'malfosse' incident which accounted for many Norman cavalry casualties in 1066.

Eustace of Boulogne and Duke William both believed that those Englishmen lining the northern side of the ditch were newly arrived reinforcements. Certainly, for a group of men to form up in an orderly way upon such a feature indicates that they may not have been part of the fleeing army, but were members of a fresh command or had been rallied by the same. Whoever the new commander was, he might have been one of the men Harold was waiting for at Caldbec Hill. Earl Waltheof is a possible candidate. Waltheof continued to feature in the politics of England in the years after Hastings. Or it might be that the earls Edwin and Morcar did in fact come down from London. John of Worcester hints that they 'withdrew from the conflict' after hearing of Harold's death and went to London. To 'withdraw' from something implies that first of all one has to have been committed to it.

The Battle of Hastings, for all its wealth of literature, still keeps its secrets from us. If we are able to entertain arguments, some 900 years later, as to the precise location of the battle, then it is an indicator of the nature of the enigma. The traditional site has yielded not a single convincing artefact or human skeleton. Somewhere between Senlac Ridge and Caldbec Hill is a small square of earth still enriched with the blood spilled in the famous last stand of the English, a spot which marks both a tremendous victory and a heroic defeat. One still hopes for an archaeological discovery to send a new generation of historians gleefully into unchartered waters.

Tinchebrai, 28 September 1106

Introduction

The autumn of 1106 was marked by violent thunderstorms and rain showers. The dark skies were to presage battlefield misery too. The Battle of Tinchebrai was the first major battle between the king of England and the duke of Normandy since their epic encounter at Hastings in 1066. There had been celestial warnings in the sky then too. However, this time the battle would be remarkably different, displaying some of the more common characteristics of Norman warfare. Duke Robert II Curthose had long since returned from the First Crusade. Within sight of the castle at Tinchebrai, near the border of what was the county of Mortain, the battle between Henry I and his brother Robert was fought. It started out as a siege action not dissimilar to many others of its time.

Henry I had been campaigning in Normandy the previous year and had come over with his Anglo-Norman army in the spring of 1106. He had recently taken the fortified abbey at Saint-Pierre Sur Dives and later set up a fortification near to the castle at Tinchebrai. Within this fortification he placed Thomas de Saint Jean. Thomas's job was to check the sorties of the men of William of Mortain and thereby prevent them from gaining any advantage from sallying from the castle. But William defied the siege castle set against him and, with a large body of knights, reinforced the castle and gathered supplies while Thomas's men timidly looked on. Henry decided to intervene directly and brought his forces to Tinchebrai so he could invest it more closely. Duke Robert could not tolerate this for long. He arrived at Tinchebrai with his own force and the stage was set for another history-changing encounter between Normandy and England.

Orderic Vitalis, the *Roman de Rou*, Henry of Huntington and an intriguing letter from a priest of Fécamp provide the source material for Tinchebrai, in addition to the words of King Henry I himself, contained in a letter to Anselm. Using all these, we can glean some evidence for the make-up and formation of the armies and the course of the battle.

The Armies

Thomas de Saint Jean had been sent ahead by Henry I with a large body of horse and foot, according to Orderic, although numbers are not known. Quite what role Thomas's men actually played or where they were deployed is also unclear. However, we are on firmer ground with the others in Henry's army. Helias of Maine had command of a mounted unit consisting of Bretons and the men of Le Mans. Our Fécamp priest suggests the number to be around 1,000. Helias's role would be crucial. Other sub-commanders were William of Evreux, Robert count of Meulan, Robert de Mellent and William II de Warrenne. In addition, Orderic describes the senior noble forces of Ranulf of Bayeux, Ralph de Conches, Robert de Montfort (some think he was on the other side), Robert de Grandmesnil and others with their vassals. There was also Alan Fergant of Brittany. It was an impressive force. But these sub-commands were not the whole picture. Around Henry was the fighting element of the *Familia Regis*, consisting of men tied to the household of the king. Alongside these were the Anglo-Norman fyrdsmen (see pages 176-178 for a discussion of the fyrd). Somewhere among all this was probably a force of archers, although this cannot be proved. Duke Robert's army may have had archers to add to its large infantry contingent. The duke's army consisted of the men of Robert de Bellême held in a mounted division at the rear of his infantry line, plus those of William of Mortain, Robert Stuteville and the Englishman Edgar the Ætheling.

There have been arguments as to whether it was the infantry or the cavalry which played the key role at Tinchebrai. It is generally thought that Henry's army was the larger, but that Duke Robert's comprised more infantry. Henry's response to the size of the enemy infantry was to demand that his knights dismount and fight on foot. In fact, Henry of Huntington says that both leaders and their lines fought on foot so they could be more resolute. It is a notion which suggests that when the stakes were high, the infantry played a more prominent role.

Deployment and Terrain

The topography of the battlefield is not certain. The fighting took place near the castle held by William of Mortain and was essentially a pitched battle resulting from an attempt to break a siege. There are no references to the difficulty of the fighting. The armies deployed after an initial parley between the brothers, according to Orderic Vitalis. A hermit (also known as Vitalis) intervened to stop the brothers from facing each other in single combat. Then messages were sent from Henry I to his brother. He told him that Robert had been planted in Normandy like a 'barren tree'. Moreover, he had mistreated the church. If Robert would hand him all the strongholds of Normandy and the management of one half of it, then Henry would give him the revenues of the other half and would pay for his own half out of the treasury of England. That way, Henry jibed, the duke could revel all he liked in feasting and sports.

Robert listened to his council and refused the offers of his brother. Henry, trusting now in God, gathered his commanders around him and set about his business. To keep William II de Warenne in good fighting spirits Henry released some prisoners, which included William's kinsman Reynold. Then, Henry is recorded by Orderic as specifically laying out his plans for the forthcoming battle, a rare reference. He directed them, says Orderic, to act as time and circumstance required – a clear indication of the tactical capability of his troops. It was probably at this moment that the mounted force of Helias of Maine was sent on a flanking march out of sight of the static ducal army now drawing up on the battlefield at Tinchebrai. The timing of the arrival of this force would be critical to Henry's plans.

Henry sent forward a first wave of troops under Ranulf of Bayeux, which comprised the men of Bayeux, Avranches and Coutances. Some people have argued that this force may have been deployed in echelon, as opposed to line abreast, but this seems unlikely given the job they were tasked with. Robert of Meulan was behind this line with the king himself and in an additional line was William II de Warenne. The rear was also supported by a line of Anglo-Norman fyrdsmen and dismounted knights. Somewhere – we do not know where – were up to 700 cavalry.

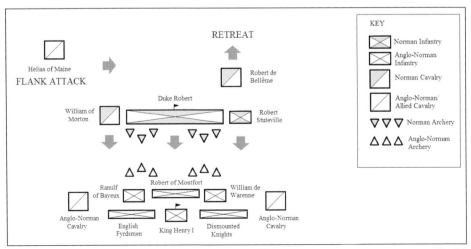

Possible deployments for the Battle of Tinchebrai, 1106   *Fig. 12*

The Battle

Henry of Huntington says the battle commenced with the sound of 'shrill trumpets' and that Duke Robert took the initiative. He crashed his infantry line into the heart of his enemy, seemingly heading straight for his brother the king. Robert had learned his tactics in the wars of Jerusalem, says Henry of Huntington. Fresh from the crusades Robert seems to have tried to repeat a successful tactic of charging at the enemy standard to deliver a fatal shock to the leader. This was not new. The tenth-century *Praecepta Militaria*, written for the Byzantine emperor Nicephorus Phocas in around 963, recommended that Imperial cavalry do exactly this. The difficulty in the Tinchebrai context is that it smacks of a cavalry action rather than an infantry one. But it seems that Henry I was expecting the onslaught. The result of this coming together would have pleased Henry, for it locked in place the important units of Robert's army. Orderic says:

> When the two armies came together they were so densely packed and stood with their weapons so closely locked that they could do nothing to each other, and all attempted in turn to break the solid line.

The battle was already becoming an old-fashioned infantry tussle. However, William of Mortain is described as attacking Henry's force from point to point, indicating a manoeuvrability associated with cavalry. But with the armies locked in combat, something had to give. Henry's plan of sending Helias of Maine on a flanking attack paid off. The battle was only about an hour old when Helias arrived at the rear of the ducal forces and surrounded the units already engaged to their front. As Helias went into the fray, Robert de Bellême gazed upon the scene from his position further to the rear. He did not strike a blow in anger. His duke was surrounded and engulfed by the Anglo-Norman army. Robert de Bellême quickly fled the battlefield, leaving the duke to be seized by one of Henry's chaplains, a man named Gaudry or Waldric. The swift Bretons seized William of Mortain, who along with Robert Stuteville would face a long imprisonment. The arrival of Helias on the battlefield accounted for 225 casualties in a short encounter in which the prisoners taken outnumbered the casualties. Henry I would write that the battle was won without any great slaughter of his own men, and 400 knights were taken prisoner along with a seemingly improbable 10,000 foot. The letter of the Fécamp monk suggests that Henry lost only two men and had one wounded – Robert of Bonnebosc. Of his enemy's casualties, however, the king himself is somewhat more bellicose: 'of those killed by the sword there is no reckoning'.

The battle may have been short, but it was decisive. It was not a battle of annihilation, nor a battle to the death. The goals of Henry I were achieved with the capture of Duke Robert. Unlike the Ætheling Edgar, who was later released into a life of obscurity, Duke Robert began a long incarceration. It was an ignominious end. However, the Battle of Tinchebrai stands as a testimony to the tactical skill of his brother Henry I.

Alençon December 1118

Introduction
The Battle of Alençon has received less attention than other battles in the reign of Henry I. This may well be because he lost the battle, but also because the fullest account of it comes not from a Norman or Anglo-Norman source, but from the *Chronicle of the Deeds of the Counts of Anjou*.

The campaign centred on the enmity between the count of Anjou Fulk V and Henry. Alençon had been the focal point of antagonism between Normans and the men of Maine for years. But in 1118 the castle was held for Henry by his nephew Stephen of Blois (the future King Stephen I of England). Stephen's rough treatment of the local people had prompted them to call to the Angevin count for aid. And so Fulk came to Alençon to besiege the castle, setting himself up in a defendable park nearby.

The Armies
The Angevin source says that Henry went out to challenge the besiegers at Alençon with a mixture of knights and foot which 'covered the face of the earth like locusts'. We do not know its exact component parts, but it is most likely to have consisted of combined arms: cavalry, infantry and archery. In fact, Henry is said to have launched attacks with both bowmen and crossbowmen. Fulk's Angevin army was similarly organised, with archery playing a significant part in what was to follow. Orderic Vitalis describes his forces as divided into milites (knights), sagittarios (archers) and pedites (infantry). Within the park on the Angevin side were Hugh of Mathéfelon, Rainald of Castro, Hugh of Amboise and Fulk V of Anjou himself.

Deployment and Terrain
Fulk's forces remained in the park area when Henry's forces arrived. The battle took place beneath the walls of the castle, but the role of the defendable park was key. Quite how it was defended and how Henry's army arrayed itself when it arrived, we do not know. The ground was fairly flat, however, and there are no hints of any difficulty in topography for either side. Henry's army split into two or more divisions, with Theobald and Stephen leading the first, which is thought to have comprised some of the younger and more enthusiastic members of the king's *familia*. This first division, somewhat 'greedy for glory', advanced ahead of Henry's main division. Stephen's later reputation during the period of the English anarchy (1135–1154) for a precipitous approach to tactical level fighting might appear to be in early evidence here.

The Battle

The battle started as a series of skirmishes, with Fulk sending out from his enclosure small combined arms parties of mounted knights and archers. Hugh of Mathéfelon led the first group with 100 knights and 200 archers or sergeants. There were two more such sorties, which made no impression on Henry's forces and each group in turn was forced to retreat to the park. However, there was another Angevin force in the field, and the arrival of this force was the undoing of King Henry in what was one of his few defeats.

The new force was commanded by Lisiard of Sablé. On his arrival Lisiard could hear the commotion of the skirmishes and taunts of the knights on both sides, even from four miles distant. He decided to dismount his men in a nearby wood, had them put on their armour and then mustered them together. From here Lisiard himself led the first line against Henry's army and it consisted of the dismounted knights, other infantry and archers. At a pre-arranged signal the Angevins charged the enemy line and the archers did much damage, including wounding Theobald of Blois, causing temporary blinding in one eye as the blood from his wound seeped into it. Fulk of Anjou chose this moment to spring forth from the enclosure. He exhorted his men, urging them to copy him. A mixture of cavalry, foot and archery hurled itself at the Anglo–Normans. The result was a disaster for Henry. His army fled in disarray and he lost numerous men. The Angevins lost only four archers and twenty-five infantry. Alençon surrendered to Fulk and the Angevin count was able to negotiate a favourable peace.

The lessons of Alençon would soon be learned by Henry I. However, the battle was an example of what is so often ascribed to the Normans in victory but in this case was shown by the Angevins: strong leadership, tactical organisation and firm discipline. Moreover, the effectiveness of organised infantry over rash cavalry cannot have escaped Henry's notice.

Brémule 20 August 1119

Introduction

The Battle of Brémule is another example of King Henry I's ability to deliver a very 'typical' yet consummate battlefield performance, displaying all the common characteristics of a Norman pitched battle where the key opponents shared the same religion and similar social disposition. Our accounts of it vary from one to the other, making it hard to discern unit formations and sequences of action. However, there is enough for us to be able to conclude that once again the capture of prisoners was more desirable than the annihilation of the enemy.

The battle was fought between King Henry I of England and King Louis VI 'the Fat' of France. We rely on Orderic Vitalis, who gives a colourful account of it, but loses some detail in the actual battle itself. We also turn to Suger's *Life of the French King*, the *Hyde Chronicle* (which provides useful additional detail) and Henry of Huntington's *Historia Anglorum*.

King Louis came to Normandy from Étamps, about a day's march south of Paris. Meanwhile, King Henry I was at Noyon-sur-Andelle (modern-day Charleval), a few miles south-east of Rouen. Henry was stripping the district of its crops to store at Lyons castle when he received news from his scouts above Verclives that the French army had been sighted moving towards Noyon. The accounts suggest that the encounter that subsequently took place had therefore happened more or less by accident. A nervous King Louis, whom Orderic describes as repeatedly complaining that he could not hope to match the forces of the king of the English, was unaware of the proximity of Henry's army. He had hoped to take the castle by treason instead of meeting Henry in the field. In fact, Burchard of Montmorency tried to persuade the French king not to take on the English force and his pleas would have been heard had it not been for a bellicose intervention from the 'turbulent' knights of Chaumont. There were similar mixed opinions in the Anglo-Norman army. William the Chamberlain had tried to persuade King Henry not to seek battle, but William II de Warenne and Roger of Bienfaite took the opposite view. The waverers notwithstanding, the armies closed upon one another and, as messengers ran in haste amid the units of both armies, the unexpected battle had become inevitable.

The Armies

The forces ranged against each other at Brémule comprised on the Anglo-Norman side about 500 knights including some *familia* troops. Orderic Vitalis gives the names of Robert and Richard (sons of Henry), the earls Henry of Eu, William II de Warenne (who is strongly represented in the *Hyde Chronicle* account) and Walter Giffard. Also present in the Anglo-Norman ranks were Roger FitzRichard, Walter of Auffay, William of Tancarville, William of Roumare, Nigel d'Aubigny and, carrying the royal standard, Edward of Salisbury. Added to these knightly squadrons was a large contingent of archers. No mention is made of them in the sources, but their presence at other stages in the same campaign suggests a role for them here, particularly when we look at the way the battle played out. The French army comprised the division of King Louis VI himself and another division under William Clito and the Norman rebel William Crispin. By all accounts, this force was entirely mounted.

Deployment and Terrain

When King Henry's four scouts at Verclives looked south towards Andelys they saw before them a wood from which the French army was emerging: a splendid sight with helmets gleaming and standards flying in the wind. To the west of this vantage point lay the wide plain known to locals as Brémule. This flat plain was ideal for both cavalry and infantry. As the French army approached Noyon, they burnt a barn belonging to the monks of Bucheron, providing the Anglo-Normans with a good visual marker as to their whereabouts. Henry came into the plain and is said to have 'wisely disposed the mailed ranks of warriors'. The *Hyde Chronicle* suggests four divisions in the Anglo-Norman Army, others just three, but the idea behind the Anglo-Norman deployment was consistent in each account. Of Henry's 500 or so knights, up to 400 were dismounted. The remaining cavalry were placed forward of the dismounted infantry either side of one another or one behind the other in echelon. These were commanded by William II de Warenne, Walter Giffard and Henry of Eu and possibly also by Roger FitzRichard.

The key to the Anglo-Norman deployment was once again the fact that many of Henry's units were on foot. There were two separate distinct lines of heavy infantry, one including Henry's sons and the other behind it was accompanied by the king himself. However, Orderic Vitalis provides some contradictory evidence that Henry's boys remained mounted. Also, Henry of Huntington specifically states that Henry was on his horse. It is possible that the reason for the confusion is that the king and his sons remained mounted amid a sea of infantry. The general picture that emerges supports Orderic's description of a 'wise disposal of forces' on the part of the king. In front of the Anglo-Norman force, two divisions of French knights prepared for the first assault.

The Battle

The battle began to the sound of battle cries. The French division launched the first cavalry attack. It is not clear where they directed the attack on Henry's army, but they were 'beaten off', says Orderic. These French had charged 'in disorder' as well, committing the cardinal sin of a lack of cohesion at the crucial point of impact. William Crispin's unit charged with eighty knights, seemingly going straight through his mounted opponents, but some of his horses were quickly killed, indicating the presence of archery in Henry's army. Crispin's force, chased by the cavalry of the *familia* through which it had passed, moved on in two separate units to ride around the first line of infantry and headed towards the king's own line at the rear. As Crispin headed towards the king he became sandwiched between the first line of infantry and the one to which he was heading. Although it is not easy for a medieval infantry line to turn about on command, even a few men rushing back from the first line could easily cut off and surround Crispin's cavalry as they increasingly became unhorsed. Burchard, a man named Otmund and Aubrey of Mareil were captured despite the fight-back, led in the throng by Godfrey of Serrans. 'The victors', says Orderic, 'captured a hundred and forty knights and chased the rest to Andely'. There is a hint here and in the writing of the Frenchman Suger that the Anglo-Normans may have held a mounted unit in reserve for this eventuality.

The French pleaded with Louis to withdraw from the fight after this disastrous charge to the enemy lines. He fled in disorder, his army breaking up and finding different paths to escape. While William Crispin had been surrounded by the Anglo-Norman forces, his recklessness had not deserted him. Crispin caught sight

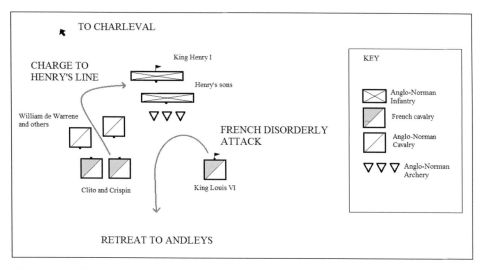

The Battle of Brémule, 1119

of the English king and launched at him, tearing through the ranks. He struck two fierce blows at King Henry with his sword. Henry of Huntington says that the blows were aimed at the king's head, but his mailed hauberk saved him. The blows pushed the coif into the king's head, causing bleeding but little more. King Henry struck back at the Norman rebel, according to Huntington, catching him with such a blow that Crispin fell from his horse to the ground. Orderic ascribes this riposte to Roger FitzRichard and not to the king, but all agree that William Crispin was captured thereafter. In an act which speaks volumes for the conventions of the Norman battlefield, Roger flung himself over the prostrate body of the Norman rebel to prevent others from killing him on the spot. He was clearly more valuable to the king as a prisoner than as a dead man.

The French had lost at Brémule due to a remarkable lack of command and control discipline. King Louis's ignominy did not end there. The English had captured his standard, which King Henry purchased for twenty marks of silver from the knight who had seized it. The French king was left wandering in the woods to plead with a local peasant to help him get back to Andelys. The English king returned in triumph to Rouen accompanied by chanting clergymen, praising God for his victory.

Orderic had clearly heard of this battle from someone who had been there. He says that he was told that only three men were killed. There had been 900 men engaged. Orderic gives the reason for the low casualty count: 'as Christian soldiers, they did not thirst for the blood of their brothers', but there were also the bonds of lordship to consider. King Henry displayed extraordinary largesse after the battle. He returned the French king's horse to him and William Clito received his palfrey back. The king divided his captives among different castles, but he also freely pardoned and released Burchard and Hervey of Gisors and some others 'because they were vassals of both kings'. The Battle of Brémule reveals much about the conventions of warfare in the Norman world. Although it was a chance encounter, casualties were kept low for social and political reasons. The victory Henry secured was achieved by better deployment, better discipline and by the recklessness of his enemy.

Bourgthéroulde, 26 March 1124

Introduction
Although the Battle of Bourgthéroulde was a relatively minor battle, it is a good example of the Anglo-Norman *familia* demonstrating an independent command and control capability. Once again, Orderic Vitalis provides our account, but Robert of Torigny and William of Jumièges provide additional detail. The battle was fought against the background of another Norman rebellion against the English King Henry I. Chief among the rebellious lords was Waleran de Beaumont of Meulan. He had taken his forces on a raid as far north as Vatteville to the south of Rouen, not far from where the Battle of Brémule had taken place a few years earlier. The battle was essentially a blocking action. The men of the king's household under Odo Borleng had gathered troops from neighbouring garrisons and blocked Waleran as he emerged from the forest of Brotonne on his return journey to his main castle at Beaumont-le-Roger.

The Armies
Numbers at Bourgthéroulde were small. On the Anglo-Norman side, the leaders mentioned were Odo Borleng, William of Tancarville the king's chamberlain, and Ralph of Bayeux, the castellan of Evreux. The troops themselves were made up of knights of lower rank, professional fighting men attached to the king's household. This fact alone drew derision from Waleran, whose noble birth placed him above the knights he faced, or so he thought. Alongside Waleran's division of knights was that of Amaury of Montfort.

It is clear that the Anglo-Norman army, although small at around 300 in number, consisted of a combination of arms. Cavalry and dismounted knights would play a part in what was to follow, but so too would archers, both mounted and dismounted.

Deployment and Terrain
We know less about the landscape at the battle of Bourgthéroulde than we would like, but what is fascinating about the deployment of the Anglo-Norman force is the discussion Odo Borleng had before it took place. Odo, a professional captain of the king's forces, told his men that the best plan was for one section of his men to dismount and fight on foot, while another remained mounted. He would also

place a force of archers in the first line with the express intent of wounding the enemy horses in order to slow them down. The other knights around Odo urged him to dismount as well. And so he did. The exact deployment is not known, but Odo's plan of a blocking line of infantry and a mounted reserve was put into place. The role of the archers and their disposition would therefore be crucial.

The Battle

Robert of Torigny contends that the Anglo–Norman force sent forward a band of mounted archers. If true, this is a rare example. They were sent against the enemy right, which would be unshielded. As the rebels under Waleran charged forward some forty archers shot at their horses, causing predictable carnage and preventing the charge from reaching the dismounted infantry. Waleran's men were thrown from their horses before they could reach the enemy line. The shooting was rapid and without interval. The result was that the rebels fled the field. It was an expertly organised deployment. Waleran was captured and imprisoned, indicating that the cavalry reserve may well have played a part in the battle after the confusion of the opening charges had passed.

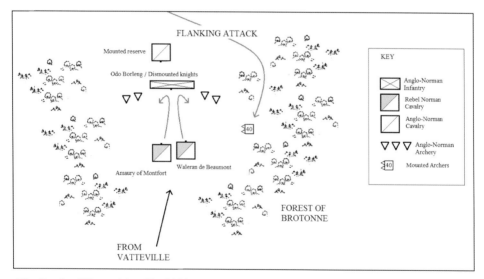

The Battle of Bourgthéroulde, 1124   *Fig. 14*

What little we know of Bourgthéroulde is enough. The Anglo-Norman *Familia Regis* was capable of campaigning independently of the king and was captained by people whose tactical abilities were of a very high standard. Once again, a rash cavalry charge at a well-organised infantry line had proven fatal to the enemy of the Anglo-Normans. As for the king, Henry I had been at Caen during the battle. Robert of Toringy says that when news was brought to him of the great victory, he was so surprised and pleased that he rode to the field itself to see it with his own eyes. Waleran, Hugh de Montfort and Hugh FitzGervase were imprisoned and later transported to England. Waleran was jailed first at Bridgnorth and then Wallingford. Hugh FitzGervase was held at Windsor. At the same time long-standing prize prisoner Duke Robert II Curthose was moved from Devizes to Robert of Gloucester's castle at Bristol. Geoffrey de Tourville and Odo du Pin, both rebel sub-commanders at Bourgthéroulde, were blinded for treason. By 1126, when King Henry I returned to England from Normandy with his daughter Matilda, English castles were full of important political prisoners, many of them captured by the exploits of the king's household in the field.

Chapter 13

In the South

The Three Battles of 1041

The Norman adventure in southern Italy had started as a mercenary story, with men selling their swords to the highest bidder. By 1041 the Normans had established some legitimacy at Aversa and it would not be long before their involvement in the region would go far beyond the mere mercenary. In this respect, the battles of 1041 were pivotal.

The castle at Melfi was a superb place from which to dominate the countryside. We might recall Ardouin, the smooth operating Lombard at the head of his Norman mercenaries (page 20). However, Ardouin's men would rise up against the catapan Michael Doukeianos, the man who had put him in this seat. Melfi, which Amatus rightly called the 'gateway to Apulia', was well placed. Whoever controlled it would be in striking distance of both Byzantine Apulian territory to the east and Lombard cities to the west. However, the catapan would not give up the fertile grounds of Apulia so easily.

When Ardouin had come back to Melfi from a visit to Aversa with his twelve Norman commanders, the ravaging began. Venosa would fall first, then Lavello and Ascoli. The Norman ravaging was as much as Michael Doukeianos could stand. He quickly gathered a force from Bari and headed out towards Melfi. The population had not recovered from the demands of the recent punishing Sicilian campaign and there are hints that Doukeianos did not have as large an army as he wanted. Near Venosa he met the Normans and their Lombard allies. He sent a messenger to them offering them a chance to leave Byzantine territory. This was a forlorn hope, one might think. Geoffrey of Malaterra has an amusing, if disturbing, account of it:

> They [the Greeks] sent an envoy ahead of them to inform them that they should choose what they preferred, either a battle with them next day, or they would be granted a truce to cross back over the border unharmed. The envoy who had been sent on this mission rode a particularly handsome horse. One of the Normans, Hugh Tudebusis [Tuboeuf, one of the leading twelve commanders], started to pat this horse. He wanted the Greeks to be

told something amazing about him and his fellows which might terrify them, and so he struck the horse in the neck with his bare fist and with one blow knocked it down as though it was dead. The other Normans rushed forward and picked up the Greek, who had been thrown to the ground with his horse and was laying there as if dead, although he himself was not injured, but merely afraid. The horse however they dragged to a cliff and threw off. The Greek, who had only just been restored to his senses by the Normans' assistance, received a better horse from them and reported back to his compatriots that they were prepared for battle. But when he told the leaders of his people all that had happened to him, they were struck with fear and admiration.

The Battle of Olivento commenced on the banks of the river bearing that name on the morning of 17 March 1041. This river flows into the Ofanto a little under ten miles to the north-east of Melfi. Amatus says that both sides agreed on the day and the hour at which the battle should be fought. The Byzantines had hurriedly brought with them some Varangians and Thracians. The numbers are not known, but William of Apulia says the Normans had 500 infantry and 700 knights. He says that 'only a few were protected by hauberks and shields'.

The Normans deployed their infantry on the wings and these were reinforced by small units of cavalry. They were ordered to hold fast and to regroup if forced to retreat. They employed a counter-attacking tactic every time they were attacked by large numbers of advancing Greeks, whose method of attack was well known to William of Apulia. A column of Norman cavalry was sent out and met by a column of Byzantine forces. William of Apulia is careful to deliberate on the Byzantine method of attack, which he says was a slow introduction of units into the battle by their commanders as they would look for weaknesses in the enemy and seek to exploit them. Amatus has the introduction of three Byzantine divisions – one by one – each encountering annihilation at the hands of the enemy. We are missing the crucial detail of the battle, but the ultimate result was that the Byzantines were pushed back and then in flight, found themselves pressed against the river – a disastrous event for any army. Malaterra says:

> Once the victory had been secured they pursued them, killing the stragglers, and many of the enemy were drowned as they tried to swim across the River Olivento.

The catapan licked his wounds. He turned again to the impressment of men from Apulia. He also received some men returning from the Sicilian campaign and some fresh reinforcements from the Byzantine army. The Normans for their part – always outnumbered – had gained more cavalrymen from Salerno and Aversa, including Count Rainulf and some additional Lombard auxiliaries. By May 1041

Michael Doukeianos was ready again. By the River Ofanto at Monte Maggiore the two armies met again. Numbers wildly vary in the sources. The *Bari Annals* have it this way:

> Then all the Greeks were gathered together, and a battle was fought on 4 May at Monte Maggiore on the River Ofanto, where many men from Anatolicon and Thrakesion, Obsequiani, Russians, Calabrians and men from Longobardia and the Capitanata perished. Angelus, priest and Bishop of Troia, and Bishop Stephen of Acerenza were killed there. Indeed it was said by those who were present at this battle that there were more than two thousand Normans there, and eighteen thousand Greeks, not counting servants. Michael returned with a few disorganised survivors, who were stupified with fear of the Normans.

The moral support of those accompanying bishops had not been enough. Nor had the presence of the Varangians. However, the battle had been a decisive one, resulting in the total defeat of the Byzantines. The Normans attacked the Greeks in a spearhead formation, thrusting themselves into the enemy who were drawn up in two lines. The result was that the first line fell back on the second, causing confusion and, once again, the enemy was smashed into a river. Amatus says that the River Ofanto broke its banks in a supernatural flash-flood when the Byzantines fled across it, causing untold numbers of dead. One of the many Norman cavalry charges might have been attributable to William 'Iron Arm' de Hauteville, a veteran of the Sicilian campaign. William is said to have been suffering an illness and was sitting it out for a while, watching events from a nearby hilltop. In Malaterra's imaginative account, he is said to have leaped from his seat and entered the fray, sweeping all before him.

Whether or not the story of William's curious burst of energy is true, the Normans' reputation for battlefield prowess was growing. Their numbers were small, and yet on horseback they would appear to have been lethal. This latest reversal was too much for Constantinople. For his part in confronting the Normans twice with a river at his back, Michael Doukeianos was lucky only to be shipped off again to Sicily and tasked with retrieving the remnants of Greek forces there. His replacement in the Capitanata was Exaugustus Boioannes, the son of a former catapan. He resolved to besiege the Normans in their seat at Melfi. The Normans had returned there after their previous victories, laden with booty. At Melfi, according to William of Apulia, Atenulf, a member of the ruling family of Benevento, bribed his way into the leadership of the Lombard revolt. The Normans wasted no time in scouring the principality of Benevento for warriors with Atenulf's help.

The rebels moved out to a fortification at Monte Serico near Montepeloso, where the Byzantines had fortified themselves. After operating a policy of

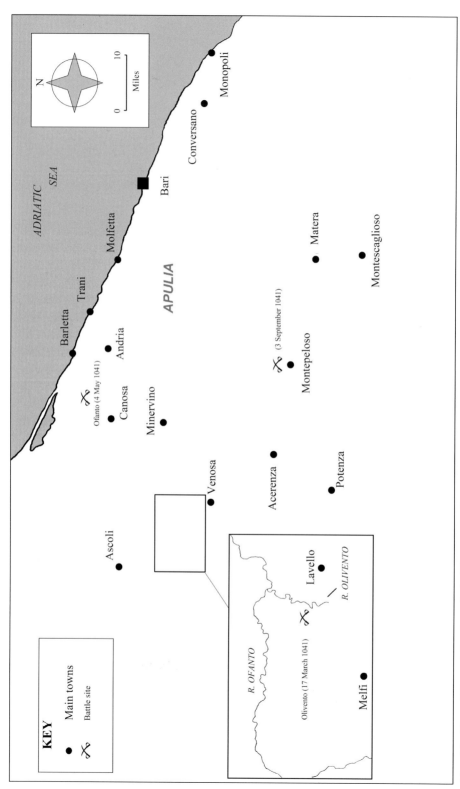

Map 11: Map of Central Southern Italy Showing the Campaigns of 1041

stealing animals and hay from under the noses of the Greeks, the Normans managed to entice their enemy out of his fortification. On 3 September 1041 yet another defeat was inflicted on the Byzantines at the Battle of Montepeloso. The new catapan, however, very nearly won this third battle of 1041. Attack after attack came at the Normans. William of Apulia says it was the actions of one of the twelve commanders, Walter, which turned the tide. He got among the retreating Norman cavalrymen and somehow rallied them. At one stage the Normans raised their banner as though they were requesting an engagement. The fleeing Greeks responded by returning to the fray and were cut down. The Greeks had once again lost out. Boioannes, whom Amatus says saw a lance coming for him and shouted out 'Catapan! Catapan!' was taken prisoner and handed to Atenulf, who paraded him in humiliating circumstances through his home town. Greek morale was collapsing across the south as cities began to come over to the rebels. Among them were Bari, Monopoli, Giovenazzo, and Matera deep in the south.

There would be many twists in the long struggle between the Lombard rebels and the Byzantine Empire. But the battles of 1041 had left nobody in any doubt of the Normans' intention to remain in Italy, and the extent of their military capabilities. Just twelve years later, all the enemies of the Normans in Italy came together to try to rid themselves of the threat.

Civitate, 17 June 1053

Introduction

One summer morning in 1053 a giant army crossed the snaking River Fortore at Ponte Di Civitate and began to set its tents at the banks of the river's tributary, the River Staina. The army consisted of troops summoned from across Italy and parts of Germany by Pope Leo IX. Its commanders' intentions were to join with a Greek army under the catapan Argyrus and combine with it to confront – once and for all – the Normans of the south. The battle which followed took place near the settlement of Civitate, northwest of Foggia. The encounter is surprisingly well recorded in near contemporary sources. The writer who gives us the most is William of Apulia. He is almost matched in detail by Amatus and Geoffrey of Malaterra, who add important facts and names. There is little variation in the general accounts, leaving us with a consistent picture. Even Herman of Reichenau, the great German chronicler and intellectual, generally agrees with the pro-Norman accounts, and the result of the battle is not contradicted. Add to this the writings of the Pope himself and we might make some sense of what happened on the day the Pope was humbled by the Norman army. Deployment, terrain, the evolution of the struggle and its immediate aftermath are all accounted for in the sources.

The Armies

William of Apulia tells us the Normans consisted of three main commands under the Commander-in-Chief Humphrey de Hauteville. Humphrey led his own command while the other two were led by Richard (then of Aversa) and Robert Guiscard. To these names he adds Peter and Walter, the sons of Amicus; Aureolanus; Hubert; Rainald Musca; Count Hugh commanding a detachment of pro-Norman Benevantans; Count Gerard commanding the men of Telese and the wise and skilled at arms Count Radulfus of Boiano. The division of this army into three is also stated by Amatus. It is likely Robert's command comprised mainly mounted knights. Also, Count Gerard would have been with Robert, along with what Geoffrey of Malaterra had earlier described as a force of up to 200 knights. Robert also had a small contingent of Slav infantry who had experience of Calabrian campaigns. From William of Apulia's account of the opening stages of the battle, it seems clear that Humphrey's command also contained bowmen of some sort, although the origin of these men is unclear.

William of Apulia specifies that the Normans came to meet the Pope with infantry as well as cavalry. If so, we are missing some details of these infantrymen. However, he does say that the Normans could muster around 3,000 cavalry and 'a few infantry', so we might assume that the infantry numbers were low.

The make-up of the papal coalition, on the other hand, is not so easy to define. William of Apulia tells us who was in it, but we must accept that a great recruitment drive led by Leo IX's chancellor Frederick, brother of the duke of Lorraine, amassed vast numbers under minor leaders from around the whole of southern Italy. The Pope's own recruiting campaign in Germany had finally netted him (thanks to Frederick) around 700 Swabian swordsmen, about whose abilities William of Apulia waxes lyrical. Werner and Albert (or Rainulf and Renier if Amatus is to be believed) were their leaders. Were it not for the intervention of Gebhart, the bishop of Eichstätt, a large force of presumably high-quality German warriors would also have added to the numbers in the imperial contingent. But this force was re-called by the emperor before it even reached Italy. The motive for Gebhart's plea is not entirely clear, although he may have been looking to the future, as he eventually went on to become Pope himself.

By way of contrast to the poorly trained multitudes in the Italo-Lombard force, this smaller number of Swabian knights might seem to be worth their weight in gold. William of Apulia – not usually enamoured with the Germans – says of them:

> ... proud people of great courage, but not versed in horsemanship, who fought rather with the sword than with the lance. Since they could not control the movements of their horses with their hands they were unable to inflict serious injuries with the lance; however they excelled with the sword. These swords were very long and keen, and they were often capable of

cutting someone vertically in two! They preferred to dismount and take guard on foot, and they chose rather to die than to turn tail.

However, Herman of Reichenau has a slightly different slant on the origins of the Germans in the allied army:

Many Germans followed him [the Pope], some on the orders of their lords, some spurred by hope of gain, but many were scoundrels and violent men, who had been expelled from their homeland for various crimes. The pope welcomed them... their skills seemed to be required for the forthcoming campaign...

There are hints here that although they were skilled and courageous warriors, the actual contingent that came south was perhaps not the ideal force the Pope had in mind after all. William of Apulia certainly seems impressed by them, but may have been writing of the martial prowess of the Germans in general as opposed to those of the force which Herman of Reichenau describes.

From Mantua to Benevento this giant army tracked across Italy, multiplying as it went. The papal call for help to expel the Normans from southern Italy was gathering pace. The duke of Gaeta, the counts of Aquino and Teano and Peter, Archbishop of Amalfi, were to join with a vast force that included those recruited from across Apulia, from Valva, Campania, the Marsi, Rome itself, Ancona, Capua and Spoleto. Count Transmund III of the Chieti, Atto V, Oderisius, son of Borellus, Roffred the lord of the castle of Guardia and Count Madelfrid of Larino also answered the call. Rudolf, the papal rector of the duchy of Benevento, and Gerard the duke of Lorraine, also played a leading part in the command and organisation of this great combined army.

Deployment and terrain
As the Normans headed out onto the Apulian plain, they would have been painfully aware of Pope Leo's appeal to the emperor Constantine Monomarchos and his call for help from the catapan Argyrus. The Normans had already rejected Greek bribes offered by Argyrus to have them dispersed as mercenaries to far-off places. It was then essential for the Normans to prevent a link-up between the Papal-Swabian-Lombard force and that of the Byzantines. No Norman military prowess, or astute generalship, could possibly achieve a victory if this happened. The whole future of their life in southern Italy rested upon Humphrey's men winning the strategic battle in the early stages. The allied arrangement had been that the twin forces would meet at Siponto in northern Apulia. This is probably why the sources hint that Humphrey and Peter son of Amicus delivered a pre-emptive strike against Argyrus's forces at Siponto sometime earlier in the year. Argyrus probably sailed from Bari to Siponto, within sight of Peter's ports of

Bisceglie and Barletta, hence Peter's prior knowledge of the move. For the Pope to get there from Benevento, where his force had arrived in June 1053, he would have to avoid a patchwork of Norman strongholds such as Troia and Bovino. And so the papal army set out to go around the north route and east around the region of Monte Gargano. Humphrey's Normans intercepted the giant army on the banks of the Staina, just north-west of Civitate, near to the ruins of the old Roman settlement of Teanum Apulum.

The Pope's vast columns of men appeared before the eyes of the Norman commanders. It was a fantastic sight. The Normans sent messengers to the Pope to seek peace with him. William of Apulia says that the first sight of the papal army made the Normans think twice. 'Although famous for their deeds of arms', he says, 'the Normans were, on seeing so many columns, afraid to resist them'. The message was that they would offer to hold their lands from the Vicar of Christ himself and they would give incense and tribute annually as well. They wanted Leo IX to be their lord and they were willing to swear '*fideles*' (loyalty) as part of this recognition. The envoys even showed the banner the Normans had been given by the German emperor many years ago. There was, however, a spirit of resistance in the allied camp and William of Apulia puts it down to the haughty attitude of the German advisors to the Pope. Amatus mentions Chancellor Frederick's bellicosity in these exchanges. The Pope said nothing to the envoys according to the south Italian sources, although Herman of Reichenau records that he flatly refused the Normans' proposals. The chancellor commanded them to flee, and the Swabians exhorted the Pope to command the Normans to leave Italy once and for all, or feel the edge of the German swords. The Germans, tall, fair and good-looking, despised the stocky Normans and were at pains to point this out to all present. The Pope made some half-hearted counter-arguments, but the mood of the allies was clear: there would be a battle.

The next morning, on 17 June 1053, on a plain which lies south-east of the confluence of the rivers Fortore and Staina, the battle took place. But after three days without proper food, the Normans were racked with hunger: they had suffered hardship in the field as they had no bread and were forced by the lack of support among the Italian peasantry to dry green corn over fires and eat the burnt grain.

The allies had set their camp on the banks of the Staina, although the Pope would view proceedings either from the ramparts of Civitate itself, or more likely closer to the field. He had given the job of standard-bearer to Robert Octomarset, about whom we know very little. Robert and the papal knights and the smaller group of Germans were shown the sign of the cross, absolved of their sins and made ready for battle.

There was a hill between the Germans and the Normans. In fact, to the west of Civitate the ground falls away dramatically. Humphrey climbed the hill, which was far shallower on his side. What he saw, despite the multitude facing him, must

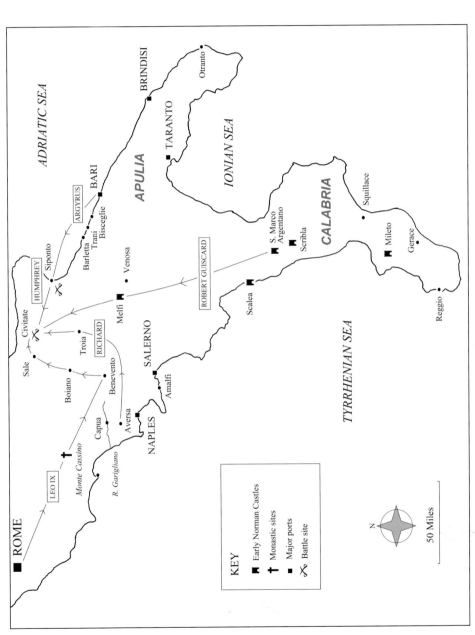

Map 12: Map of the Civitate Campaign – the approach

have pleased him. The allied disposition sprawled along the banks of the Staina. As Humphrey began to form up his three divisions on the side of the hill, the Swabians responded by stringing themselves out in a relatively thin line to cover the flat ground before the camp and to face Humphrey's knights. To their left (and to Humphrey's right) a multitude of Italians under various Lombard leaders were struggling even to form up. Humphrey had already set himself in the middle of his battle line. Richard of Aversa's 'picked squadrons' of knights were on Humphrey's right flank. Set slightly in reserve and to the left of Humphrey's command was that of his brother Robert Guiscard with his cavalry and his Calabrians, Normans and Slavs. His orders were to hold until he was required to assist.

The Battle

> In the meantime, as we were trying to shatter their [the Normans] pertinacity with saving admonition and they, in return, were pretending to promise complete subjection, they attack our company in a sudden onslaught but they still lament more than rejoice in their victory. *From a letter to Constantine Monomarchos from Pope Leo IX*

The Italo-Lombard hordes bunched in confusion on the allied left flank. The image of what happened next must have stuck with the Pope for the rest of his life. Whether the subsequent rout of this giant force was down to the enigmatic entry in an anonymous *Life* of the pope, which attributes the entire loss of the battle to the treachery of Count Madelfrid of Larino, is not possible to say. The implication is that Madelfrid took Norman silver in return for precipitately fleeing from the field of battle. The Lombards are said to have been 'cowardly' by William of Apulia. Certainly, it seems they were unable to draw up a battle line in a proper manner, but these accusations of cowardice might be masking a collapse in morale brought about by something which we cannot find, although we might suspect it. The Pope, for his part, insisted to Constantine that the parley, or negotiations between the Normans and their would-be lord and master, was still ongoing when Richard of Aversa crashed into the Italians on the field of Civitate. The Pope may have been mulling over the offers made the previous day, but everyone else seems to have known only too well that a battle was about to start, and even the Pope appears to have given this his blessing, according to Amatus. So it is difficult to see the release of Richard's chosen squadrons of knights as being anything more sinister than military opportunism, and it is the timing of this release which may be the reason for the plummeting morale of the Italo-Lombard hordes.

Richard of Aversa's cavalry charge against the Italians was very effective. The enemy turned and fled, and a mixture of troop types and qualities, still in confusion, fell back against the shock impact of the Norman horsemen. Amatus describes Richard dividing the Germans at this stage and passing into their midst, which is a difficult point to reconcile unless we assume he is mistaken. As the vast force fled, Richard's men cut down the stragglers in numbers. However, in the middle of the battlefield a very different struggle was taking place. Humphrey's division had begun to soften up the Swabian lines with missile fire from his bowmen. However, he received the same response from the Germans, who had brought their own bowmen with them. There followed a mighty clash between the steadfast Swabians and the furious Normans, as William of Apulia tells us:

> Finally both sides charged sword in hand, and their swords inflicted some incredible blows on each other; you could see human bodies split down the middle, and horse and man laying dead together.

It is not clear whether the two opposing forces were dismounted at this stage. One would expect the Swabians to have dismounted to bring greater effect to their swordplay, but quite how Humphrey's Normans faced the threat is unknown. The mention of horses lying dead with their riders could point to the Normans charging mounted, not with lances but with swords in hand, in order to prosecute close-order fighting with the German infantry from the saddle. Whatever the tactical choice here, Robert Guiscard was looking on. He launched himself at the flank of the Swabian line as he perceived his brother to be making no gains against the fierce swordsmen. William of Apulia, in the forgivably flowery language which befits an epic verse, describes the scenes of horror of a Norman battle in full swing:

> Then Robert, seeing his brother so fiercely attacked by enemies resolved to yield not an inch, charged fiercely and proudly into the midst of the hostile ranks, aided by the troops of Count Gerard and followed by the Calabrians whose leadership had been entrusted to him. He speared them with his lance, beheaded them with his sword, dealing out fearful blows with his mighty hands. He fought with each hand, both lance and sword hit whatever target they were aimed at. He was unhorsed three times, thrice he recovered his strength and returned more fiercely to the fray. ... He cut off feet and hands, sliced heads from bodies, ripped into breasts and chests, and transfixed those whose heads he had cut off. Cutting off the heads of these huge men he made them the same size as those smaller, proving that the greatest bravery is not the prerogative of the tall, but often rests with those of shorter stature. After the battle it was known that none, victor or vanquished, had inflicted such mighty blows.

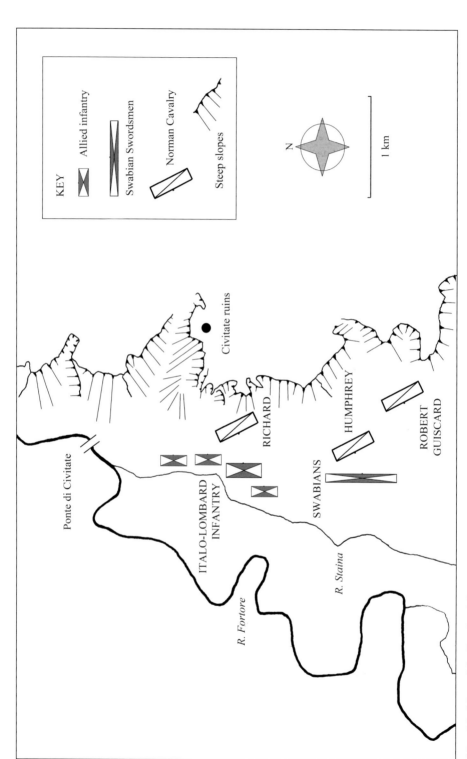

Map 13: Map of the Battle of Civitate, 1053

The Germans fought harder as the odds stacked up against them. Amatus tells us they looked behind them for support, but there was none. As Guiscard's men began rolling up the flank of the unshielded right side of the German lines, Richard of Aversa, far over on the right side of the battlefield, had seen that behind him to his left the Swabians were still holding out against the combined forces of the de Hauteville brothers. He disengaged from prosecuting the rout of the Lombards and crashed into the rear of the Swabian line, whose men were now surrounded. There is no reason not to believe Amatus when he says that no Germans escaped save those the Normans pardoned out of pity. The proud Swabian swordsmen were cut down, although Herman of Reichenau writes that the first Norman line was actually near to defeat by the Germans when supporting troops ambushed them and surrounded them.

And so in one pitched battle on the dusty fields of southern Italy, the myth of Norman military invincibility had become a stunning reality. Pope Leo IX knew what it would mean. So too did the townsfolk of Civitate, who decided after the Normans had surrounded the place and thrown up earthworks, to hand over the forlorn Leo IX to the victors, while helping themselves to the papal baggage train. For a little while to come, although the Normans prostrated themselves before the Pope, they would have him exactly where they wanted him. A whole generation of victories would be theirs as they escorted the most valuable prisoner in Christendom back to Benevento. The Normans, at long last, had conquered all they surveyed. And yet there were two notable groups absent at the Battle of Civitate. The men of Salerno, whose recently murdered prince had based his entire career on Norman prowess, did not attend. Nor did Argyrus, the Lombard nationalist turned Byzantine catapan. His failure to appear did his political future no good at all. He sailed from Bari to Constantinople, bringing news to his emperor of Norman mastery. His fate is poorly recorded, but he stayed in his position for some time. What he could not deny, however, was what he had always expected. The Normans were never going home.

Cerami, June 1063

Introduction

It may seem impossible to reconstruct anything from the biased account of the Battle of Cerami. Parts of Geoffrey of Malaterra's narrative draw upon the supernatural. However, some tentative conclusions are not out of the question, since the Battle of Cerami shares something in common with other pitched battles of the period.

By the middle of June 1063 Roger de Hauteville's campaigns in north-east and central Sicily had suffered a number of setbacks from which he had barely recovered. Roger had just returned from Calabria with fresh supplies in horses and other goods to bolster his small force at Troina, but was still remarkably short of manpower. His dream of a Sicilian conquest looked very much in the balance. In fact, had it not been for the recently successful action fought by Roger and his brother Robert Guiscard against Ibn al-Hawas's forces outside of the fortress at Enna in which the Normans secured a multitude of booty, the whole Sicilian project might well have petered out.

On the day that Roger rode out from his fortification at Troina the count knew he had to find out the size of the enemy. He headed west to survey the valley of the River Cerami from one of its many surrounding hilltops. What he saw from this position will have convinced him of one thing. He and his army would be hopelessly outnumbered by the force which had been sent out from Palermo.

The Armies

The force ranged against Roger de Hauteville on the other side of the River Cerami was said by Malaterra to consist of Africans, Arabs and Sicilians. The North African Zirid Prince al Mu'izz had already tried sending a fleet to Sicily in 1061, which had dispersed due to adverse weather conditions. His son Temin had subsequently sent his own two sons with reinforcements to Sicily and these appear to have been the men who suffered the defeat at Enna earlier in 1063. The troop types are not recalled by Malaterra but are likely to have been a mixture of cavalry and infantry with a contingent of archers and slingers. The numbers given by Malaterra seem preposterous. The Saracen cavalry numbered a seemingly plausible 3,000 or an unlikely 30,000, depending on the translation. This was not counting the infantry, whose numbers were 'infinite' or at least not less than 20,000. At the head of them all was the emir of Palermo, whom Malaterra calls Arcadius.

As for Roger's tiny force, we assume that those who are mentioned are mounted knights. Roger only had around 100 of these. Among them were probably the sub-commands of Roussel of Bailleul and Arisgotus of Pucheil (or Puzzuoli), not counting an additional *conroi* of thirty-six men belonging to the distinguished nephew of Count Roger, Serlo II de Hauteville. With Roger's own unit these horsemen cannot have numbered more than about 136 mounted knights. If there were any infantry at all on the Norman side – which is by no means unlikely – then they are not mentioned by Malaterra.

Deployment and Terrain

The landscape around the small town of Cerami is craggy. The river winds its way through the numerous hills, carving out a landscape in which there is scarcely a flat plain. On a June morning Roger looked across the valley and saw a huge Saracen army. Neither side approached the other at this stage. It was the Saracen army who blinked first in the early stand-off. They moved back to their nearby camp, still not crossing the river. Roger returned to Troina briefly while the stand-off continued. For three days no one moved to cross the river. On the fourth day the Saracen army moved back to the hilltop on which it had first been observed. Roger ordered the advance. However, when he was only halfway towards the enemy news reached him that the settlement at Cerami itself had been attacked. He diverted his force to deal with this new development, sending ahead his nephew Serlo, already a master of the advanced guard role and veteran of Messina (1061) and Enna (1063).

The Battle
In Malaterra's tendentious account Serlo de Hauteville let nobody down. He had been instructed to gain entry to the enemy camp and hold until Roger's force arrived. This might seem an unlikely and dangerous assignment for one *conroi* of thirty-six knights against a host of thousands. Serlo rode to the enemy camp and is described as crashing through the gates 'like a raging lion'. The upshot of this extraordinary assault in the first stage of a battle riddled with impossibilities was that the enemy fled. Roger soon arrived to find Cerami still in his own hands and his dashing nephew ready for action. But there were others in the army who were unsure. The giant Saracen army had fled, but to chase it into the wilderness would surely invite disaster, since there were so many of the enemy out there. Roger turned to Roussel of Bailleul, whose military advice he clearly valued. Malaterra's account of Roussel's response gives a clue as to the enemy formation:

> But when asked by the count [for his opinion] Roussel de Bailleul replied fiercely that he would never again help him, either here or anywhere else, unless he brought the enemy to battle. When the count heard this he was angry and sternly reprimanded the faint-hearted. He marched in haste towards the enemy's camp (where they had taken refuge) to offer battle to them. The latter took heart once more and, dividing their forces into two, charged forth bravely against our men.

Roger responded to the enemy's tactical evolution by splitting his own small force into two. Serlo, Roussel and Arisgotus led the first division and Roger remained with his own men in the second. We know nothing of the dispositions but we are told that the one Saracen division anxious to gain a hilltop overlooking the Normans outflanked the first Norman division, including Serlo's men, and fetched up at the rear of Roger's own division. At the sight of a vast force to their rear Roger's men became understandably afraid. However, just when the account of the battle at its peak might be expected to elucidate something of the tactical approaches of both sides, Malaterra introduces divine intervention to explain to his audience what happened next:

> They were hastening towards the battle when there appeared a knight, splendidly armed and mounted on a white horse, carrying a white banner

surmounted by a brilliant cross fixed to the top of his lance. He rode in front of our line as if trying to make our men more eager for battle, and then he made a mighty attack upon the enemy just where their ranks were thickest. When our men saw this they were overjoyed, and cried out repeatedly to God and Saint George. They were overcome with emotion and burst into tears at such a sight, enthusiastically following the figure in front of them. Many of them saw the banner with the cross hanging from the top of the count's lance, which could not have been placed there except through Divine power.

As thick clouds are broken up by a furious wind, says Malaterra, Roger rode into the heart of the enemy and his warriors fought furiously to disperse them. The emir Arcadius had also been in the thick of it. Some 15,000 Saracens perished. Roger had clearly defeated an army while heavily outnumbered. Something remarkable – worthy indeed of Saint George's intervention – had happened at Cerami in June 1063. It is possible that a direct charge at the enemy leader had brought about the implausible result. After the battle the Normans scoured the craggy landscape, slaughtering infantry in their thousands. Eventually the stench of the rotting corpses would put an end to the bloodlust as the Normans triumphantly headed back to their hilltop fortification at Troina. They took great spoils from the deserted enemy camp, including camels and prisoners who were sold into slavery. The Pope received four camels as a gift from Roger. The conquest of Sicily was beginning to feel a little bit like a crusade.

Roussel de Bailleul

Roussel, who had distinguished himself at the Battle of Cerami in 1063, had a long and distinguished military career. After serving in the household of Roger de Hauteville, he had found service as a mercenary commander in the Byzantine army by the late 1060s. He had been present at the Battle of Manzikert in 1071 but had not engaged the enemy. His career continued to develop as the Byzantines saw the usefulness of his force of heavy cavalry. But Roussel wanted his own patrimony. In the early 1070s he set up an independent state in Galatia and rebelled against the empire, but the Byzantines persuaded the Turks to crush him. He set up again at Amaseia in Anatolia, where he was even admired by the people. They only consented to Alexius Comnenus's demands to take him away after he paraded Roussel blindfold in front of them, pretending he had been blinded. He was subsequently imprisoned and later released, only to fight once more against the rebel Greek Nicephorus Botaniates whom he then joined after defeating him. Roussel was finally defeated in 1077 by the Turks, handed to the emperor and executed.

Misilmeri, 1068

Roughly ten miles to the south-east of Palermo stood a settlement known to the local population as 'the emir's village'. Here, at what has become known as the Battle of Misilmeri in 1068, something happened which struck fear into the hearts of the Saracens of Palermo. This goes a long way towards demonstrating the Norman knowledge of the psychological aspects of warfare, or at the very least Geoffrey of Malaterra's knowledge of it. The Zirid commander Ayub, one of the sons of the Zirid sultan who had been sent to Sicily to bolster Muslim forces before the Battle of Cerami, had recently overcome and defeated the forces of another Muslim leader, Ibn al-Hawas. As a consequence, Ayub felt ready to take the battle to the Normans, who were still devastating the countryside from their seat at Petralia. As the people of Agrigento, Enna and Palermo recognised Ayub and gave him the support he needed, he gathered a considerable army and took to the campaign trail to restore Muslim fortunes.

Roger de Hauteville was once again on the march. The size and make-up of the Saracen army that blocked Roger's path at Misilmeri is not known. It was drawn 'from every possible place', says Malaterra. We can only assume that it was considerably larger than Roger's small force. It seems the Saracens attacked the Normans first. Roger had made a stirring speech to his men encouraging them to trust in God. Then, in the only hint of any kind of tactical deployment 'he carefully drew up the battle line'. The subsequent clash, as we have become accustomed to hear, went in favour of the Norman force. Malaterra is keen to point out that so many Saracens perished that there was no one to carry news of the disaster back to Palermo; Roger himself found a way to communicate. The results, Malaterra says, were devastating:

> It was the Saracens' custom to bring with them, when they went on a journey of any length, pigeons, which at home were fed on corn mixed with honey. The male birds were kept in cages, and when there was some change of fortune which they wished to make known at home, they wrote the news down on pieces of parchment which they hung round the birds' necks, or under their wings. They then let the birds loose, and the latter would hurry home bringing the news of what had happened to their absent friends and whether they were successful. The little birds could not read, but would hurry home, bringing the parchments with their messages, in search of the sweet honeyed grains on which they were so often fed. The count captured the cages with these birds along with the rest of the spoils. Dipping the parchments in blood, he released the birds, and thus informed the Palermitans of the misfortune which had occurred. The whole city was thunderstruck; the tearful voices of women and children rent the air and rose to the heavens. Our people rejoiced, theirs brought forth sadness.

If we chose to believe it, Ayub was broken in one extraordinary moment. He fled to Africa, leaving behind a demoralised population and a great city at the mercy of Roger, the man who broke its heart. But Palermo was huge. Roger's small force could not hope to take it, so he bided his time. He knew his brother's help would be imperative. However, Duke Robert Guiscard was in Apulia and his eyes were firmly fixed on Bari, the last great Byzantine city in the region. The capture of Bari was by no means inevitable, but it was to be the first of the truly great sieges in the south. As for the scantly-recorded Battle of Misilmeri, perhaps the town's modern coat of arms, with its forlorn dove fleeing a tower, is the most poignant reminder of the power of psychological warfare in the Norman age.

Dyrrhachium, 18 October 1081

Introduction
Duke Robert Guiscard began his preparations in Salerno in the summer of 1080. The treaty of Ceprano made between Pope Gregory VII, Robert Guiscard and Prince Jordan of Capua had finally settled a turbulent period of Apulian uprisings and put to rest the papal misgivings about Norman depredations and their great sieges against the Christian people of Italy. The way was clear for Robert to launch a much longed-for expedition, but he needed an excuse to attack Byzantium. His true motives were not the ones he publicly promoted. The governor of Dyrrhachium had sponsored the duke's Apulian rebels. But Guiscard had greater things in mind than the neutralisation of this one threat. He was bent on conquest and his son Bohemond, who would surely benefit, shared his passion.

It was portrayed as a restoration mission. Nicephorus Botaniates had seized power in Constantinople. The deposed Byzantine Emperor Michael VII Doukas (whose son Constantine had been offered in marriage to Duke Robert's daughter Helena) would be restored to the throne. But he had been imprisoned in the city. Even the Normans knew this much. However, a man appeared in Salerno conveniently claiming to be Michael VII. He was probably an ambitious monk, but he was paraded as the 'cause' and many contemporaries fell for the ruse as he climbed aboard ship with the invasion party the next year.

The duke sent Bohemond to the Albanian coast in March 1081. He had just fifteen ships and was instructed to occupy Avlona and reduce its surroundings. Then he must take Corfu. Bohemond did not let his father down. He took Avlona and also the fortifications of Kanina and Orikon, important coastal forts on the southern approach to Dyrrhachium. He was not successful against the citadel at Corfu, however, and retired to Butrinto on the mainland to await his father.

In May 1081 the main force set sail from Otranto. William of Apulia says that some of the ships were of Ragusan origin. This was a semi-independent Slav region on the north Adriatic coast and it seems likely Robert Guiscard had garnered their support against Byzantium. Anna Comnena says the force was

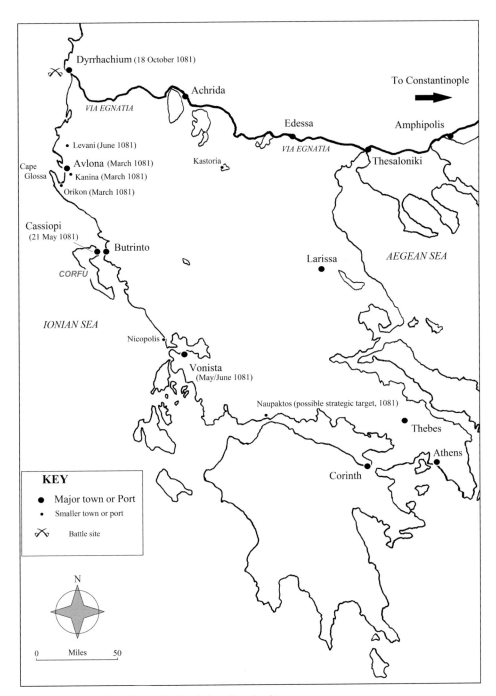

Map 14: Map of the Campaigning before Dyrrhachium

30,000 strong, comprising 150 ships – a probable exaggeration. Orderic Vitalis has it at 10,000 men, while Malaterra for once gives a more plausible 1,300 horsemen ('as those present have testified') and Romuald of Salerno just 700 of the same. Malaterra also has the force supported by a poorly armed mob, and Anna goes into detail about the duke's impressment of men of all ages who had never seen armour, even in their dreams.

Robert landed not at Avlona, but at Cassiope on Corfu. The city fell on 21 May 1081. Part of the fleet sailed further south to Vonista on the gulf of Amvrakikos. According to Anna Comnena there was initially a plan to capture Nicopolis and Naupaktos in the south, which might have paved the way for attacks on Athens, Corinth and Thebes and given access to their lucrative silk markets. Father and son consolidated their hold on Avlona before heading north to the intended target of Dyrrhachium. Bohemond went by land and took the fort at Levani en route, but Robert was less fortunate as he sailed his fleet out to Cape Glossa. A storm blew up and wrecked many ships. It cost the duke a week as he sat out the heavy weather at Glabinista. If he had time to reflect at all, he may have given thought to the recent takeover of the Byzantine imperial throne by the very capable military commander Alexius Comnenus, Anna's illustrious father. Alexius had encountered the Normans before, in the form of the rebellious mercenary Roussel de Bailleul whom he had captured in 1076, although this is unlikely to have helped him understand the Normans' capabilities in a pitched battle situation. Nonetheless, for Robert, it would now seem that the trumped up 'restoration' excuse for the invasion was fast losing credibility.

The new emperor wasted no time. Dyrrhachium's defences were improved, and its governor George Monomarchus was replaced by a friend and confident of Alexius named George Palaeologus. Monomarchus may even have begun negotiations with Robert when the latter had heard of the new emperor's rise to power. Alexius also set in train a web of political agreements and alliances designed to confound the duke of Apulia's every move. He also appealed to the Venetians, whose Doge, Domenico Silvio, gathered a fleet.

By 17 June Robert Guiscard was beneath the walls of Dyrrhachium. The town is described as being hemmed in from all sides. A siege tower was built, termed a heliopolis, a multi-storey mobile tower with catapults and drawbridges built on classical precedent, and covered with protective hides. In fact, during the siege Guiscard's machines would suffer repeated counter-raids from the city. The siege dragged on until August 1081, when a Venetian fleet arrived. Accounts vary as to what happened next. Malaterra has the fleet being energetically attacked by Robert's ships, which had prevailed by sunset on the first day. He then says the Venetians promised to surrender the next day, but spent the night refitting their vessels, building fighting tops on their masts. On the second day the Normans' advanced squadron sailed out to receive the surrender and was attacked. They declined even to offer battle because they were too few in number. Thus the

Venetians were able to sail into Dyrrhachium and reopen communications with the city. That night, the Venetians prepared their ships with 'Greek fire' (naphtha siphons) and sailed out to attack the Norman fleet, managing to sink one ship. The Normans retaliated and bravely destroyed a large Venetian vessel, responding to stratagem with valour. The result was a draw and the Venetians retired to port.

Anna Comnena tells it differently. On the arrival of the Venetian fleet at Pallia (possibly Cape Palit to the north of the city), Duke Robert sent out Bohemond with a squadron to seek the Venetian acclamation of Anna's pseudo-'Michael' and himself. The inhabitants of the city, according to more than one source, had already jeered at the imposter with howls of laughter. William of Apulia says that when he was paraded before them, the citizens did not fall for the ruse one bit, saying 'this man used to wait tables with jugs of wine – he was one of the butlers of lowest rank!'

The Venetians had promised to acclaim the pseudo-Michael the next day. Meanwhile, at nightfall, they lashed their bigger ships together to form a classic fighting 'sea harbour' (a naval formation recommended in the tenth century *Taktika* of the Emperor Leo VI). Wooden towers were made at the top of the masts by hauling the ships' skifs on cables and placing armed men within them. Improvised artillery projectiles were made by hammering spikes into large pieces of wood forming giant blocks which were lifted into the skifs. At daybreak, Bohemond came to make his demand of the enemy fleet, but they laughed at him and made fun of his beard. Bohemond therefore led his squadron towards the bigger ships and a battle followed in which his ship was holed by one of the improvised missiles and he had to jump aboard another to remain alive. Bohemond's squadron was routed by the Venetians and then pursued to Robert's camp, where the enemy crews disembarked and attacked the camp, ably assisted by George Palaeologus, who had sortied from the city. The Venetians retired to their ships and the sortie returned to Dyrrhachium. These naval battles had lasted a full three days. Many of the Venetians in the end sailed off with numerous riches for their Doge, as they had been promised.

Word of the naval defeats reached Corfu and the surrounding coastal towns who had submitted to Robert and the resulting turbulence may have forced the duke to spend many weeks at Orikon. At this time, the Emperor Alexius was in Thessaloniki, having left Constantinople in August. He had written to his Megas Domestikos Gregory Pakourianos, the redoubtable commander-in-chief of his army, to join with him. Pakourianos then appointed Nicholas Branas as hypostrategos, his sub-commander. Nicholas departed from Adrianople with his heavy infantrymen and headed west.

The emperor sent messages to a commander called Basil Mesopotamites who had 2,000 Turcopole horse-archers. William of Apulia alone mentions this engagement. William says this force was defeated in the far south near Butrinto when a Norman force turned upon it. This was where the duke still had his main base. By capturing Basil and closely questioning him, Robert realised that the force he would soon face at Dyrrhachium would be immense. He knew the Emperor must surely arrive soon. Robert moved his siege engines closer to the walls, at which point George Palaeologus countered him by throwing open the gates and attacking fiercely, although he received an arrow wound in the head for his troubles. The great siege tower was moved into position. Palaeologus had been preparing a counter-tower throughout the night, with a giant beam designed to swing against the exit door of the siege tower and thereby prevent its drawbridge from opening. He positioned his counter-tower opposite Robert's and the beam swung into action, while the men on his walls fired Robert's tower with a mixture of pitch, naphtha and burning dried wood. The Normans subsequently fled out of the bottom door of the tower and Anna's heroic and injured Palaeologus sortied once again with his axe men and destroyed the mighty tower.

It was said that Robert tried to set up a second tower before the emperor arrived. But on 15 October Alexius did just that. Malaterra says the duke's scouts saw the imperial banners in the distance. The army covered the hill and plain like locusts, says William of Apulia. But what did these armies, who were about to face each other, actually consist of?

The Armies
Robert's army is said to have encompassed a great many impressed men from his Apulian and Calabrian domains. Anna Comnena scoffed at their abilities, saying they were both young and old and scarcely knew how to hold a bow and arrow. But these were not the main body of the fighting troops. Behind this poorly armed mob were the experienced sailors of the Ragusan ports and those of Calabria and Apulia. These were far more capable men. In addition, there were the heavy cavalry of Bohemond, and Amicus (probably the former rebel Amicus II of Molfetta, now restored to favour). It is probable that there were also contingents of light cavalry and numerous archers in the army.

The imperial army comprised a variety of elements. Anna goes into some detail about the leaders of individual units. For the sake of consistency we shall keep to Anna's Greek spellings of their names (except for the more commonly Latinised version of her own father's name). Constantine Opos led the Exkouvitoi unit (the Excubitae Tagma), Antiokhos led the Macedonian men, and Alexander Kabisilas led the Thessalians, a combined force believed to be in the region of 5,000 men. Also, there was Tatikios, the son of a Saracen. Xantas and Kouleon led the Manichaeans (religious dualist heretics) who numbered nearly 3,000. The emperor's household units were commanded by Panoukomites and another unit of Frankish mercenaries were led by Constantine Houmpertopoulos, a man almost certainly of Norman background and possibly even related to Robert Guiscard. Also in the army were Constantine Porphyrogennetos (son of the emperor Constantine X) and Nikephoras Synadenos and a man called Nampites, the commander of the Varangian guardsmen who were by now composed largely of Anglo-Saxons who had fled England after the Norman Conquest. Alexius had also appealed not only to the Turks, but also to Bodin, the leader of the Dioclean (Montenegran) Serbs, who in theory had been Byzantine allies since the mid-1040s. There may also have been an Armenian contingent in the imperial army, although its numbers are unknown.

Deployment and Terrain
Alexius brought his giant army to the banks of the River Charzanes (Erzen) on 15 October 1081. He camped on the opposite side of the lagoons which at the time separated the citadel of Dyrrhachium from its hinterland. The Norman camp was on the other side of these lagoons, closer to the walls of the city, and a bridge led to the open ground to the east.

Alexius reconnoitred the landscape by visiting the Sanctuary of Saint Nicholas and began thinking about his deployment. Messengers were sent to Duke Robert and also George Palaeologus, who came to the emperor only after some persuasion. There were arguments among the imperial commanders about whether to offer immediate battle. The more experienced commanders and Palaeologus suggested a policy of patience and starvation. But others were insistent that a move should be made. These included Constantine Porphyrogennetos, Nikephoras Synadenos and Nampites, the keen Varangian commander. The hawks won the argument. Alexius formed a plan to attack Guiscard's camp at the rear in a night surprise by sending the Serbs and Turks on a circuitous march around the marshes to the north of the city, while he would engage the enemy to the front. In a move which smacks of prior intelligence, the Norman duke moved out from his camp and burnt it, crossing the bridge and finding an area closer to the enemy in which to deploy, near to the sanctuary of Saint Theodore. He also burnt his transport ships after a rousing speech in which he demonstrated to his men that they were there to stay and the final decision would be God's alone. The bridge was demolished too, thus rendering the Byzantine flanking attack impotent.

On the morning of 18 October 1081 Robert Guiscard formed his line about 800 meters from Alexius's army. William of Apulia says the ground was constricted at the point of deployment and that the nature of this constriction broke up the duke's formation. However, this is difficult to reconcile with the other sources. Robert deployed his heavy cavalry in the centre of the line, with his infantrymen probably to the rear of these. To his left was his son Bohemond's cavalry and to his right was Amicus with his cavalry. On seeing this deployment the emperor adapted his own line to suit. The units who had gone on the flanking march around the salt marshes were not re-called. He ordered Nampites to dismount his men and walk forward. Alexius positioned himself in the centre of the line. To his left was Pakourianos's division and to his right Nicephorus Melissinos's division,

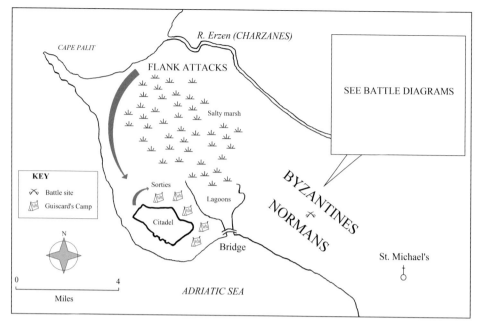

CAPE PALIT

R. Erzen (CHARZANES)

FLANK ATTACKS

SEE BATTLE DIAGRAMS

Salty marsh

BYZANTINES + NORMANS

KEY
⚔ Battle site
⛺ Guiscard's Camp

Sorties

Lagoons

Citadel

Bridge

St. Michael's

N

0   4
    Miles

ADRIATIC SEA

Map 15: Map of the Battle of Dyrrhachium, 18 October 1081

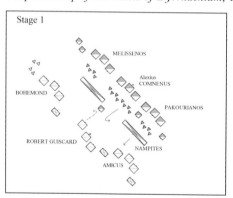

Stage 1

MELISSENOS

Alexius
COMNENUS

BOHEMOND

PAKOURIANOS

ROBERT GUISCARD

NAMPITES

AMICUS

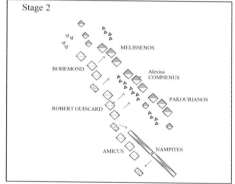

Stage 2

MELISSENOS

BOHEMOND

Alexius
COMNENUS

PAKOURIANOS

ROBERT GUISCARD

AMICUS   NAMPITES

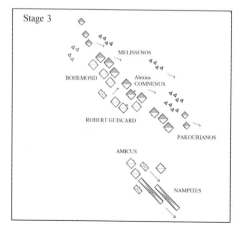

Stage 3

MELISSENOS

BOHEMOND

Alexius
COMNENUS

ROBERT GUISCARD

PAKOURIANOS

AMICUS

NAMPITES

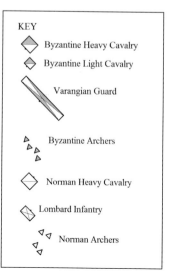

KEY

◆ Byzantine Heavy Cavalry

◇ Byzantine Light Cavalry

▬ Varangian Guard

▷ Byzantine Archers

◇ Norman Heavy Cavalry

◈ Lombard Infantry

◁ Norman Archers

each consisting of smaller companies. Alexius had placed a large body of archers behind the advancing Varangians with instructions to fire at Guiscard's line. The Varangians were required to split their ranks right and left to allow the archers to come forward and to do the same to facilitate their retreat.

The Battle
The battle opened with Alexius moving himself forward with his archers and Varangians in front of him. At this time, his flanking troops arrived at the Norman camp, finding it half burnt and abandoned. Another sortie from the city arrived at the camp to discover much the same thing. Robert Guiscard sent out a cavalry unit ahead to perform a feigned flight and entice the Byzantines from their line, but these men were countered by Byzantine light cavalry. Anna Comnena says the infantry and cavalry of Amicus's division spotted a weakness at the end of the Varangian line and tried to attack it, but fell back towards the sea in disorder, some of them wading up to their necks and receiving no help from the Byzantine and Venetian ships' companies.

Into the fray like a Valkyrie from Germanic legend galloped Sichelgaita, the Norman duke's wife. In a passage in Anna's account which borders on the incredible, this redoubtable Lombard woman was able to rally those in flight as she screamed her instructions at them. She had already been wounded, according to William of Apulia, though God had preserved her. But there had been a development for the Varangians. Buoyed by success, they had over-stretched themselves. With a papal banner to help him reinvigorate the troops, the duke saw tiredness in the Englishmen. He ordered an infantry unit into their unprotected flank. The result was a massacre of the Anglo-Saxons. The exhausted survivors of this attack fled to the sanctuary of the archangel Michael, further to the south-east. But it was no sanctuary at all. Some rushed into the building, while others climbed the roof, which then caved in. The pursuing Normans torched the building and burned it to the ground. Amid these flames died the brave men of Anglo-Saxon England, some of them suffering perhaps their second miserable defeat to the armies of a tenacious Norman duke.

Back on the battlefield Robert's cavalry saw an opportunity to charge. He led them like some 'winged horseman' and his men pushed the emperor back. In some places they even tore his line apart. Alexius stood firm, but the Norman cavalry charges were killing many around him. The Normans knew who to target. Constantine Porphyrogennetos was killed. So too was Nicephorus Synadenos, among others. Then, with just three men, Amicus, on seeing the emperor, charged at him with lances at the ready. Amicus's horse swerved and he missed his target. A second Norman had his arm cut off by the emperor. The third struck a blow with his lance to Alexius's head. He fell back on his horse, but remained saddled, his helmet toppling to the ground. As the emperor drew himself back up, he could see the Turks fleeing the field. He also saw Bodin's Serbians beating a hasty retreat and he would have known that these men had not even committed themselves to the battle, despite the fact that he had put them in the perfect position to attack the Normans from the rear.

It was over for Alexius. Thousands in his army lay dead. Many citizens were left unburied. The Manichaeans were 300 men short of their starting number. Alexius must now do what King Harold had failed to do at Hastings in 1066: remain alive. As Robert Guiscard headed to Alexius's camp at the Sanctuary of Saint Nicholas he sent out a detachment to capture the fleeing emperor. They pursued him to a place called Kake Pleura, where nine horsemen surrounded him. He escaped their attack as his horse leaped onto a rock. Later still, he was surrounded again by Normans and he charged at one of them, knocking him to the ground and killing him. Alexius fled to Achrida, where he was able to reorganise amid an atmosphere of bitter defeat.

George Palaeologus had been unable to get into Dyrrhachium after the battle. The emperor therefore took it upon himself to appoint some Venetians to care for the citizens and placed the town under an Albanian native official who occupied a position called *komes kortes*. For months the city remained loyal to the emperor, but Anna tells us of its final betrayal by its Amalfitan merchant community (more probably by a Venetian called Domenico, according to other sources).

Alexius Comnenus was, for the moment, undone by Norman superiority on the battlefield. The emperor was a wise and experienced commander, but despite his experiences with Roussel de Bailleul, he would never have seen anything quite like the repeated cavalry charges he had faced at Dyrrhachium. The Byzantine military manuals such as the *Taktika* and the *Praecepta Militaria* had warned against taking on the 'Franks' in a pitched battle. Now Alexius knew why. It would take a very long time for the Byzantines to handle the 'Franks', or Normans, as a mounted enemy. They were no more or less fierce in the saddle than the Turks, but it seemed that their approach to warfare was different. But what were the details of their methods? Were they so different from other military cultures?

Part 4

The Norman Way of War

Chapter 14

The Nature of Warfare
Across the Norman World

Norman warfare has some distinctive characteristics which, while they are not unique to the Normans, serve to place their style of warfare in the context of the medieval world. Warfare was dominated by strategic concerns. These included reducing an enemy's land and nullifying his ability to live off it, the reliance upon the small fortified place as a position from which to dominate a landscape and the execution of and relief of sieges. If there was to be a battle, the employment of a combined-arms approach was usually (although not universally) adopted. The overall desire to avoid set-piece encounters is something we have observed in the first part of this book when considering some of the individual commanders. William of Poitiers, writing about William the Conqueror, even says that the duke went out of his way to avoid set-piece battles with the French king whenever the king invaded Normandy. The risk and uncertainty of a commander's fate in battle might well be the reason why so many leaders of the era, Norman or others, placed their faith more in God than themselves when it finally came to such an encounter. That said, there were plenty of battles throughout the period. It might be through absolute necessity that battle was sought. Or it could be when a commander perceived that the odds were stacked in his favour (such as at Varaville in 1057, where Duke William observed the French army split in two when crossing a ford). But there is more to Norman warfare than the pitched battle.

As we have seen, the taking of prisoners of rank in battles was preferred to their slaughter. Two examples from Amatus serve to illustrate the point. In or around 1075 a battle occurred on the banks of the River Melfa between the men of the prince of Capua and Duke Robert Guiscard. The goal of the engagement that followed was the capture of high-profile prisoners for ransom and the carrying away of property. When William of Pont-Echanfray arrived on the field with an infantry force he threw himself at the battle, which had already been lost by his side in an earlier cavalry engagement 'in order to win back the lost battle'. He 'freed the prisoners and forced those who had been victorious to fight'. The knights took heart and those who had been prisoners attacked those who were taking them to prison. Amatus also says that William searched the battlefield in the morning and carried off the enemy's property. Thirty of the prince's squires were captured and seventy knights (VII.24). This obscure engagement might be regarded as a typical 'Norman' battle. The second example from Amatus (VII.31) concerns Robert of Loritello's ambush of the men of Count Transmund, in which he says:

> The Normans stayed their hands so as not to draw blood, nor did they capture the poorly armed ones but the better armed ones. Bernard's sons and Transmund's nephew were taken, also the bishop of Camerino and many others....They took 4,000 horses; however, it is not necessary to speak of the other animals and equipment.

Clearly then, the purpose of a typical Norman battle was not necessarily to fight to the last man. One of the arguments that has interested historians about medieval warfare in general – and the Normans are certainly no exception to this – is whether or not some of the great military treatises of the late Roman and contemporary Byzantine ages were available to the western commanders of the day. If leaders such as Robert Guiscard and William the Conqueror knew of these great works, to what extent did their style of warfare pay homage to the classical notion? One of the works which is frequently cited in this respect is the *De Re Militari* of Vegetius. The question might equally be posed of the Byzantine Emperor Maurice's *Strategicon*, Leo VI's *Taktika*, the *Praecepta Militaria* of Nikephoras Phocas and the *Taktika* of Nicephorus Ouranos. Each of these manuals or treatises were widely read in the Byzantine Empire and conceivably also in the West. However, it is with Vegetius and his common-sense approach to warfare that the historians draw many parallels and comparisons when discussing medieval warfare.

Pleading for army reform in the later Roman period, Vegetius wrote in the late fourth or early fifth century. He looked back to a bygone age of Roman military dominance. How to fortify camps, how to train troops, how to instil discipline and how to fight, march and employ tactical and strategic measures, were all covered in the four books of the work. Book I concentrated on the recruitment, organisation and training of soldiers, while Book II was more or less a manual of infantry. Book III contained useful military maxims, some of which echo those first penned by the influential Sun Tzu, who wrote in the sixth century BC. Book IV contained a feast of material for the historian of siege and naval warfare. There is little doubt that the work was influential in the Middle Ages. There are too many versions of it for anyone to suggest otherwise. In fact, the work was used by Rabanus Maurus Magnentius, a Frankish Benedictine monk, when he wrote his own *De Procincta Romaniae Militiae* for Lothair II of Lotharingia (855–869).

The question posed is whether the Norman approach to warfare was in anyway 'Vegetian'. It is suggested that the Normans did not command the same types of armies that Vegetius was talking about and could not have followed many of his instructions due to differences in resources and political organisation. This might seem to be supported by the argument that many of the maxims within the treatise were common sense anyway, and would probably be understood by an illiterate Pecheneg camp follower, let alone a king of England or duke of Apulia. One Vegetian principle often referred to is the idea that a prudent commander should look for methods other than battle to achieve his goals. This would bring great riches if things went well, but not too much harm if things did not. It is impossible to argue that on the whole the Normans did not do this. But we should not miss the subtlety. 'Vegetian' warfare was an option for the Normans and not a doctrine.

The arguments about the importance of Vegetius to our Norman commanders are intractable and distracting. From what we have seen, leaders such as William the Conqueror certainly embodied a 'Vegetian' style of warfare when they wanted to. Perhaps one can imagine a monastic library somewhere in northern France with a manuscript of *De Re Militari* waiting for a visiting count to refresh his boyhood training. Medieval commentators such as Orderic Vitalis drop hints that they knew of these classical military writings. William of Poitiers (*Gesta Guillelmi* 54–62) also alludes to Vegetius and was keenly aware of the maxims himself. It cannot be the case that the Norman leaders were ignorant of such writings. However, as we shall see, not all of Vegetius's work could be followed to the letter by Norman commanders, simply because they lacked the imperial scale of resources to execute it all, particularly in respect of infantry matters.

Chapter 15

Recruitment, Organisation and Mercenaries

There is always a danger that the term 'feudal' can drag us into a still-ongoing debate about what feudalism is, who invented it, what the social and economic status of a 'knight' really was, and what a knight's fee actually looked like. These issues have been widely explored, with results not always conclusive. In short, the historical debate over feudalism in England centred on the argument that it was William the Conqueror who brought the system to the country in 1066. Against this argument ran a counter-argument that the Anglo-Saxons prior to 1066 actually had a system of obligations based on personal lordship ties and land tenure, which looked suspiciously like the 'feudalism' of the later period. And so, for a while, the Anglo-Saxon system of military recruitment became more 'feudal' and the Anglo-Norman less so. Continuity across the famous dateline of 1066 became a focus once again. The debate carries on today because the evidence shows that the reality is very complex.

For the sake of simplicity, the most important thing to understand is how and why troops found themselves 'serving' in the armies of our period. For this, the term 'feudal' can be misleading, the concept being imposed by posterity and only pertaining to one aspect of the overall subject. The word 'feudal' in a military sense is more specific than its wider literary sense. It was the military service owed by the holder of a fief to his lord, as part of the obligation accepted during the act of homage. The service was unpaid and was usually expected to last for forty days a year. A royal or princely summons was issued for the service. One such famous recipient of a writ of summons for military service under William the Conqueror was an Englishman, Abbot Æthelwig of Evesham, who was asked to summon all those under his authority who owed knights and to send them to Clarendon, where he too must appear in person along with the five knights he owed in respect of his own abbey. This may have been in response to the planned expedition to Maine of 1073 in which Englishmen featured, or the Conqueror's invasion of Scotland in the previous year. But the word 'feudal' would not have been heard by the men of the eleventh century. For the senior lords of Normandy, Norman Italy, Norman

Sicily and Anglo-Norman England their response to a summons was their fulfilment of the *servitium debitum*, or military obligation.

How a Norman commander put his army together has its roots in the early medieval past. Then, great warriors attracted young men into their service with promises of wealth. In this respect there was not a great deal of difference between the Dark Age warrior leader of the age of Beowulf and the Norman lords of the eleventh century. By the 'Norman'period there were numerous additional methods of recruiting, but the fundamental principles remained. Despite the varieties of troop types and recruiting grounds it is perhaps best to note that by the late eleventh century there were in fact only two major groups or 'pools' of troops recruited into the service of a senior lord, duke or king. These were those men who owed service in return for their lands (the enfeoffed knights and also the territorially obliged fyrdsmen in the case of England) and those who were paid to fight as stipendiaries or as true mercenaries. So, on the one hand there is the 'obligated' pool of troops and on the other there is the 'hired' pool.

To make what seems simple a little more complicated, the boundaries between the obligated troops and the hired troops were often blurred. Fyrdsmen and enfeoffed knights could quite easily be selected and paid to serve in the *familias* of the senior nobles of the era, providing them with extra pay and their paymasters with uncomplicated mercenaries instead of men bound by the feudal rules of service. Such were the aspirations of the knights of the era (who were always looking for advancement both in social status and material wealth) that the enfeoffed knight and the stipendiary warrior might be one and the same man.

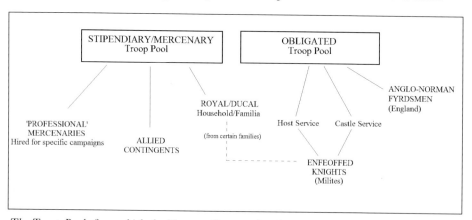

The Troop Pools from which the Norman Commanders drew   *Fig. 15*

Obligated Troops

Let us take the first category of obligated troops such as the enfeoffed knights and fyrdsmen. In England, the resource pool was massively enhanced by the existence of the fyrd, an ancient territorially based Anglo-Saxon institution that remained large in number despite the exodus of elite English warriors in the aftermath of Hastings. The Normans made good use of the system, and the fyrd were very loyal in their service, with such loyalty to the king mentioned consistently by the sources during the reigns of the first three Norman kings of England. In fact, they turned up for service in 1068, 1073 and 1074 (a year in which they accompanied William the Conqueror to Maine), 1078, 1094 (when they were dismissed early), 1101, 1102, 1106 (in support of Henry I on the Normandy Campaign) and again in 1117.

Armed with shields and spears and some degree of body armour, the Anglo-Norman fyrd provided the bulk of the infantry for the army if it was required. There were many thousands of them theoretically available, with Orderic Vitalis reporting that a seemingly unlikely 30,000 showed their support for William II Rufus in facing down the rebellions of 1088. The service was owed either by thegns recommended directly to the king (a lordship obligation) or by those who held 'bookland' from the king. Its territorial method of recruitment was recorded in a famous passage in the Domesday Book, 'Customs of Berkshire':

> If the king sends an army anywhere, one soldier goes from every five hides, and 4s. are given to him from each hide for his food and pay (ad victum vel stipendium) for two months. This money is not sent to the king but given to the soldiers.

In 1094, in what is seen as an abuse of the system, William II Rufus, while in Normandy, ordered Ranulf Flambard, his ingenious money-raising bishop, to raise 20,000 fyrdsmen. These men gathered at Hastings to set sail to Normandy but Ranulf (on the order of the king) took from them 10s and turned the men away. The money was sent to the king and used to hire mercenaries. The implication here is that the 10s which was collected was the money given by the estates for the soldiers' food and provisions when on campaign. The other outstanding 10s, which was not collected, would have represented the pay for their services on their return from their campaign. Despite such clever accounting, this seemingly phantom fyrd did indeed continue to serve its Norman masters. The *Leges Henrici Primi* of Henry I's reign imposes a 120s fine for failure to perform fyrd service (not a new imposition), and it is also clear that in some cases service could be commuted in advance for the sum of 20s, the same amount as a fyrdsman was supposed to receive for the two months of his service.

The fyrd certainly saw some action under the Norman kings. William II Rufus used Englishmen to take the rebel castle at Tonbridge in 1088, and later in 1095 he used them to besiege Robert de Mowbray at Tynemouth and Bamburgh. In 1102 Henry I used them to take Arundel from Robert of Bellême. Moreover, many Englishmen found themselves campaigning in France, probably for the first time in their lives, throughout the period.

And so the bonds of lordship (with the English now transferring their allegiance to their new overlords) and the five-hide system might appear to have 'survived' the Conquest. However, there was another pool of troops, the enfeoffed knights of Normandy and England, whose calling was also based on a form of obligation. Arguments persist over whether the knight's fee was based around the five-hide unit or a system of decimal calculations based on the constabularia of ten knights. Often termed 'miles' in the sources, the enfeoffed knight certainly served subject to feudal limitations. He served in the royal or ducal host and also provided Castle Service.

In France and Normandy the enfeoffed knight would expect to meet his obligations in a number of ways. The *arrière-ban*, for example, was an emergency call-out of freemen, similar in spirit if not in execution to the English emergency call-out system which was resorted to in 1016 by Edmund II Ironside during his Danish wars. It was the remit of kings and princes. It did not have 'feudal' obligations based on land tenure at its core. Because of its very nature this method was probably not often used. In Normandy, where tensions were often strained between the duke and his subordinates, it would have been considered a dangerous imposition. However, a more formal arrangement was the *service d'host* (*expedition*). Here, the Norman duke was summoning the feudal quotas of his domain as owed by his tenants-in-chief. This was the forty-day *servitium debitum*. Enfeoffed knights serving in this way were thus obliged to serve within the borders of the duchy under the duke's banner. After the Norman Conquest this was of course complicated by the fact that various lords had lands on either sides of the Channel. Among those answering the *servitium debitum* were the feudal knights of the realm. They were equipped with lance, sword, shield and hauberk and were trained to fight on horseback. Because of the bonds which tied them to their lords, they were usually quite loyal to their overlord, and the king of England relied on their support (along with that of the fyrdsmen) on a number of occasions, not least when they stood by Henry I in 1101. The size of the enfeoffed knights' resource pool varied in size over the years, particularly in England where in the years after the Conquest the numbers were small and the barons and leading churchmen who owed contingents bought in mercenaries to meet their obligations. Also, not every enfeoffed knight owed military service for their tenure, although many in England did. Overall, it is thought that the pool in England could have amounted to around 5,000 knights.

Towards the end of our period came the gradual introduction of scutage. This was where a payment was made in lieu of military service levied on a knight's fee. From around 1100 it appears, and was often levied on ecclesiastical tenants-in-chief who had difficulty fulfilling their quotas. By the end of the century, however, its usage was causing political headaches for the Plantagenet kings.

The next level of obligation was the *service de chevauchée* (*chevalchia*) which was based on the duty of a vassal to his lord. Here, an enfeoffed knight would serve his lord on whatever expedition that lord had either chosen to go on or was obliged to go on as part of his own duty. It is tempting to see the whole group of obligated troops serving in Norman Italy and Sicily as similar in essence to the situation in the north. But we know less about those areas, and it could well be the case in England that we have one system grafted onto another in the aftermath of the Conquest. If the twelfth-century *Catalogus Baronum* of Roger II of Sicily's reign (1130–1154), which lists the feudal obligations of Italian nobles, is anything to go by, the enfeoffed knight was of fundamental importance to the recruiting system across the southern Norman world.

One other area of obligation for the enfeoffed knight was Castle Service. Castles had begun to spread across Christendom throughout the tenth and eleventh centuries. In Normandy by the 1020s there were strong ducal castles at Mortain, Brionne-sur-Risle, Fécamp, Saint-Lô, Ivry, Evreux, Eu and Exmes. More were added under the reigns of Duke Robert I (1027–1035) and William the Conqueror (1035–1087). In Apulia, however, we hear frequent mention of the 'castella'. In addition to these, there were the older enclosed cities of the Byzantine east coast, which under Norman rule usually experienced a smaller Norman inner fortification within its walls, manned by a Norman garrison such as those at Troia and Bari. A similar phenomenon occurred in English urban contexts after the Conquest and there was also a proliferation in England of the distinctive motte-and-bailey style Norman castle, built first in timber and then later with stone keeps replacing the previous wooden ones.

Much like the field army, the troops who garrisoned the castles were a mixture of mercenaries and those who owed the duty as a condition of the knight's fee. During periods of peace, castles ran on skeleton crews containing janitores and vigiles (non-military offices). There might be only a minimum of knights and missile troops to hand. However, during the many periods of conflict this would change. Numbers, however, might still be small in the smaller castles. In England and Normandy (when it was under the English king) the *Familia Regis*, or king's household, was responsible for organising castle ward in both the smaller castles and the larger royal ones. For our obligated pool of troops, whose service was dictated by the holding of a fee, the administration was quite complex. Their service was limited to a period of time which would have caused difficulties should a castle require year-round manning. Consequently, the sheriff organised the ward by grouping fees together and assigning segments of the year to each group, and it fell to the castellans to enforce compliance.

Inevitably, the 'feudal' service in castles was heavily supplemented by the mercenary. In 1061 Geoffrey of Malaterra says Roger de Hauteville garrisoned Petralia after its capture with both '*milites et stipendiarii*' (II. 20), indicating that such arrangements were by no means a peculiarity of the Norman north. In Normandy during the volatile early twelfth century the inclusion of mercenaries in castle service was often the case, as the feudal pool was small and the loyalty of the men questionable. In England, mercenary provision fluctuated throughout the period and according to need.

Stipendiary/Mercenary troops
The stipendiary pool of troops was vast and varied. The troop types themselves ranged from the mounted knight, with his destrier (war horse), lance, sword, shield and hauberk to specialist archers, slingers, crossbowmen, sailors, engineers, lightly-armed javelinmen and many others. The *familias* at royal, ducal and baronial level formed a core to most of the armies featuring in the period. These were the household troops of the leading figures of the age. They were drawn from various sources including landless adventurers, second sons of senior magnates or even the sons of rebels hoping to regain favour and power with the lord who had prevailed against their fathers. In King Henry I's *Familia Regis* these men could be of high birth indeed. Engenulf and Geoffrey of l'Aigle and Jordan of Auffay are identified as such. At a level beneath them were men such as Henry de Pomeroy, Odo Borleng and Bertrand Rumex, who could assume military leadership roles.

The *familia* had its own code of behaviour, its own internal command and administrative structure and its pockets were usually very deep, especially in Anglo–Norman England. As we have seen, the Anglo–Norman *Familia Regis* could take to the field entirely by itself without the king present and still prevail in a pitched battle, such as at Bourgthéroulde in 1124 (pages 142-144) and at Lincoln in 1069, where a detachment sallied out from the town and defeated a foraging force under the Anglo-Saxon rebel Edgar the Ætheling. On campaign too, the *Familia Regis* could operate on its own, as it did in 1084–86 in Maine on behalf of William the Conqueror. Again in Maine in 1098, the *Familia Regis* under Robert de Bellême, the '*princeps militia*' of William II Rufus, achieved the conquest of Maine and even held it against Fulk of Anjou the next year.

But before we look at the workings of a *familia*, it is important to look at another stipendiary option open to the Normans, although it was expensive and politically dangerous. This involved the employment of allied contingents within the Norman army, such as that supplied by Helias of Maine in 1106 to Henry I at Tinchebrai. Special arrangements had also developed between the kings of England and the counts of Flanders. In 1101, Henry I came to an arrangement (renewed in 1103 and 1110 and periodically revisited) with Duke Robert of Flanders. In return for a fee or money fief of 500 pounds of silver a year, the count would agree to provide Henry with 1,000 mounted knights (*equites*) for service in England or Normandy or with 500 knights for service in Maine. He would serve the king against all men excepting his fealty to King Philip I of France. Henry would effectively be purchasing the count's loyalty by way of contract. Henry would supply the ships, but the count would have responsibility for them during active operations. Henry would maintain the Flemish knights and compensate them for any losses, just as he would do with his own household. If the French king tried to invade England the count should seek to dissuade him. If this was unsuccessful, he should provide the French king with only a small contingent. Should Normandy be invaded by the French king, the count of Flanders was to provide only twenty knights to assist. The later money fief reduced the numbers to 500 knights in England and 250 in Normandy and brought the contingent of twenty knights to the French king down to just ten. Also, the new French king mentioned in the text was Louis VI and not his predecessor Philip I.

Such an arrangement had already existed in some form during the reigns of William the Conqueror and his son William II Rufus. The Conqueror had paid 300 marks a year for Flemish service, and in 1093 William II Rufus had reactivated the agreement on a new footing, paying for the Flemish leader's personal appearance within forty days. Some have seen these sorts of arrangements as the forerunners of the military indenture system of the later medieval period, although this is a complex claim to prove. What it does show, however, is the strength of the diplomatic capabilities of the Anglo–Norman kings and their concern to provide their armies with quality troops.

It was in the deliberate hiring of true mercenaries, as we might understand them – directly paid troops for specific campaigns – that a leader's wealth spoke the loudest. These men came from almost everywhere in the Norman world. Knights from Normandy, Anjou, Maine and the Low Countries were such examples. Infantrymen from the vast pool of demoted Englishmen in the post-Conquest period were another. Breton cavalry and Welsh infantry formed other groups, too.

What drove the mercenary into the household of a baron, duke or king was the hope of reward. The greater the achievements of the leader, the more swollen his *familia* might be. This accounts for the small numbers of Normans in Italy and Sicily during the period of the conquests in the south. Much of the military success in this period in Apulia and Calabria, and also in Sicily between 1016 and 1072, was carried out by the *familias* of the Norman lords with the occasional augmentation of true mercenaries. The need for Robert Guiscard to financially support his *familia* as it galloped across the plains of the Mezzogiorno drove further expansion and further exaction of tribute from regional towns. Moreover, it was to the household of leaders such as Robert Guiscard, Humphrey de Hauteville and Rainulf of Aversa that the newly arrived Normans would flock, seeking service. Even Roger de Hauteville had started his career in the household of Guiscard with just sixty eager and hungry knights. Later, in 1061 and 1063, just 300 landless yet ambitious knights, whom Geoffrey of Malaterra calls '*iuvenes*', accompanied Roger on his successful Sicilian campaign, about which the stronghold of Gastrogiovanni (Enna) was the pivot. Such men are also called '*bacheliers*' in the Romance literature of the era. William II Rufus had been one such in his own father's household.

Of all the *familias* in the Norman world, that of the Anglo-Norman kings is perhaps best known, thanks to the document written in around 1136 known as the *Constitutio Domus Regis*, which outlines the make-up, organisation and pay structures within the king's household of the latter part of Henry I's reign. The Anglo-Norman army literally revolved around the *Familia Regis*. Its close links with the governmental system were inevitable. Around the king himself we find a *hosticum* – an immediate group of close followers, possibly even a personal bodyguard. Within the *Domus Regis*, at the very heart of government, were the *familia* officers, the constables, master-marshal and deputy master-marshal. The master-marshal was the paymaster and the constables possibly his quarter-master generals. The constables and master-marshal outside the king's household would receive two shillings a day, one salted simnel loaf, one sextary of ordinary wine, one small wax candle and twenty-four pieces of candle. Serving within the household they received fourteen pence, half a sextary of ordinary wine and a candle. The marshal got eight pence a day, a gallon of ordinary wine and twelve pieces of candle if outside the household and three pence a day and a candle when he was within it. His serjeants, when on the king's business, would also receive three pence a day. The *Constitutio* also mentions the royal hunt's bowmen who received five pence a day, possibly the same figure as the military bowmen of the era. Other members of the *familia* would have received an annual retainer wage and also been paid when on campaign. The amount of payment is not known, but is believed to be in the region six to eight pence a day.

Men would have been compensated for the loss of equipment and horses when in service. But it was not just this security which attracted them to the *familia*. An active king, duke or baron could provide rewards based on his monetary and landed wealth. If you served long enough and did good things for your paymaster, you might expect rewards greater than you got elsewhere.

In southern Italy the hiring of mercenaries was widespread. The incoming waves of Normans were themselves mercenaries for many decades. When mercenaries were employed for various campaigns, they fell into the structure of the *familia* of the lord who hired them. In England, however, Henry I was judicious in his employment of true mercenaries, seeming only to employ them when strictly needed. This can be compared to the reign of King Stephen in England (1135–1154), when the mercenary knight reaped the benefit of anarchy and widespread internecine warfare and, as a consequence, did very well for himself.

Men from the stipendiary pool of warriors were just as likely to exhibit professionalism as those bound to their lord by feudal obligation. This occurred at the siege of Bridgnorth in 1102. Robert de Bellême was besieged by King Henry I and his garrison consisted of a mixture of obligated troops and hired mercenaries. The troops who owed their service to their lord began to waver during the siege and sought to strike a deal with the men of King Henry. On learning of this, the mercenary contingent attempted to prevent the surrender of the castle, but were shut up in a part of it by the others. The royal forces were subsequently handed the castle. The king then granted Robert's mercenaries the right to leave freely with their horses and their arms, but as they rode through the ranks of Henry's men they complained loudly that they had been let down by the plotting garrison. They did this for the explicit reason, as Orderic Vitalis recounts '...so that their downfall might not bring contempt on other mercenaries.'

The key to successful recruitment was to continue to produce the wealth or promise of wealth a leader would need to reward his followers. Men would come to the service of a lord in a number of different ways, some obliged by the way in which they held their land, others by hope of reward or forgiveness for their family's misdeeds. For example, the two sons of Roger, Earl of Hereford, fought in King Henry I's household in the hope their father's confiscated lands might be restored to them. Whatever the reason, the deeper the purse of the Norman commander, the stronger his army.

At the centre of it all was the Norman knight. He might be young, relatively poor, landless, without a wife and hungry for action. He might be older, richer, landed, married and accomplished. He always wanted more. The Norman knight is perhaps better judged not by his actual wealth in terms of lands and possessions, but by his aspirations. Without him, the whole system of feudal obligation and stipendiary service would have fallen to pieces. He galloped into battles and sieges over the muddy fields of England, the craggy hills of Wales and the scorched ground of Apulia and Calabria. And beneath his saddle was the greatest weapon of the Norman age.

Chapter 16

The Normans and Their Horses

What made the Normans such a renowned cavalry force? In a widely cited paper on the subject of the Norman warhorse, historian R.H.C. Davis uncovered the secret, concluding that both a consummate understanding of horse management and a passion for importing the finest stallions were at the heart of it.

A glance at any geological map of Normandy will reveal that it is roughly divided into two contrasting geological regions. In the west, sandstones and granites and schist gradually give way to younger rocks of clays, limestone and chalk belonging to the Paris Bassin in the east. Haute-Normandie lies north-west of the Paris Bassin. Basse-Normandie, more similar in character to the lands of its Breton neighbour, encompasses most of the west of Normandy. In plain English, then, you have an Upper and Lower Normandy. Generally, the whole duchy was good country for breeding horses, but it is thought that the areas of Upper Normandy, particularly in the valley of the Seine, where the limestone and the chalky soil provided grasses rich in calcium ideal for strengthening the bones of the young horses, were the key areas for this enterprise. Here, on the banks of the Seine, during the earlier Carolingian period, there were many royal and ecclesiastical studs. The banks were lined with woodland for the forest mares, the soil was rich in the right ingredients and the governmental apparatus as it existed on the royal estates in the region was well equipped for horse breeding.

Horse management is a delicate business. There is no doubt that the matter was taken seriously and was rigorously controlled. We should remember that without human intervention, the horses of this part of Europe would be little more than ponies. It is clear that the Norman horse was much more than this, however. The knight's destrier, as he became known, was so-called probably because he was led on the right side or the animal itself led to the right. The natural aggression displayed by this animal was possibly further enhanced by the training of the animal itself. The knight would not ride this mount to battle, however, for fear of it becoming blown too early. He would ride a lesser mount. There would be a horse for his squire and also one for the baggage they would bring together. Already, it is clear that the supply requirements, even for a small mounted force, would be considerable.

Experts on equestrian history have tried to calculate the height and build of a

Norman horse at around the time of the Battle of Hastings. The evidence presents itself in the form of surviving horseshoes and, of course, the pictorial evidence provided by the Bayeux Tapestry, which among other things shows the beasts to be stallions with unmistakable clarity. The upshot of all this work has been the suggestion that the Norman warhorse was a medium-sized animal of stocky build of around 14.2–15 hands in height. The estimated weight of the animal is said to have been around 800–1,000 lbs (360–455kg). The capability of such a horse in terms of load bearing and stamina is of interest too. Comparisons with the modern, slightly lighter Arabian horse of 14.2 hands, weighing 750–850lbs (340–385kg) shows it is capable of carrying a quarter of its weight over a journey of 100 miles travelling at 6.7 miles an hour. This is presumably without any training or breeding for such tasks.

Duke William is presented with his horse at Hastings, from the Bayeux Tapestry. The full inscription above reads HERE THE SOLDIERS HAVE GONE OUT FROM HASTINGS AND COME TO BATTLE AGAINST KING HAROLD.

Judging by the Bayeux Tapestry the Norman horse was unarmoured, but carried on his back a warrior clad in a mailcoat (hauberk). The warrior held a spear or lance in one hand and the reins with another. He had a sword at his side, and a kite-shaped shield. The burden on the Norman warhorse thus came from its rider and his equipment. So, if the Norman warhorse was such a well-adapted beast, how did the horse breeders of northern France and elsewhere get from the native pony to the sort of animal we see on the Bayeux Tapestry? The answer lies both in the management practices at the breeding centres across Normandy and in the connections which the Normans had with Spain, a country where horses of

Arabian and Barb stock dwelt in numbers. Through gift-exchanges these horses made their way to the Norman ducal and baronial households and they would have been highly prized and cared for. Spanish horses were so highly thought of that William the Conqueror himself had been given one as a gift by Walter Giffard. The Normans who visited Spain and campaigned there must have been impressed by the mounts they found. Roger and Ralph de Tosny both experienced mounted warfare in the peninsula and Robert Crispin returned to France with much plunder in the 1060s. Later still, Robert de Bellême brought back horses from Spain which were later said to have provided the basis for the medieval stock of horses at Powys.

Horse breeding was a science and an art at the same time. The idea is simple enough. You have to find a stallion who exhibits the qualities you desire. These qualities could be anything from docility to outward aggression in terms of temperament, not to mention physical build. The offspring of this stallion should start to exhibit similar tendencies and traits and you would be able to select those individuals who showed these characteristics the most strongly and use only them for breeding. This approach can result in the breeding-in of certain characteristics and the breeding-out of others. If you cannot keep your mares separated from the stallions, or you allow feral or unwanted stallions to get in with the mares in your herd, your work might have to start all over again. With a gestation period of eleven months and a two-year period for foals to run with their dams before you can separate them, a herd will quickly decline in quality in just a few short years if the breeding programme is disrupted. This is exactly what happened in northern France and in England when the Viking raiders of the ninth century took horses from the rich breeding areas of East Anglia in England and the Seine Valley in northern France. It might only take a hole in a fence to allow an alien stallion to ruin a breeding programme, but this level of harm pales into insignificance when compared to the consequences of a Viking raid.

Such vital concerns were not lost on Charlemagne (800–814), France's emperor before the arrival of the Northmen. In his *Capitulare de Villis*, a document describing the management of royal estates, he saw the importance of removing foals from herds at an early age so as to avoid them going feral and dying somewhere in the unmanaged wilderness. He also knew of the importance of providing a territory for the herds which was properly fenced off and maintained. He demanded his stewards told him of the poor-quality horses before it was time to send them into the mares for breeding, so they could be weeded out. Furthermore, the importance of properly feeding the mares through the winter months was acknowledged.

Royal breeding farms existed in England during the Norman period. In the 1130 Pipe Rolls is mentioned one Swein, a shield bearer to the king, whose job it was to look after the breeding of the king's mares at Gillingham. Such farms, of which there were probably many (both lay and ecclesiastical) would provide the replacements for the casualties accrued on campaign and in battle for members of the *Familia Regis*.

There is plenty of evidence from across the period that the breeding of horses was also a profitable business. The abbeys of Fécamp and Jumièges clearly dealt in horses, with the latter being recorded as selling a horse of a 'very great price' between 1020 and 1030 to Hugh, the bishop of Bayeux, in return for land and privileges at Rouvray. Similarly, Drogo, count of Amiens and the disputed Vexin region, received six horses of 'a very great price' for lands at Genainville. A Norman destrier was an expensive animal indeed. It could fetch between £20 and £30 compared to 14s or so for a workhorse. The religious establishments could and would use their valuable equine resources in their dealings with the laity. Similarly, tithes of mares were often given to the monasteries and the noblemen of Normandy played their part here. Examples include William FitzOsbern's 1050 donation to the abbey of Lyre of half the tithe from his stud at Glos-la-Ferrière, near Saint Evroul, and the knight Gerold's giving of the tithe of his mares in Roumare to the nuns of Saint Amand in Rouen in 1067.

It is perhaps little wonder that the horse was such a prize, being at the heart of the Norman way of war. In the campaigns of southern Italy and Sicily, where the main bulk of the fighting was carried out by the mounted *familias* of the Norman leaders, the capture of horses from the enemy must have been of equal value to the capture of and subsequent ransom of prisoners. In fact, when Richard of Aversa demanded riches from the Salernitans in the early 1050s, Amatus says that 'rather than [being given] horses arrows were shot at him' (III.46). After the Battle of Enna in 1061, in which Robert Guiscard and his brother Roger defeated a Saracen army, a reward of equine riches was reaped. Amatus says that 5,000 cavalry were taken. Geoffrey of Malaterra however, (II.17) has it this way:

> They [the Normans] pursued the defeated towards Castrogiovanni [Enna] and killed up to ten thousand of them. So victory was gained and they secured such great spoils that a man who had lost one horse in the battle received ten for one; undoubtedly the army as a whole similarly enriched itself.

The needs of the Norman horse – this prize asset – when on campaign were clearly great. A whole logistical network was built around it. The subject of military supply in the Norman period is our next area of focus.

Chapter 17

Logistics and Supply

How a Norman army was supplied with food, water, replenishments and weaponry was inextricably linked to the role of castles as supply depots and to the organisation of ducal and royal *familias* with people given specific roles in this regard. Existing road networks and newly built routeways would also be of vital importance for the distribution of food and weaponry. We are far better off for evidence in the northern Norman world than we are in Italy and Sicily, although the arrangements must have been similar.

Supply in the Anglo-Norman army was a function of the *Familia Regis*. An army on active campaign may choose foraging as a supplementary method of provisioning itself. Costs for other supplies were met by the king's chamber in England when the army was on the move. However, there needed to be a properly organised advanced arrangement for supply, particularly within one's own patrimony. In the royal household in Anglo-Norman England the buying and distribution of supplies was under the jurisdiction of the constables. In charge of the accounting for both supplies and troops' wages was the master-marshal. In Normandy, the system of purchasing, distributing and keeping guard of supplies was similarly organised by ducal officers. One such officer existed at Caen and another at Le Vaudreuil: these were the Maréchal de Venoix and the Maréchal de Prés respectively. The equine connotations implied by the name Maréchal have a heritage going at least as far back as Charlemagne and indicate the importance of maintaining and provisioning a cavalry force. There were five main depots in Normandy for the storage of '*le foin de roi*' (the king's hay). As well as the two sites mentioned in connection with their officers above, there was Rouen itself, Avranches and Bonneville-sur-Toques. Further impositions were placed upon villagers near to the supply depots in order to ensure harvest and cartage. The same sort of carrying service was also expected in England. It would seem also from the English evidence (primarily a forged charter of King Henry I freeing the Canons of Holy Trinity in London of various services) that the 'vehicles' of the distribution were indeed carts, packhorses, and, of course, shipping. The advantage of the latter was that ships did not consume some of the goods en route.

During peacetime, or at least when the supply depots were being filled as part of routine administration, the county farms in England would bear the brunt of the supply burden and the accounting was done by the exchequer. At this level, the sheriff played a role. A Pipe Roll of 1130 gives an idea of the sort of produce transported: wine, grain, oil and bacon, wooden building materials and pepper all appear. Wine and grain were carried from Woodstock (an important depot in Henry I's reign) to Clarendon, although the pepper is thought to have been specifically for royal use, rather than used by the garrison. We learn of other produce from the Pipe Rolls of King Henry II (1154–1189). Although his reign is later than the period covered by this book, the preparations made for the king's invasion of Ireland in 1171 show the produce needed by an Anglo-Norman army when campaigning. Some £550 was spent on food, of which £320 was for bread alone. Bacon once again features heavily at £120, and beans, salt, cheese and wine also feature, as do oats for the horses. We know little about the cooks and bakers who accompanied the armies, except that they must have been there. Orderic Vitalis provides an example of when it could all go wrong if food was not prepared correctly. When the Angevins invaded Normandy in 1137, they slaughtered animals and 'ate the meat raw or half cooked without salt or bread…[and] there were not enough cooks and bakers to serve such a multitude… as a result of foolishly eating uncooked food… almost all suffered from dysentery and plagued by diarrhoea left behind them a trail of filth.'

Those supplies in England which were transported to various castles by cart or packhorse were brought along the existing road system, mainly Roman and Anglo-Saxon in origin. It was an offence to destroy or alter the king's roads and this was known in Old English as *stretbreche*. Infringement prompted a 100s fine. The *Leges Henrici Primi* (the legal treatise of King Henry I, compiled in 1115) states that royal highways should be a certain width, wide enough for two wagons to pass, for two herdsmen to touch with their goads (spiked driving sticks) outstretched and for sixteen milites to ride abreast.

The supply and maintenance of the horses of the Normans was a great logistical concern. There cannot have been a castle in England, Normandy, Italy or Sicily, where horse maintenance was not a priority. Fodder was a great concern. Orderic Vitalis tells us that in western climates there was a great need for oats for the horses 'without which', he says, 'it is almost impossible to keep up the strength of horses'. A horse requires around ten pounds of hay a day plus eight gallons of water. This is just basic maintenance. When actively campaigning, and indeed fighting, the requirement would virtually double, as well as needing a number of nutritional additions. This is not the end of it either. If the Flemish money fief of 1100 was expected to provide the king of England with three horses for each man it brought along, we might assume that an army of around 1,000 mounted men meant that around 3,000 mounts accompanied them on campaign. These would include the destrier, its replacement, and at least one packhorse. One can imagine the size of the fleet King Henry had to raise. This fact alone might explain why the size of Norman armies was somewhat limited, especially in Italy and Sicily where the numbers rarely seem to exceed 500 except on major campaigns. The reliance on cavalry in the south in particular would tend to support this theory and the difficulties of provisioning horses in Sicily during the early years of Roger de Hauteville's campaigns in the 1060s might explain the almost negligible size of the armies, said sometimes to be only around 100 or so in number.

Difficulties in supply were of course very common, not least on winter campaigns where fodder was in short supply. William II Rufus's campaign in 1098 around Le Mans, despite occurring in the summer months, ran into difficulties because of lack of supply due to it being the period between harvests. How supplies were dished out to the troops over a long campaign was another problem. William the Conqueror's colossal logistical efforts in the Hastings campaign show that there were daily rations. William of Poitiers tells us that while the duke was waiting at Saint Valèry for a good wind to come, in a risky move he increased his daily rations to disguise the shortage.

Supplies were so important to Norman warfare that they could form the focus of a campaign between protagonists. For example, in 1053 the revolt of Count William of Talou at Arques against the young Duke William of Normandy centred on the duke's hasty attempts to prevent supplies reaching Arques. It was the Duke's milites from Rouen who attempted to intercept the French King Henry I's efforts to supply Arques. Part of the relieving force was ambushed by William's men and Count Enguerrand of Ponthieu perished in the fight. The French king succeeded in fighting his way through the blockading force with mixed success, but some supplies did get through. However, eventually the garrison was starved into submission (page 42).

For William, the tables were turned on him in 1055 at Ambrières, deep into Maine, where he had built a castle in the lordship of one of Geoffrey Martel's vassals. Geoffrey came to attack the castle. While the assault was a failure for the Angevin count, he did succeed in preventing the duke of Normandy's army from foraging for supplies. William, due to lack of supplies, therefore had to withdraw. This concept of placing one's force in a position so as to prevent the enemy from harrying or foraging was a particular feature of the warfare of the period. For example, when Abbot Suger wrote about the French King Louis VI and his allies raiding with impunity around Gasny in the Vexin in around 1117, he specifically stated that this was 'an almost unprecedented occurrence when the English king [Henry I] was there'. Moreover, the English king's subsequent construction of two counter-castles was designed to cut the French supply lines and force them to fall back on their own territory for plunder. In the end the policy did not quite work for Henry, as the French king destroyed the forts in a typical example of measure versus counter-measure.

There were occasions when the besieged were equally aware of the supply problems of the besiegers themselves and openly looked to capitalise on it. In 1075 at the siege of Santa Severina the besieged nephew of Robert Guiscard sent his men out from the fortification to hunt, and he specifically ordered them to pillage the besiegers' supplies. 'Although he was running low on wine and grain,' says Amatus (VII.18), 'his men sated themselves with the meat which they stole, even though it was unsalted'.

We should not forget that the stipendiary troops were actually paid. Those '*ad victum regis*' (in the king's maintenance) would find markets to purchase their food and other items, thereby augmenting the army's food and drink even if it was consumed soon after it was bought. There are even examples of commanders deliberately arranging for markets and fairs to be held to help support their troops (page 195).

It is clear that no Norman army – wherever it was – could embark upon a campaign of any length without giving consideration to the concerns of supply. It is testimony to the success of the military leadership of this era that there are so few references to any real disasters above and beyond those which would be expected in times of famine or poor harvests. It is clear that the Norman commanders knew very well how to provision and supply their forces, and doing so successfully would engender the good morale needed to obtain victory in the field.

Chapter 18

Training

> They began to imbibe military skills, to practice the use of horses and weapons, learning how to guard themselves and strike down their enemies.
> *Geoffrey of Malaterra (I.4)*

Malaterra speaks of the sons of Tancred de Hauteville learning military skills as they grew up in Normandy. Tancred's boys were brought up in a tradition familiar to many young men in a world of warrior leaders. It was a life mirrored by their Anglo-Saxon and Scandinavian cousins, and the skills of warfare were taught from an early age. It is abundantly clear that Norman military commanders were masters of their work at both tactical and strategic levels. But for each Norman knight, his individual militarism was part of his upbringing; it was literally bred into him.

The training of a Norman knight would have fallen into roughly three categories. These were individual activities, group activities and the tournament. First, there was the training which Malaterra hints at: the martial abilities of a young man being honed over and over in weapons handling and riding. A young knight could begin his training at seven or eight years of age. The kind of training would depend upon whose household they were attached to. It could be a royal household, a baronial one, or that of a minor noble lord. The skills and games these boys were taught came under the tutelage of a *nutricius*, a chosen trainer who would perfect these skills. There is evidence that boys were taught physical hand-to-hand combat and how to throw spears. The biography of Abbot Hugh of Cluny (d.1109) tells of his father forcing him to learn the schooling of his horse, the wielding of his spear, the management of his shield, how to strike and not be struck back and how to take spoils and plunder, a cornerstone of the warfare of the age. But such training was not conducted in a safe environment by any means. Orderic Vitalis tells us that casualties were common. Two of the seven sons of the Giroie family were killed in their youth during such exercises. One boy, Arnold, was killed when he was hurled against a rock while practising wrestling, and another, Hugh, was killed by a wayward javelin during practice.

As well as the personal skills, there was the concept of training together in groups, for which much experience would have been gained on active service within a lord's *familia*. As far as the training on horseback was concerned, there is also the obvious question of how horses themselves could possibly have performed their tactical battlefield roles without some sort of training of the animal itself. But there was another group activity which the Normans loved: the hunt. Riding together the young knights learned to perfect their horsemanship in conditions similar to those on campaign. Communication with scouting parties and weapons handling (with bows for stags and spears and nets for the wild boar) would also have been honed in the hunt. The Anglo–Norman kings' sometimes dangerous passion for the New Forest bears testimony to the importance of the hunt.

The gap created by the absence of regular parade ground drills like those employed by the Byzantines was filled by these group activities and also by the phenomenon of the medieval tournament. The extent of the usefulness of the tournament as training for warfare has sometimes been questioned. It is argued that it was not embraced by the Anglo–Norman monarchy either, since they appear to have banned the tournament on several occasions. Against this should perhaps be set the evidence from Galbert of Bruges, who recounts how Charles the Good, the count of Flanders (1119–1127) kept his knights fit for war by tourneying in Normandy and France with 200 of them.

There are some examples of the commanders themselves offering training under what would appear to be last-minute conditions. King Henry I's impromptu training of his English infantry in 1101, teaching them to face cavalry attacks, is an example of a Norman king having the foresight to spot a training need in his infantry. Another example of what we might call a summary refresher training course is given by Orderic Vitalis when he recounts how, before the Battle of Ascalon (12 August 1099), the Christian leaders instructed their infantrymen 'how to shout war cries, how to stand firm, how to break through seemingly impenetrable enemy lines, and told them to fear nothing, frequently look bravely at their banners and steel themselves to withstand the blows of the enemy'. Again, when he was preparing for his great assault against Byzantium, Robert Guiscard found it necessary to personally oversee the training of his impressed infantrymen at Salerno on a daily basis until, Anna Comnena says (I. 13), he had hammered them into a disciplined force.

What is clear is that training varied depending on the troop type. The knightly classes would have had their personal and group training nurtured from an early age, their martial qualities bred into them. Their mounted skills were honed by a mixture of the tournament and group practices within the *familia* of their lord, baron or king, depending where they served. On another level, when we consider massed ranks of infantry, the training they received was more practical and immediate and it seems to have been a concern of the commanders of the day that such training was given immediately before these men saw action. Once in the field, there was no hope of performing the intricate tactical manoeuvres drilled men could execute. The commander of infantry would have to rely on his own leadership skills and the discipline he had instilled in his men.

Chapter 19

Leadership and Discipline

Discipline is a frequently repeated theme in the *De Re Militari* of Vegetius. It was important to regulate the army's relationship with the outside world as much as it was to keep internal discipline. Norman armies seem to have had a structure to instil discipline when the army was on the move, although it could still go wrong on occasion. The *Familia Regis* in the Anglo-Norman army and the ducal and baronial *familias* elsewhere approached this issue with codes of conduct of their own. Sometimes it required legislation. In Henry I's *Leges Henrici Primi* offences such as breach of the peace and murder committed within the king's *familia* or any army would place the perpetrator at the king's mercy and he would risk losing his property and even his limbs. Deserting the field of battle either on land or at sea was also punishable.

The importance of the personality of the leader himself cannot be underestimated. Skilled and strong leaders such as William the Conqueror and Robert Guiscard were able to strike a balance between the threat of punishment for anyone stepping out of line and the promise of great rewards for victory. Moreover, both of these leaders have rousing speeches placed in their mouths before battles and campaigns, as if the medieval commentators are trying – by comparison with the ancients – to show the extent of each leader's personal influence over their troops.

With each success these leaders grew stronger and found it easier to obtain the obedience of those under their command who were in search of lucrative reward. The last thing any leader wanted was dissident elements in the ranks, as Duke Robert II Curthose discovered to his cost at Vignats in 1102 (page 84). The main disciplinary problem when an army was on campaign was how to curb its natural propensity to turn the strategic art of ravaging into wholesale plunder and destruction where it was not militarily or politically required. Ravaging and harrying could have specific strategic and political goals. However, when an army was in its own leader's territory some degree of restraint was needed. William the Conqueror, waiting with an impatient invasion army in the harbour at Dives in 1066, managed to prevent widespread looting and loss of discipline with the promise of magnificent riches. He also kept the money coming. When he became king of England, he was quick to legislate against plundering. King William II

Rufus, on the other hand, had not fully addressed the issue within his own army. Henry of Huntingdon says that when Rufus's army was travelling through England it plundered as if it were an enemy. It was clearly a fine line. Even the strongest of leaders could not prevent excesses. William the Conqueror at Mantes in 1087 could not stop the burning and destruction meted out by his own forces in what was his last fateful campaign, although letting his men off the leash in this instance may have been deliberate.

Duke Robert Guiscard found a practical solution to keep the troops happy in his first Sicilian campaign in 1061. The Christians of the Val Demone came to him after his initial successes and paid him tribute in gold and provisions. Amatus says (V.25) that he then 'arranged for a fair and market where all sorts of things might be sold, and on account of this the knights took heart and had no great desire to return home.' He even repeated the arrangement when camped outside Naples in 1076–77. Here, the duke liaised with Sergius V, who ordered a market and fair to be set up where 'those things necessary for man and beast were sold' (Amatus, VII.15). He did it again outside Salerno during the siege of 1076 (Amatus, VII. 14). It is clear that both William the Conqueror and Robert Guiscard knew the importance of keeping their men happy. There is no reason to believe that the same sort of discipline was not instilled at baronial and comital level.

Chapter 20

Strategy

The Role of Castles and their Garrisons

> The prince [Richard of Capua] placed the castello of Argento under his [John of Maranola's] authority so that [from it] he might be able to overcome or withstand his enemies. *Amatus (VI.1)*

This comment from Amatus demonstrates at once the importance of the castle for both attack and defence. Without such a stronghold any lord would be vulnerable in the landscape. Orderic Vitalis, however, provides us with lengthy accounts of Anglo-Norman warfare based around the besieging or relief of castles. He sees castles as instruments of public order, as dens for brigands, as a tool of conquest in a wider landscape and as administrative centres and homes for the elite of society. Above all, he acknowledges them as fortifications in their own right.

The Norman castle is a fascinating subject to study for both archaeologists and historians. However, we are not concerned here with the role of the castle as the centre of a private estate, nor as the focus of a cultural revolution in the medieval period as a whole. Similarly, the morphology and design of castles, whether of timber or later of stone, is a separate study in its own right. The main types of castle in the northern Norman world were the ringwork type with its cultural antecedents in Anglo-Saxon England, and the more famous motte and bailey works, which comprised an earthen mound on top of which was placed a timber tower (and later in most cases, a stone donjon or keep), surrounded by an outer bailey with its ancillary buildings. In Italy, Sicily and the Levant the types were also varied and owed much to Lombard, Byzantine and other traditions. The point is that wherever we go throughout the Norman world, and whatever it looked like, the role of the castle in warfare and of its garrison was more or less the same. It was a fortified place dominating the local landscape, providing a base from which garrison forces could operate. It also provided an ostensibly defensive refuge for a select few people and acted as a supply depot for armies on the move.

Orderic Vitalis recalls what happened to Robert de Comines at Durham in 1069. Robert was caught inside the bishop's own lodgings, having not heeded warnings about the anger of the local people against the Normans. In a night surprise the house was torched and his men slaughtered. Had they been inside a castle, the outcome would surely have been different. Little wonder then that during periods of weakness in Norman ducal or royal authority the appearance of 'adulterine', or unlicensed, castles became widespread. The most notorious period for this phenomenon in England was during the anarchy of the reign of King Stephen (1135–1154), but it also happened when Duke William was in his minority up to his victory at Val-ès-Dunes in 1047, and again after his death in 1087 and once again during the ducal reign of Robert II Curthose up to 1106. The need for barons to operate from a castle, licensed or otherwise, was clearly overwhelming.

There are very few accounts of warfare in the Norman period in which a castle does not feature, either at the heart of events or somewhere in the background. Even the pitched battles of the period have a fortification somewhere in the picture, such as the pre-fabricated motte-and-bailey castle rapidly erected by William the Conqueror at Hastings in 1066, or the castle at Tinchebrai in 1106, the siege of which was the focal point of the battle. The reasons why castles featured so heavily in Norman warfare is that they could dominate their locality to such an extent that their occupiers could act with impunity until challenged by a force capable of neutralising their effect. A good hint as to the role of a castle is provided by the *Anglo-Saxon Chronicle* in its entry for 1074, where it is stated that King Philip of France offered the Anglo-Saxon exiled prince Edgar the Ætheling the castle at Montreuil 'so that afterwards he could daily do ill-turns to those not his friends'. Such was the potential power of the castle in its immediate landscape.

Although it would seem that the defensive role of the castle was key, this is not entirely true. The castle's garrison was able to operate offensively in the landscape. This is why it was said by Suger that the motte-and-bailey castle at Le Puiset could not be approached to within eight or ten miles when in hostile hands. This amounts to a distance equivalent to half a day's march. With a fortification exercising such an impact in its immediate district, it is easy to see why these castles were strategically placed along lines of communication and in border zones. This is as true of the Italian Norman examples as it is of those in the north. Robert Guiscard was given the castle at Scribla in Calabria because of the importance of its situation in the landscape. The fact that this desolate and isolated place was surrounded by malaria-infested marshland was secondary to its strategic importance. This area of Calabria at the time was nominally a Byzantine-controlled region. Moreover, it controlled the Roman Via Popila, the main routeway through that part of the country. Similarly, after the fall of Palermo in 1072 Roger I began a campaign of strategic castle-building across Sicily, of which the castle at Paternò in the Simeto Valley is a fine example of a fortified tower designed to counter Islamic movement in the area.

The idea of castle-building was to either neutralise the enemy's ability to operate from within his own castles (hence the siege or blockade), or to extend one's own power through the proliferation of friendly or directly-controlled castles. Therefore the denial of movement was paramount for each side. This is shown by Robert of Bellême's pleas to Helias of Maine for his assistance in support of Duke Robert II Curthose as recorded by Orderic Vitalis. Robert directly pleaded with Helias to join him, saying to him that he (Robert) still had thirty-four strongly fortified castles under his control from which he could harass his enemy. More evidence is provided by Amatus (II. 40) when he recalls how one William Barbote rebelled against the Lombard Prince Gaimar of Salerno. William Barbote had entered the castello of Belvedere 'and did as much damage as he could in the principality of Salerno'. Drogo de Hauteville was called to aid the prince and he 'placed his army and tents around the castello, and he kept William within its walls so that he could do no more damage'. The ability of William to operate from Belvedere was therefore nullified. Eventually, the castle was taken by a ruse whereby a peasant infiltrated the fortification and burnt it to the ground.

When an enemy was at large in the countryside, the garrison forces – swollen in numbers during times of war – would need to sally out to operate against the enemy. This might be in conjunction with forces from other castles or as a desperate attempt to relieve the pressure of a siege. Being prepared for enemy incursions was important for the commanders of the era. William the Conqueror knew only too well that he needed to get fresh supplies of arms and armour to his castles in the east of England in preparation for an expected Danish invasion in 1075. In 1079, before the siege of Gerberoi, William also flooded his border castles with troops specifically to prevent the enemy plundering the territory with impunity.

Although siege warfare was a common way of taking castles (pages 199-205), it was not always the first resort. Taking a castle by treachery or bribery was less resource-intensive. William II Rufus, for example, used such tactics to control Upper Normandy in the aftermath of his father's death in 1087 to take Aumale, Eu and Gournai. His brother King Henry I of England, in his Norman campaigns, placed royal garrisons in the castles whose castellans he had corrupted in the run-up to the Tinchebrai campaign. In 1068, when Robert Guiscard was faced with rebellion in Italy, he secured the castle at Montepeloso by the mere offer of a fief to one treacherous Geoffrey.

How castles fell other than being taken in sieges is a curious subject. Sometimes the mere threat of siege and starvation could be enough to induce capitulation. If an invading force was strong enough and had won its battles in the landscape against the defending field armies, there would not be much point in those castles' occupants resisting and therefore suffering a siege. It was more prudent under these circumstances to simply surrender. It is the nature of that surrender that seems to have been governed by convention, provided there was no real bad blood between the protagonists.

Orderic Vitalis once again provides insights, this time into the convention of castle surrender. A truce might be agreed between the attacking force and the castle force, but this would only be for a few days while the garrison was allowed to send to their lord for help. If he did not come at once, then the garrison's surrender was expected. Robert of Bellême's men found themselves in this position at the siege of Arundel Castle in 1102. When their lord could not come to their assistance they surrendered to the king. Henry I had allowed the Arundel garrison to appeal to Robert, who was in his castle a great distance away at Bridgnorth.

Some garrisons might wish to surrender honourably rather than suffer a siege. At the time of the death of William II Rufus in 1100, his household troops were besieged by Helias of Maine at Le Mans. On hearing of the English king's death, the men appealed for help to Duke Robert II Curthose and the new King Henry I of England. It was a tricky moment for the garrison as they did not really know from whom they held the castle. They received no help from either of the brothers, Robert or Henry, and so they surrendered to Helias. Consequently, this garrison of 200 knights was escorted from Le Mans by Helias, who protected them from the ire of the citizens who had suffered at their hands and took them all into his own service. This example shows the extent to which surrender was governed by the perception of feudal obligation. Orderic's tale of Bishop Odo's overbearing demands at the surrender of Rochester in 1088 shows how a strong personality might seek to push the boundaries somewhat, although the king fell for none of it (page 70).

All this convention and feudal custom notwithstanding, some castles and indeed cities were not spared in quite the same fashion. It all depended on who the defenders were. They could be rebels on their second chance (having once pledged never to rise against the lord who had accepted their surrender), or they could be infidels in Sicily or the east. Here the consequences of holding out against the attackers were different and were not governed by feudal concerns. As we shall see, siege warfare could be a very unpleasant business if it needed to produce a result.

So castles, a vital part of warfare in the Norman landscape, were often besieged, blockaded, surrendered or betrayed. On a larger scale, the same applies to cities, both in the north and south of the Norman world. It is the siege to which we now turn. The accounts of sieges range from the mundane to the downright harrowing.

The Nature of Sieges

The siege was a key feature of strategic warfare. Castles were not their only focus. Citadels within cities also provided a target. These were important fortifications from which Norman lords dominated the townsfolk. The number of sieges during this era – leaving aside for the moment the colossal sieges of Bari, Palermo, Salerno and Dyrrhachium – are almost uncountable, so common was the employment of the strategy.

Sieges were conducted in a variety of ways. One method was to blockade the enemy fortification with a counter-castle. This had the effect of preventing movement from the target stronghold and effectively neutralising its control of its own environs. With just a few men inside such constructions, the besieging commander was in theory able to release other forces to actively campaign in the enemy region. In 1079, William the Conqueror erected four such structures against his enemy Rémelard, and in 1088 William II Rufus erected similar castles at Rochester when he faced his rebellion. He also built the stronghold at Bamburgh which went by the name of 'Malveisin' or 'bad neighbour' (pages 74–75). Such constructions were often given nicknames by the Normans. In 1119 Henry I built such a structure near Eu, whose lord, Stephen of Aumale, had been persuaded to rebel against the king by his wife Hawise. The counter-castle was thus called 'whore humbler'. The approach was also common in the south, being adopted by Richard of Capua around his own city in 1062 and by Robert Guiscard outside Troia in 1060 and at Enna in Sicily in 1061 where he constructed four counter-castles from which his forces laid waste the fields and orchards. As if to press home the point about the frequency and usefulness of such counter-castles, the last stages of the conquest of Sicily saw no fewer than twenty-two counter-castles established around Taormina in 1079, supported by a naval blockade which forced the emir there to submit to the Normans.

The counter-castle could, of course, be attacked itself. One spectacular example of this comes in the build-up to the Battle of Bourgthéroulde in 1124. Here, the rebel Waleran de Meulan attacked the men of the English King Henry I in their structure outside the besieged castle at Vatteville and dragged the besieging commander from the rampart using an artificial hand with iron hooks.

If a decision was made to actually assault a stronghold there were a number of ways to do it. Mining or undermining was one way. William the Conqueror did just this at Exeter in 1068. Attacking a fortification with bombardment engines such as the earlier forms of stone-throwing trebuchets was perhaps a more common method. The Normans in the south realised the importance of these engines very early in the campaigns around Reggio and Troia in 1059–60. Moreover, Amatus says that trebuchets (his words are translated by a later medieval writer who may be using this term anachronistically) were the focus of both sides' attention at the siege of Trani in 1073. Here, after a quick capitulation Robert Guiscard went on to the town of Corato, ordering his men to go back to Trani and fetch the 'trebuchets and other engines'. However, when these men arrived at Trani, they were captured by the men of Robert's arch enemy Peter, along with the trebuchets. Only the intervention of Prince Guy of Salerno on behalf of the duke re-established possession of the war machines and captured Peter. So important were the engines that sieges could not often be successfully prosecuted without them. Simple siege ladders were not enough. In 1061 in Sicily, at Centuripe, slingers and archers from the enemy walls prevented a Norman assault. It was said that the walls were too high and the ditches too deep for an assault (Amatus, V.21).

One of the great exponents of siege warfare in the northern arena was Robert de Bellême. He used a variety of engines against fortifications including a siege tower against Courcy in 1091 and stone-throwing catapults against the town and inhabitants of Breval in the following year. The idea behind such towers, which sometimes had a *ballista* on top (a large tension-based, crossbow-like device), was to gain a height advantage over the enemy walls. Henry I built one such tower twenty-four feet higher than the walls of the rebel Waleran of Meulan's castle at Pont-Audemer in 1123 so that the archers within it could fire into the fortification.

Preparatory fire with burning arrows was another tactic adopted at sieges and had the effect of destroying many of the wooden structures so common in this era, especially shingle roofs. Duke Robert II Curthose employed the method (page 230) and Henry I also used this tactic extensively during Waleran's rebellion of 1123–24. Direct infantry assault might then be brought into play using scaling ladders.

Sieges were basically an infantry affair, with the cavalry being held in reserve around the fortification in order to counter the sallying forces who rode out to try to relieve the pressure. However, because of the missile firepower inherent within the castles and citadels of the period it was important not to get the besieging cavalry too close to the walls. At Chaumont in 1098 William II Rufus is said to have lost a seemingly unlikely 700 horses to enemy bowmen in just such a disaster. One clearly had to be careful in the vicinity of a fortification. Robert Guiscard's army pitched its tents too close to Ajello in 1065 and as a result suffered a damaging sortie from the inhabitants of the town, which cost the duke some of the good men of his *familia* (Malaterra II.37).

The length of sieges varied depending on the size of the fortification, the resilience of its inhabitants, the political outlook of its lord or castellan, and the amount of supplies it had in storage. Rufus's siege of Tonbridge was concluded on only the second day in 1088. Duke Robert Guiscard took Trani in 1073 'within a few days' due to the townsfolk being in the grip of famine and 'other afflictions', as reported by Amatus (VII.2). That same year Cannes fell to the duke 'very shortly' because 'there was no rain and it lacked cisterns', says Amatus (VII.6). These examples where provisions were low inside the besieged castle are given a clearer meaning when compared to the fate of Sujo in the early 1070s at the hands of the prince of Capua. He laid siege to the town, which had no provisions to begin with. Within two days, says Amatus, everyone was starving (VI. 28).

Fulk of Anjou was able to take La-Motte-Gautier-de-Clinchamp from King Henry I's supporters in just eight days in 1118. Henry I's siege of Pont-Audemer in 1123, mentioned above, saw a surrender after seven weeks and an honourable capitulation of the garrison. The sieges of Norwich in 1075 and Arundel in 1102, however, lasted three months, and are considered in the northern Norman world to be at the other extreme, with an average duration for sieges being about four to six weeks (such as the 1088 siege of Pevensey Castle). Perhaps because of the more complex urban make-up of southern Italy sieges there were a little longer. For example, the siege of Ajello mentioned above lasted around four months, as did those in 1086 at Syracuse and Agrigento. At Benevento it was five months. Santa Severina held for an impressive two years from 1075. However, a large-scale siege at Capua in 1098 lasted just forty days. Of course, the colossal sieges of Palermo (1071–72), Bari (1068–71) Salerno (1076–77) and Dyrrhachium (1081) were on an altogether greater scale and were examples of what happened when the stakes were very high indeed.

It was a gruesome experience to be on the wrong end of a siege. Guiscard's siege of Troia in 1060 was all about his desire to build himself a citadel inside the town. The townsfolk offered him gold and horses, but it was not enough to satisfy the duke of Apulia. Nobody was allowed in or out. The bread ran out. The fires stopped burning for lack of wood. The wine ran out, and then the water. Outside the walls, the townsfolk's own harvest was reaped by others. In the end they had no choice but to surrender. Robert entered the town and the citadel was built.

Richard of Capua's investment of his own city in 1062 was also based on his desire to take the fortifications and towers which remained outside his control after his earlier successful siege some years earlier. It is an example of the suffering which could be caused even when a town was besieged by its own prince. Bows and crossbows were used to begin with. Inside the town women carried stones to their men, says Amatus (IV.28). A twelve-year-old boy named Auxencie had been trained in bowmanship and slew many Normans, although he later perished. Richard brought his engines up and battered the walls and destroyed the towers. All the while the citizens were receiving foodstuffs via small boats coming up the river, but Richard countered this with boats of his own. A Capuan plea to their overlord the Holy Roman Emperor brought no good result. Eventually the gates were opened to Richard and the city's fortifications were his. Siege warfare, while a common feature of Norman warfare, was no easy undertaking. Time and effort was put into it and the results for the defenders could be devastating.

The great sieges of Bari (1068–71), Palermo (1072), Salerno (1076), Naples (1077) and Dyrrhachium (1081 and 1108) were conducted with a 'must-win' mentality. The first siege of Dyrrhachium (1081) is discussed above, pages 162–170. The others also deserve further inspection.

The siege of Bari required an immense naval and land based effort by Robert Guiscard. Raising the manpower had caused rebellion across Apulia. The siege began on 5 August 1068 and involved an encirclement on the naval side (borrowing from Byzantine practice) whereby each of Robert's ships was shackled to the other and at each extremity of the semi-circle thus created, the last ship was tied to a fortified jetty. On the landward side of the city, the walls were surrounded. But the blockade leaked. Inside, the Greek leader Byzantius managed to escape to Constantinople to raise the alarm. Early in 1069 Greek ships appeared to relieve the city, but the Normans managed to sink twelve of them in a naval battle. Even so the cordon could not hold. The ships broke through with supplies accompanied by Byzantius, a new catapan, and Stephen Pateranos, a Greek commander. The siege dragged on through 1069 and 1070 with the duke's towers being burnt down whenever they were brought up. These months were only punctuated by the assassination of Byzantius. At one point Stephen Pateranos sent an assassin to the wooden siege hut of Robert Guiscard beneath the walls of Bari. The would-be killer aimed his poisoned spear through the gaps in the wood, but the duke bent down to spit on the floor and the spear missed him. The Normans then rebuilt the hut in stone.

Again the cordon around Bari leaked. Pateranos got to Constantinople. Robert had sent for the fleet of his brother Roger in Sicily. Within the city a pro-Norman faction under a man named Argirizzo was handing out food to convince people to switch sides. In early 1071 the Sicilian fleet arrived. The citizens had been told to light fires on the ramparts if they caught sight of a relieving fleet, and they did so, but far too early. They gave Roger the signal to prepare for a naval battle. When it came, the relieving fleet was led by Joscelin, Lord of Molfetta, a thorn in Robert's side. Roger sailed into the enemy fleet, heading for the lead ship with twin lights on the masthead. It was a hard-fought battle with heavy losses for the Normans, but Joscelin was captured and brought to Robert. No ships got through to Bari, and nine were sunk. Within the city, so nearly relieved, the spirit was dying. Weeks later, Argirizzo seized a tower and the citizens capitulated. This last Byzantine

Palermo, Sicily, from Utveggio Castle. In the eleventh century the city's population was around 200,000. The city was besieged and taken by Robert Guiscard and his brother Roger.

stronghold finally fell on 16 April 1071. The citizens, probably to their surprise, were treated with some degree of dignity, so important would the city be for the duke's future plans.

Palermo was the next great project. The duke had sent Roger back to Sicily and went to Otranto to prepare. In late July 1071 fifty-eight ships left Otranto for Reggio, with the duke going overland to meet them. After the crossing to Sicily the brothers Robert and Roger decided first to detour to Catania. From Catania Roger proceeded to Palermo by land and Robert by sea. In mid-August 1071 Roger arrived on the eastern edge of Palermo to await his brother. The subsequent siege of Palermo differed from that of Bari in that the Normans did not throw a ring around the city. That tactic had been found wanting at Bari, and Palermo was simply too vast.

Roger camped near the Oreto on the east side of the city. The first target would be the Muslim fort of Yahya, which protected the mouth of the Oreto. This would give the Normans a base for operations if it could be taken. Its garrison sallied out to meet Roger's men and was defeated in a quick battle costing them fifteen lives and thirty prisoners. Soon Guiscard's navy arrived at the mouth of the Oreto and the siege began with an immediate attack and a repulse. Then, in the autumn, a Muslim fleet arrived. Its vessels were armoured with special felt-hided tents to protect from Norman missiles, but in the event they lost a naval battle to Robert's ships. The remnants of the defeated fleet rowed back to Palermo harbour, where the citizens raised the harbour boom behind them as they entered. The pursuing Norman vessels, however, simply smashed through the raised chains and carried their fight to the shore. The result was another defeat for the Muslim fleet and a closer investment of the city.

By December 1071 Palermo was starving. News from Apulia reached Duke Robert that another uprising was occurring. He knew he could not afford the time to starve out Palermo and he had to attack quickly. The walled fortress in the Al-Qasr district was the target. On 5 January 1072 Roger's men attacked, but resistance was strong. A Muslim garrison sallied out and drove Roger's men backwards, only to be counter-charged by Robert's cavalry and forced against the now-closed gates of the fortifications. But still the Normans were not inside. Siege ladders were brought to the walls, but the few who managed to ascend them had their shields smashed from their hands. Robert then saw an opportunity to try the defences elsewhere. He sent 300 picked men to the Al-Khalesa district of the city where the walls were less well defended. Here his men succeeded in scaling the walls. They opened the gates for Robert and his men flooded through. Street fighting continued for some time and Al-Qasr held, but not for long. A negotiated surrender followed, and on 10 January 1072 Robert formally paraded through the streets of the great capital of Sicily.

In the summer of 1076 Robert Guiscard and Richard, prince of Capua, combined to besiege the Lombard Prince Gisulf at Salerno, who had long made himself a target for Norman aggression. Like both previous sieges it was to be a combined land and sea affair. Gisulf's cruel reaction to the tightening of the siege shows how the Normans might rely upon the character of a leader to hasten his own city's demise. Gisulf ordered two years' worth of stock to be stored by his citizens and then seized a third of it for himself. He could not resist extracting more from his own people and the result was a quickening of a famine, with bodies lying unheeded in the street. As the citizens ate their own dogs and cats, Gisulf sold them their own grain at extortionate prices. The city ultimately fell to treachery after six months, but might have held longer if its prince had not lacked sensibility when faced with a siege situation. Towards the end of the siege Prince Gisulf even tried to trick Guiscard, who had demanded the tooth of St Matthew (a well-loved local relic), but was instead fobbed off with a tooth from a deceased Jew.

Robert and Richard turned to Naples the following year, but this was not as successful. What occurred was an example of the success of aggressive counter-attacking against Richard's siege installations. Sorties were made out of Naples to attack the opposing forces on land and sea. Ships' crews were captured while they were sleeping. Richard's counter-castles were stormed, sacked or burnt and he was given no time or space to rebuild them properly. In the event, the siege of Naples petered out. But these counter-measures are once again in evidence again at Dyrrhachium in 1108.

Bohemond's investment of Dyrrhachium in 1108 provides examples of the different types of siege engine. There was first a hide-covered, tortoise-like battering ram. The ram was suspended from a beam inside. It was propelled by men armed with poles. The ram was set in motion like a pendulum to repeatedly batter the walls of the town, while the wheels were taken off to provide the framework with stability. But it did not work, much to the delight of the townsfolk. Then the Normans tried to undermine the city walls to the north of the town. They dug a tunnel and had their workmen protected by sheds covered in hides. But the citizens had built a counter-tunnel and when they came across the Normans they poured 'Greek fire' into it and repelled them. The last measure the Normans adopted was in fact their main plan, another heliopolis type of tower, which had begun construction the previous year. This mighty contraption, like its cousin of 1081, was brought up to the walls. It was countered by a hastily constructed higher tower within the walls of the city, upon which men tried to rain down a fire of missiles and naphtha, but the distance was too great for the defenders. The defenders then set fire to the ground between them and the attacking tower and this resulted in the tower being burnt to the ground. Of all of the great sieges of the period, this last perhaps gives the best example of measure versus counter-measure. Sieges could certainly bring a great deal of human suffering to the strategic scene. But there was another long-established strategic method of warfare which brought misery to thousands.

Ravaging and Harrying

The burning and devastation of land was often accompanied by the looting of food, supplies and the destruction of a productive landscape. It was a policy promoted by Vegetius and numerous others before and after him. The method deserves some qualification, however, for in the Norman era, as in many others, there were differing reasons for leaders to employ this strategy and it was executed to varying extents in the landscape. The term later applied to widespread devastation designed to weaken an enemy's economic strength and political will was *chevauchée*. This was a particularly popular strategy used by the English (among others) in the Hundred Years War. The root of the word indicates that the strategy was implemented by mounted men.

It was to be expected that a Norman – or any – army would supply itself from the land as it went along. For the Normans in England this sort of foraging was supplemented by the supplies they had arranged in advance and brought with them on the hoof. To the average villager across the Norman world though, it did not particularly matter whether the passing army was friend or foe; the result was the same – livestock and other produce growing in the area would be seized. The soldiers' visitations brought differing degrees of pain according to the strategic and political goals of the army's commander. If a passing army was simply supplying itself as it progressed, there would still be pain for the local population. However, if political and economic destruction was the goal the pain could be unbearable.

The methodology adopted in the ravaging of an area was not sophisticated, but it was effective. Crops were often targeted. They were either uprooted and carted away or burnt where they grew. Corn, wheat and vineyards all succumbed to flames. Whole villages, constructed largely of wood, could be destroyed by fire. Livestock was either driven off, stolen or destroyed. So common was this last feature of the strategy that in the border areas of the Norman patrimonies, such as the Scottish and Welsh Marches, it was virtually the sole form of warfare for generations, being practised repeatedly on both sides of the border. Livestock was obviously important to an army on the move and preventing the capture of animals was a rare achievement. In around 1049 Robert Guiscard cleverly captured Peter, son of Tyre, outside Bisignano and extorted great riches from him (page 27). He made an agreement with him that 'Peter's animals in times of war as well as in times of peace might move about unharmed.'(Amatus III.10).

For the most part, the invading army would concentrate on neutralising the economic life of the enemy. Wace reports that in 1101 Helias of Maine, when invading Normandy, drove the peasants from the fields and the merchants from the roads (III, 11). And yet it was the human cost of this strategy that was the greatest. The misery of death, enslavement or homelessness was certainly not lost on the northern English settlements during the particularly cruel 'Harrying of the North' during William the Conqueror's punitive campaigns of 1069–1070. Nor was the pain any less deeply felt across Calabria in 1058, when the local people endured a disastrous famine which they rightly blamed on the widespread burning and destruction recently carried out by Norman armies. In fact, these southern Italian populations were especially vulnerable. They relied upon vines and olive and mulberry trees, which once destroyed would take many years to regrow.

The destruction meted out by these armies was rarely mindless thuggery. It had at its heart a military or political goal and there were several good reasons to adopt the method. Robert de Bellême even used widespread plunder for purely selfish reasons in 1102 when he prepared his forces for a rebellion against the English King Henry I, by raiding around Staffordshire and removing livestock into Wales. Swelling one's own coffers was always an attractive proposition if it could be achieved with ease. But the politics were never far from the surface. Sometimes it seems that an area was destroyed as a form of revenge. In 1058 Richard of Capua burned around Aquino, a dependency of Gaeta, after a bid to marry his daughter into the house of Gaeta failed. But although this act was in essence an act of vengeance committed by a warlord who felt wronged, it would have been for its intimidatory effects that it was carried out. In fact, the psychological effects of harrying were profound. The method could be used to goad an enemy commander into precipitate action. This is usually the motivation attributed to William the Conqueror's burning around Hastings after he landed in England in 1066. Knowing that the area was the land of his enemy Harold Godwinson, he is thought to have adopted the policy of devastation, not only to supplement his army's supplies, but also to bring about a level of human suffering that would entice Harold into an early engagement. It was a clever strategy and one which suggests that William knew the personalities of the members of the House of Godwin surprisingly well.

When an army entered a hostile area on campaign, the strategy of burning and looting could force an entire region to capitulate. This would effectively end a campaign without any loss to the invading army; an efficient way to proceed for any commander. This was the case in 1073 when William the Conqueror invaded the county of Maine with a combined force of French and Englishmen. The force was reported in the *Anglo-Saxon Chronicle* as having pulled down vineyards and burnt cities, making 'all the county surrender to the king' before it returned home. This was a repeat performance of the destruction William had meted out to the same people in 1063, when strongholds were captured and garrisoned by men who perpetuated the misery on the land.

The fall of strongholds due to an army's destructive presence in the landscape was perhaps the best result a commander could expect. William's circuitous route around London in 1066 brought that city to surrender. Such was the power of the strategy that it was often used early on in a campaign as a statement of intent to force cities and key strongholds to capitulate. Again, the 1066 campaign provides an example, whereby the destruction of Romney seems to have precipitated the fall of Dover and Canterbury. Similarly, Henry I's destruction of Bayeux in 1105 was the catalyst for the fall of other Norman towns in the early years of his struggle against his brother Duke Robert II Curthose.

The defenders of a fortification, however, might not fall for the ploy of a simple threat. Such defiance usually resulted in the implementation of the harrying strategy in the immediate district. The result was a denial of the supply base around a fortification and a further denial of any human resources which might support it. An attacking army would therefore weaken the defenders to such an extent that if the attacking army moved away to prosecute another strategic goal, it could rely on the weakened stronghold remaining relatively subdued.

A good example of defiance in the face of the strategy comes from Reggio in 1057–58. The vital port, yet to fall to the brothers Robert Guiscard and Roger de Hauteville, prepared itself for the expected siege by bringing in great quantities of supplies from the surrounding countryside, which allowed it to hold out for so long that Roger had to ravage around Gerace to supply his own brother's besieging forces. Ultimately Robert Guiscard raised the siege, although the town would later fall in a separate campaign.

An example of the fear of such a strategy comes from Melfi in the early 1060s. Robert Guiscard's stronghold had been taken over by his Norman rival Peter, son of Amicus, while Robert was away on campaign. He returned to besiege it and set about attacking the walls, but Amatus says that the 'people of Melfi asked Peter to defend their grain which was still in the fields after the harvest' (IV.5). Clearly, the expectation of the townsfolk was that the devastation of their crops was otherwise inevitable. However, because Melfi was such an important centre to both Robert and Peter, an uncomfortable truce was agreed.

It was one thing to adopt a strategy of destruction around a fortification, but quite another to devastate an entire region. However, the motives were similar for the adoption of the method on the grand scale. The 'Harrying of the North' of England in 1069–70 was technically conducted within the Conqueror's own kingdom, but was designed to deny the troublesome region between Durham and York (which long held a politically and culturally Scandinavian outlook) to the king's Danish enemy as a base of power. The human landscape was destroyed in this massive operation, but also significantly curtailed was the capacity of that same region to support a Danish, rebellious Anglo-Saxon or Scottish leader who might choose to recruit in these once fertile grounds. Clearly powerful and effective, the strategy of harrying and destruction was enthusiastically adopted by the Normans, although they were by no means the only ones to do it. However, as with many other aspects of Norman military prowess, history suggests that they were particularly successful.

Using the Landscape

How an army moves about in the landscape is of vital importance. The nature of the terrain can affect a force's cohesion and rates of movement at a strategic level. Cleverly disposed forces can block an enemy advance (or retreat) with the judicious use of just a few troops, as was the case in 1124 at the Battle of Bourgthéroulde (pages 142-144). The denial of enemy movement in the landscape was paramount. An army which stops moving is forced to consume its supplies and is effectively neutralised. We have seen how the young Duke William of Normandy was an expert in shadowing of enemy forces to achieve this (page 43). When the French King Henry I invaded Normandy in 1054 the duke placed his forces so that there was no close engagement nor devastation of his land. The duke deliberately picked off the king's foragers when he could.

A superior knowledge of terrain at a strategic level could have a significant advantage, as it did for Helias of Maine in 1098 when he was faced with invasion by William II Rufus. Here, Helias blocked river crossings, barriers and difficult paths through the woods. Conversely, a lack of knowledge could have a hampering effect. William the Conqueror was held up for several weeks at Pontefract until his scouts could find a deep and difficult ford some miles away. Such examples show how inextricably linked the landscape was to the fortunes of the forces which marched across it.

The terrain of an entire theatre of war may have an effect on the ability of an army to operate effectively within it. In 1095 and again in 1097 William II Rufus had only limited success in Wales because of the difficulty of the terrain. Rough ground could also mean that the supplies normally expected from fertile countryside were harder to procure. Not only could cartage not reach the invading army because of lack of roads, natural foraging by the army would also yield less produce than was usual in more open terrain.

At a tactical level, the ground over which forces have to fight a pitched battle can also produce difficulties, as the steep slopes and constriction of the field did for both sides at Hastings. Here, William of Poitiers tells us of the difficulty encountered by the Normans in surrounding the English force, who were advantaged by their higher position. Later in the same battle, the presence of a huge ditch proved the undoing of many Norman knights as their lack of knowledge of it led them to charge on to disaster when pursuing the fleeing English (page 132).

The Hastings campaign tells us much about the effect of landscape. The Bayeux Tapestry shows us a mail-clad Englishman giving prior warning of the Norman host to Harold. This man is usually taken to be a scout, although he is surprisingly heavily armoured for the job. William of Poitiers writes of William the Conqueror's response to finding himself in the vicinity of Hastings, a landscape of cliffs and rocky pathways. He says that it was the ancient Roman custom 'like the generals of today, to send out scouts, rather than to go themselves, more anxious about their own safety than wishing to leave such duties to their army'. William, however, took twenty-five men and explored the locality himself, laughing off the fact that he had to come back on foot. He further distinguished himself by carrying the hauberk of William FitzOsbern as well as his own. Poitiers' remarks about William perhaps provide the exception which proves the rule. This was not the usual method of scouting employed by the commanders of the day. Poitiers is trying to show how brave the duke was. Usually a selection of cavalrymen would be sent out to reconnoitre the landscape. That said, Geoffrey of Malaterra says of Robert Guiscard that on his early campaigns around Reggio he spent three whole days on reconnaissance alone, ultimately withdrawing from the city as a result of his findings (II.18), but it is not clear if this reconnaissance was carried out by Guiscard himself or by mounted men in his army. One policy adopted by Robert Guiscard and his brother Roger on campaign in the interior of Sicily was to use the knowledge of their Sicilian ally, the emir Ibn-at-Timnah, and his men, whom Amatus specifically states provided the eyes and ears for the Norman forces (V.22).

The purpose of scouts was to protect an army from surprise attack and to give prior warning of the size, strength and movements of the enemy. Also, any information the scouts could relay about the lie of the land and any perceived difficulties for the troops would be of use to the commander. Rivers, marshes, roads, bridges, fords, rough ground and flat plains were all observed by the scouts, as each could have an effect on the movement of cavalry, infantry and supply carts. The numbers of troops given over to the job of scouting seems to have varied according to the familiarity of the countryside the army found itself in and the individual approach of the commander himself. For example, in 1119 Henry I placed four knights on high ground above Verclives overlooking the well-known routeway from Paris because he knew the land very well and wanted early warning of the arrival and movements of any enemy. However, in 1068 when William the Conqueror travelled to Exeter to put down a revolt he took with him, according to Orderic Vitalis, 'five hundred equites [mounted knights] to scout out the field and fortifications, and to find out what the enemy were doing'. This was a remarkable reconnaissance-in-force. It was an army in its own right. It serves also as an example of William the Conqueror's particular thirst for information prior to military action. This characteristic is seen as early as 1053 in the Conqueror's career. At Domfront, when he was besieging Geoffrey Martel, William rode out by day and night, according to William of Poitiers 'or lay hidden under cover, to see whether attacks could be launched against those who were attempting to bring in supplies, or carrying messages, or trying to ambush his foragers'.

It is safe to assume that scouts were a regular feature of the Norman armies, both on the move, or when at a standstill. How, though, did the armies organise themselves to move through the landscape? There has been a tendency to assume that Norman armies lacked a formal 'order of march' as such. It is a problem of terminology. Given that these forces were sometimes comprised of combined arms it is difficult to see how they could have moved about in one amorphous lump. Roman armies had their own orders of march in which the infantry marched both ahead and behind the baggage train, with the cavalry making up the van and the rear, and mounted scouting units flung out to the front and sides. This is a 'Vegetian' formation. During the crusades the crusading armies developed an order of march which again concentrated on the protection of the baggage in a hostile terrain. A hollow square of crossbowmen enveloped the cavalry, who themselves marched around the baggage train. But for the Norman armies we have little evidence. William of Poitiers gives us a probable order of march on the eve of Hastings. The following description is often taken to indicate the Norman duke's preferred deployment on the battlefield itself, but if read within the context of the wider passage the paragraph is placed at the point when William decides to advance from his camp at Hastings, several miles from the battlefield. This does not mean that the deployment on the field was any different, however, but what Poitiers is describing is an order of march. Poitiers says of William's march from his camp at Hastings that he advanced 'in the following highly advantageous order':

> In the vanguard he placed infantry armed with bows and crossbows; behind them were also infantry, but more steady and armed with hauberks; in the rear, the cavalry squadrons, in the midst of which he took his place with the elite. From this position he could command the whole army by voice and gesture.

Our lack of hard evidence for such formations elsewhere in the Norman world should not prevent us from drawing conclusions here. In organising his army as it marched out from Hastings, William was responding to the hostility of the landscape and the need for him to be able to communicate with each part of his

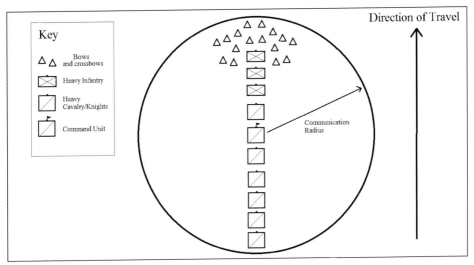

Duke William's 'order of march' before Hastings   *Fig. 16*

force. It was not a 'Vegetian' formation as such, nor was it a crusading formation. It was, however, a practical formation employed by one of medieval history's most consummate commanders, and there is every likelihood that other Norman commanders also knew exactly what they were doing when it came to organising their marching forces.

William's force, as described by William of Poitiers, would have moved out of Hastings at the rate of its slowest element, the heavy infantry. This was for the purposes of cohesion. For William, who was expecting at any minute to encounter a huge infantry force, the slowness of that advance was not so much of a problem. But for one other commander having to move at the rate of the slowest parts of the army was a notable frustration. After the Normans had taken Messina in 1061 Robert Guiscard arrived and counted his troops. He found that he had around 1,000 mounted knights and around 1,000 infantry. Amatus describes Robert as 'trusting more in God than multitudes', so he 'rode hard with the few men he had, though they continually had to wait for the infantry'. This may be evidence that large bodies of infantry were something of a hindrance to the dashing Guiscard.

The speed at which armies travelled is difficult to determine due to insufficient itineraries. There is, however, a useful example in Orderic Vitalis's description of the campaign of William II Rufus in Maine in June 1098. The king started at Alençon, spent the first night at Rouessé-Fontaine, the second at Montbizot and the third at Coulaines on the Sarthe near Le Mans. The indication here – bearing in mind that this is an invading army operating in hostile territory – is that the army was moving at a rate of ten, fifteen and ten miles over these three days. William's force was a combined arms force and this rate of movement must indicate the lower end of the scale. Entirely mounted forces were easily capable of greater distances.

The evidence from the south is also revealing. It would seem that commanders were keenly aware of strategic weaknesses in the landscape. In 1073, during the wars between Duke Robert Guiscard and Prince Richard of Capua, the influential 'sons of Borrelus' came over to the duke's cause. The duke made them commanders in his army when he came to them at Venafro. Amatus says 'they marked out their route and the castelli which were not well garrisoned or very strong. These they seized and immediately burned. From there they went to Capua'. This was a distance of some forty-one miles, dotted with fortifications which it seems were very carefully targeted for destruction.

It can thus be seen that the landscape played a dominant role in shaping the commander's responses to the challenges of campaigns and battles. Scouting, orders of march, strategic awareness and tactical deployment were all affected by the landscape. The Norman response was no better or worse than that of the much-vaunted ancient armies. It might even be argued, particularly in the case of William the Conqueror, that the evidence points to a notable versatility.

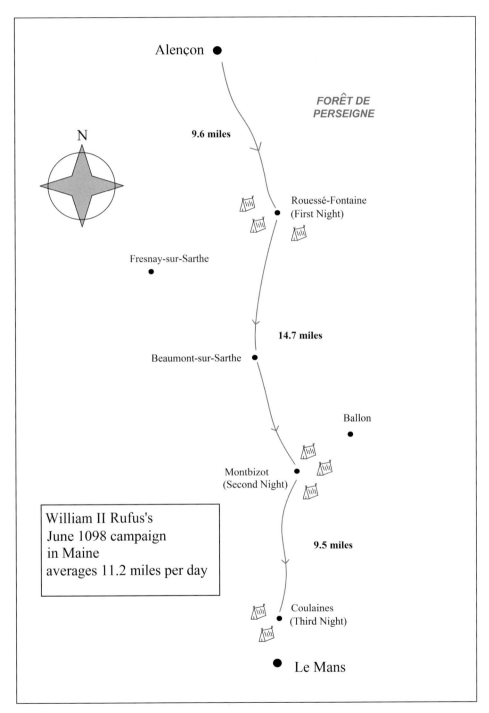

Alençon

FORÊT DE PERSEIGNE

N

9.6 miles

Rouessé-Fontaine
(First Night)

Fresnay-sur-Sarthe

14.7 miles

Beaumont-sur-Sarthe

Ballon

Montbizot
(Second Night)

William II Rufus's
June 1098 campaign
in Maine
averages 11.2 miles per day

9.5 miles

Coulaines
(Third Night)

Le Mans

Map 16: Map of William II Rufus's march to Le Mans, June 1098

Stratagems and Ruses

The use of stratagems to defeat an enemy is common to all periods and cultures. In southern Italy during the early years of the Norman involvement in Apulia, the deep pockets of the Byzantines and the venality of the Lombard princes bear testimony to the power of bribery as just one stratagem in warfare, with leaders changing sides at the sound of the rattling of a purse. When men and resources were scarce, the Norman commanders would often resort to stratagems to achieve their goals. There was no one better at it than the man whose name had the concept of cunning embedded in it. Amatus even said of Guiscard '…the astute and prudent duke would often conquer by stratagem what he could not overcome by force of arms'.

One of the more overt examples of bribery occurred when Robert Guiscard was faced in 1068 with a revolt by Norman lords Geoffrey, Joscelin and Abelard, the son of the former Duke Humphrey whom Robert had succeeded in Apulia. Geoffrey fled to the castrum of Montepeloso where Robert came and 'corrupted by his blandishments the fortress's custodian Godfrey', says William of Apulia:

> …giving him bribes and promising him more, including a fortress more powerful than the one he had. (The lordship of Montepeloso did not belong to Godfrey alone, he had conceded half of it to Geoffrey). But the duke had promised him full lordship over a more noble fortress, Uggiano. Desiring to rule alone over this, he advised Robert to raise the siege and feign a retreat; but as soon as he knew Geoffrey to be absent to return and he would enter the fortress in safety with the keys which he had been given. Then he would confer Uggiano upon him. Thus Godfrey handed over this fortress to him by a trick, and so he received Uggiano, but who would trust him thereafter? All the people of Italy called him traitor.

Bribery was not the only stratagem in the Norman arsenal. As we have already seen (page 31), Robert Guiscard employed a 'Trojan horse' type of trick, in which a supposedly dead 'body' was used to conceal weapons and gain entry to a monastery. In 1119 comes an example of another ruse, which also brings to light the intriguing evidence that battle cries were obviously well known to all protagonists and men of the countryside alike. The town of Andelys was captured by French troops who were fighting against the Anglo–Norman King Henry I. They had crept into the town overnight and hidden in a grain store until the following morning, when King Louis's army was seen outside the gates. The townsfolk ran for the castle, and the French soldiers emerged and ran with them, crying the battle cry of the English. Once inside, the Frenchmen changed their battle cry to '*Montjoie*' and captured the place. Moreover, after the Battle of Brémule had been lost by the French, Peter of Maule and some other fugitives threw away their cognizances (shields and other devices with distinctive insignia) to avoid recognition and mingled with the pursuers shouting the English war cry and praising King Henry.

Stratagems were often employed to take a fortification. In Maine in 1063 William the Conqueror is said to have used two children to slip into the castle at Mayenne and set fire to it from the inside, according to William of Poitiers (I. 39-40). However, perhaps the last word on the employment of stratagems under siege conditions should go once again to Guiscard and his remarkable approach to the siege of Cisternino in 1073. Town after town had fallen to Robert after he had crushed yet another revolt in Italy. One of the key leaders of the revolt, Peter of Trani (Robert's familiar foe) was captured and imprisoned. The little town of Cisternino, however, held out. Cisternino belonged to Robert's prisoner Peter. Robert had a giant wattle screen erected and the unfortunate Peter was lashed to it. The screen, with Peter on it, was used as a giant shield by the Normans as they advanced against the town. The citizens knew they could not fire upon their own lord and thus had no means of defence against the Normans. The rather compromised Peter cried out to his subjects to surrender. They had no choice but to do so.

Chapter 21

Tactics on the Battlefield

Command and Control

We have already observed the leadership characteristics possessed by the Norman commanders when dealing with discipline on campaign, but when it comes down to how such things can affect battlefield performance there are a number of good examples. The Anglo-Norman victories at Brémule (1119) and Bourgthéroulde (1124) demonstrate the capabilities of the *Familia Regis* in this respect and the French failings in command and control at a tactical level are also brought out in the accounts of Brémule (pages 138–142).

With strong leadership at a tactical level, a Norman army could be very effective on the battlefield. Its subdivisions into smaller units, each with a certain degree of reliability as a result of high-quality command and control, could lead to better mobility and flexibility than that possessed by the enemy. In fact, Orderic Vitalis, when mentioning an Angevin army which appeared not to have its leadership subdivided into distinct units, bemoaned these '*indisciplinati*' as being ignorant of the strictness of discipline of Roman warfare (VI:472). He hints here at a knowledge of Vegetius. However, the armies of the day were still brittle in morale outside the core of the milites and mercenaries and even here morale was dependent upon the fluctuating fortunes of battle.

The need for strong leadership on the battlefield was vital. Despite the presence in the ranks of the Norman armies of warriors who lived and breathed warfare as part of their social function, and despite the presence of men whose familiarity with war was based on hard experience, there still existed a 'crowd' trying to get out. The propensity of an army of this era to fall to pieces very quickly was well-known to the Norman leaders. The Normans, however, knew this of their enemies perhaps more than their enemies did of them. There is good evidence that they preyed upon it. Richard of Aversa's well-timed initial mounted charge at the motley collection of Italian infantry at the Battle of Civitate resulted in the panicked dispersal of thousands of men brought about by a smaller and more mobile opponent. It is a theme repeated across the south, where Norman numbers were always small compared to their enemies. At Civitate, this disciplined charge led to the clearing of the way for Richard to wheel around and hit the Pope's Swabian swordsmen in the rear. Here was an example of poor command and control on the part of the enemies of the Normans. This infantry force had only recently been cobbled together and would have lacked even rudimentary training.

The generally small size of Norman armies made command and control easier. Orders were transmitted orally or by the sound of horns or the signals given by standard bearers. This made the giving and receiving of instruction much easier to perform. It is difficult to see how at Tinchebrai the flank attack of Helias of Maine could have been achieved without clear signalling. Nor indeed can the frequent changes in the Norman approach to the Anglo-Saxon shieldwall be explained by anything other than an effective command, control and communication system.

Keeping control of things on the battlefield was the key to success. If a commander could keep control he could concentrate on breaking the enemy's will to fight. This is why tactics such as targeting the enemy commander were adopted. Catching the enemy unaware, outmanoeuvring him, charging at an opportune moment to create disorder and panic were all ways to reduce the enemy's cohesion and turn what had been an army into the crowd it evolved from. By the same token, it was equally important not to let it happen to your own side; hence the famous moment in the Battle of Hastings when Duke William was forced to quell a rumour in the ranks of his own army that he had been killed. He did this by lifting his helmet to reveal his face. Even the rumour of the loss of a leader could reduce the cohesion of an army. When it happened for real, as the English found out in the same battle, there was no hope of coming back.

Actual battlefield command structure is less easy to determine. Wace, the author of the *Roman de Rou*, writing in the later twelfth century, supplies some interesting nomenclature. A lord supplying troops to the feudal host might bring his quota along, consisting of a mixture of feudally obliged troops and mercenaries he had hired to make up his quota. They would gather around him under his banner, forming what Wace called a *compagnie* or *maisniée*. Beneath this were the much debated *conroi* and *conestablie*, the squadrons of mounted knights whose organisation may have been in groups of ten, although this is difficult to prove. The heirarchy of command appears to have been that a *chevetaine* or captain commanded the larger unit and a constable the smaller. Wace is useful here in that he does not colour his vocabulary with misleading archaic Romanisms, and perhaps reveals more to us than we think. But how did these units actually ply their trade on the battlefield itself? What were the combat tactics of Norman armies?

Mounted Tactics: Shock Cavalry, Stirrups, Couched Lances and the Feigned Retreat

> On horseback he Nicephorus, [Anna Comnena's brother-in-law] gave the impression that he was not a Roman at all, but a native of Normandy...
>   A mounted Kelt is irresistible; he would bore his way through the walls of Babylon. *Anna Comnena, Alexiad*

The Norman, or in a wider sense 'Frankish' mounted warrior of the eleventh and twelfth centuries certainly had a profound impact on those he encountered. There are, however, a number of controversial theories regarding Norman mounted tactics on the field of battle which have ranged from attributing seemingly supernatural abilities to the mounted *conroi* to the complete denial that they were any different from anyone else.

That the Norman knight could perform 'shock' tactics deserves some sort of qualification. Exactly what 'shock' means is a moot point. Alexius Comnenus clearly feared Bohemond's cavalry and sought to nullify the effects of their charges. Moreover, the *Taktika* of Leo VI (written between 895 and 908) specifically warned against taking on the Franks in pitched battle, so formidable was their cavalry charge with 'broadsword, lance and shield', at least until one's own side had the odds stacked in one's favour. At that time the Franks charged in unwieldy masses with seemingly little organisation and yet were very effective. Vegetius never saw cavalry in this way, preferring to see them in an auxiliary role, and it is probably here that the Norman knight steps out of the Vegetian warfare theorem into his own world.

Before we look at the evidence for the 'shock' impact of the Norman knight, it is worth looking at what is required from the horse itself. Only recently have historians considered this part of the argument and the conclusions are that the Norman horse must have been a very well-trained animal. In a combat environment the horse must be trained not to be afraid when galloping at an enemy line, and most importantly the animal has to be able to alter its stride and change its leading leg. This usually takes place during suspension (in mid-air) when at speed. All four feet are off the ground at this point. The rider signals to the horse with subtle indications from his spurs behind the girth on the opposite side of the intended directional change. The horse will then plant his rear legs on the ground in the reverse order from the one he is currently using, thus allowing him to lead off with the other leg and change direction. If it goes wrong and the front legs hit the ground first instead, the result is a disunited and very uncomfortable change. The animal's training for this might have been similar to modern dressage training and could have involved complex figure-eight movements, with the animal learning to respond to the rider's signals. Experts have calculated that the lateral flexion work alone (designed to enable the horse to feel 'soft' in moving from side to side) could have been up to two months before the animal was ready even for lead-change training.

The riders, as we have seen, were also trained from an early age. A glimpse of the sort of cavalry training they might have received is perhaps evident in the thirteenth century document *La Règle du Temple*. This document, which pre-dates the first vernacular translations of Vegetius by a generation, sometimes reads like a cavalry drill manual. Significantly, it contains no reference to Vegetius. It is generally thought that the *Rule*'s instructions were initially conceived at least a century earlier, after the Templar order was officially endorsed at the Council of Troyes in 1129, thus putting its contents closer to our 'Norman' period. The *Rule* describes the equipment and horses of the organisation and the rank structure from the Master down to the brother knight. Conduct on campaign and on the battlefield is also described. We cannot say if the arrangements in the *Rule* are the same as they were for the Normans, but they make thought-provoking reading nonetheless. Each brother knight was entitled to up to four horses, two of them warhorses, one riding horse and a packhorse. Around him were squires to look after and ride the horses. At the top end of the tree the Master's household would have consisted of a dozen men and horses. The Master was in charge of military strategy. Beneath him was the Seneschal, whose role included administrative and logistical duties as well as holding the famous Piebald Banner. But the allocation of horses was down to the Master. There is a reference to the performance of horses which shows a keen concern for their quality. The *Rule* mentions 'pullers', 'stoppers' and 'throwers'. Mounts with such undesirable characteristics were to be replaced. The *Rule* is insistent that on the battlefield the mounted Templar should keep formation with his comrades and must not charge or break ranks without permission. When the Marshal led the knights into a charge, the squires were to charge behind with the spare destriers. A Turcopolier commanded the lesser-armed serjeants and officers, whose individual units were reinforced by individual brother knights.

When it came to the charge itself, this was carried out on the Marshal's orders. He would take the Piebald Banner from his under-marshal and surround himself with ten knights. The timing of the charge was the Master's decision, but the *Rule* stipulates that cohesion was the important thing. After the charge and during the mêlée, no brother could leave his squadron without permission. If he were to be assisted off the battlefield for a while he was to return to his banner. The banners were hugely important as rallying points in the battle. It was forbidden for a standard or gonfanon bearer to lower his banner to strike an enemy. With this level of sophistication in cavalry organisation in the *Rule*, it is tempting, though perhaps dangerous, to imagine the Normans adopting something similar.

What then, of the 'shock' issue? The capability comes not so much from the physicality of the impact (which could sometimes falter if an enemy line held), but from the psychological effects suffered by the receivers. Anyone who has ever faced a cavalry charge will say that it is very much a test of nerves. Alexius

Comnenus and his predecessors clearly knew of the potential effects. People have sought to explain the success of medieval 'shock' cavalry by attributing it to three developments which seem to appear midway through the Middle Ages. These are the emergence of the stirrup, the increasing use of the rider's lance from the 'couched' position and the development of the saddle with a high rear cantle, or back. The general theory says that it was the stirrup that made the rider more stable at the moment of impact. He could present his lance in the couched position and his saddle with its high back would absorb the shock of impact. In this way, the Western horseman was different to others, or so it seemed. Having resisted the impact, he could charge on into the mêlée and cause untold damage.

There are a number of problems with this interpretation. The stirrup's function was not to support the rider in his seat at the moment of impact. In fact, experiments have shown that at this moment the rider's feet are more likely to be jerked out of the stirrups. Where the stirrups are most useful is in providing lateral support for the rider and therefore making it easier for him to fight from horseback in the mêlée, following on from the charge. Thus, the chances of exploiting the success of the charge are increased. This mêlée fighting was often carried out from the saddle using the sword, as frequent depictions in the Bayeux Tapestry show.

Too often the repeated success of medieval military groups such as the Normans is put down to technological change. This is a very modern 'industrialised' view. If we accept it, we allow ourselves to obscure our view of the skill of the horsemen, the quality of the mounts and, above all, the command abilities of the commanders and sub-commanders, their tactical positioning, the specific timing of their charges and so forth. In respect of the couched lance and high-backed saddle theory, it is best to consider what actually happens at the moment of impact. How this moment is handled is as much down to the rider's skill as it is to his equipment. He uses the muscles in his chest, arms, back and hips to translate the force of impact into his seat and legs, with which he grips the horse. It is true that the saddle with its high pommel and cantle will brace the rider in this respect. It is important to recognise that between the lance and the horse, there is the rider. His body is the shock absorber, not the saddle. His skill in weapon handling and in general horsemanship dictates the effectiveness of the impact.

The idea that the couched-lance style of fighting was gradually being adopted in our period is misleading. A twelfth-century depiction of charging cavalry from the *Miscellany of the Life of Saint Edmund* (see colour plate 15) certainly shows in beautiful detail compact units of cavalry with lances in the couched position. The earlier Bayeux Tapestry only shows a few horsemen adopting this style and thus it has been argued that in 1066 the technique was in transition. This theory does not take into account the opponents of the horsemen in each depiction. The cavalrymen in the *Miscellany* are chasing down mounted opponents, for which the couched-lance style is eminently suited. The horsemen on the Bayeux Tapestry are attacking a solid wall of infantry, for which the overarm style of fighting is more suited. Wace, writing in the twelfth century on the subject of the eleventh-century Battle of Val-ès-Dunes, says the couched lance was present there. Some regard this with scepticism, preferring to see it as a description of contemporary practice, but it makes perfect sense in a cavalry versus cavalry situation.

Norman cavalry attack the English shieldwall at Hastings with a mixture of 'couched' and 'overarm' lances. Bayeux Tapestry. The lead 'Norman' is probably sporting a gonfanon from Boulogne.

The preferred method of a mounted attack on an infantry line with lances raised overarm. Harold's shieldwall is attacked at Hastings. Bayeux Tapestry.

Once again, we look too narrowly when we try to explain Norman success. A couched lance and an accommodating saddle design are only a very small part of the picture. These were very sophisticated horsemen. There were a number of ways to fight on horseback with a spear or lance and it is probable that each Norman knight knew all of them. One could throw the missile as a javelin (for which one would require a lighter weapon). Also, one could thrust the spear downwards with a raised arm, or forwards with a swinging action underarm. Alternatively, a two-handed thrusting motion could be used. And then of course, there was the lance being held in the couched position. None of these techniques were culturally unique to the Normans.

A word of caution is needed, however. The much-vaunted Norman cavalryman was not invincible. Against a well-organised infantry line he was in dire peril, as the failed charges at Hastings show. Against well-placed archery his unarmoured horse was vulnerable, as events at Bourgthéroulde show. Over difficult terrain his horses would stumble and be picked off by the enemy, as the 'Malfosse' incident at Hastings clearly showed. One fine example of cavalry's vulnerability to well-organised infantry comes from an attack upon the city militia of the Syrian town of Shaizar by Tancred (the then prince of Antioch) in 1111. Here, a cavalry charge was launched against the infantry with no good result. Tancred then chastised his men, who replied to him that they were afraid for their horses. Tancred's response was revealing. He told them that the horses were his property and he would replace them if they fell. And so his cavalry tried again and again. They lost seventy horses. But let us not be confused. As a weapon of decision on the battlefield the Norman knight did indeed have his successes, the clearest of which is probably Richard of Aversa's well-timed charge at Civitate.

The impact of the Norman cavalry on the battlefield is indisputable. However, there is one controversial characteristic assigned to Norman horsemanship which is still argued over today. This is the notion of the feigned retreat. It is argued that the Normans' discipline in the saddle was such that it was possible for them to command a unit to wheel away from an engagement, pretending to flee from the battle line, and thus draw the enemy out, only for the cavalry to wheel once again and return to pick off their hapless pursuers, or for other friendly units to take on the exposed enemy. This tactic is attributed to the Norman cavalry at Hastings in 1066 and it is loosely argued that the same tactic was in evidence at Arques in 1053 against the French and again against the Saracens at Messina in 1060. However, what evidence do we have that the Normans, or for that matter anyone at all, could achieve such manoeuvres?

There is a great deal of evidence for the use of the tactic down the ages. However, the evidence shows some important variations in its employment. Let us first examine the Hastings references. William of Poitiers is the key figure here. When the Battle of Hastings was raging and the English numbers seemed most daunting for Poitiers' mounted Normans, the cavalry adopted a tactic which appears to have been designed to pull apart an otherwise impenetrable line. Here is what he says:

> Seeing that it would be impossible for them to overcome, without great loss to themselves, such a numerous enemy which offered a cruel resistance, the Normans and their allies turned their backs, pretending to take flight. They remembered how a little earlier, flight had led to the success they desired. Among the barbarians, who hoped that they were victorious, there was the greatest rejoicing. They urged each other on with cries of triumph while they abused our men and threatened to hurl themselves as one man on them. As before, several thousands were bold enough to rush forward, as if on wings, to pursue those who they took to be fleeing, when the Normans suddenly turned their horses' heads, stopped them in their tracks, crushed them completely and massacred them down to the last man.

Poitiers's reference to an earlier event in the battle is probably the episode in which the entire left flank comprising Bretons and others yielded to the enemy and had to be rallied in what was probably the most perilous part of the battle for Duke William. William of Malmesbury writes that the Anglo-Saxon army's tight formation would have served them well 'had not the Normans, by a feigned flight, induced them to open their ranks, till that time, according to their custom, closely compacted'. Later still, Malmesbury tells of the frustration of Duke William and hints that a feigned retreat could have a prearranged signal assigned to it:

> Finding this [the unyielding opposition] William gave a signal to his party, that, by a feigned flight they should retreat. Through this device, the close body of the English, opening for the purpose of cutting down the straggling enemy, brought upon itself swift destruction; for the Normans, facing about, attacked them thus disordered, and compelled them to fly. In this manner, deceived by a stratagem, they met a horrible death in avenging their country...

So what of the history of this tactic? In the last days of the Roman Empire the feigned flight was encountered by the Romans when facing the Alans. Later, the Byzantines encountered it with the Huns, according to Byzantine historian Agathias. The Alans had been so good at the manoeuvre that the general Arrian had to put quill to parchment in order to design a defence against it. He allows for a part of his own cavalry to chase the 'fleeing' Alans, whilst the remainder come on in good order and the infantry are instructed to remain firm. So the tactic is to be countered by a cavalry response and in no circumstances will the cohesion of the infantry be sacrificed. The lack of such a mounted counter-measure at Hastings perhaps underlines the Normans' ultimate, if somewhat attritional, success.

The steppe cultures of Eastern Europe (predominantly cavalry forces) were well acquainted, as one might expect, with a whole toolkit of mounted tricks. Moreover, tenth-century historians attribute the feigned flight to the enigmatic Magyars, Hungary's much-vaunted cavalrymen, who gave the Germans such a hard time on the battlefield. Regino of Prüm goes as far as to say that the Magyar tactic was very similar to that of the Alans. It is believed that the tactic found its way west through Visigothic contact with the Russians and from the Visigoths it became known to the Franks. The Normans will either have picked it up from their Frankish contemporaries or, as seems equally likely, their Breton neighbours, whose heritage was closely aligned to that of the Alans, who had been settled by the Romans in ancient Armorica. There is simply too much evidence to allow us to entertain the tired old arguments that a feigned retreat was not a credible manoeuvre for cavalry of the Norman period. These arguments were based by generations of military historians on the maxim that once a force is committed to an attack and is engaged, it cannot change direction. This does not account for the fact that Norman cavalry units were perfectly capable of breaking off an action at the tactical level.

That the feigned retreat was acknowledged by contemporaries is not in dispute: the Byzantines had even advocated the tactic for their own mounted troops. The reason for the wide adoption of the measure was because of its success. Both the Romans and the Byzantines had seen it done to them and added it to their own manuals. One cannot help but wonder, if King Harold had survived Hastings, whether mounted warfare in Anglo-Saxon England might have been significantly changed as a result of his contact with the Normans.

Hastings, of course, was a very unusual battle fought in difficult terrain. It is probably not wise to serve the Hastings evidence as 'typical' of the Norman approach. So, what are the other examples of the feigned retreat carried out by the Norman cavalry? The action at Arques in 1053 as elucidated by William of Poitiers, Orderic Vitalis and William of Jumièges is sometimes put forward as an example of a feigned flight. Let us have a look at it. The Normans set their siege castle against Arques, while the French king arrived and set his camp at Saint Aubin. Jumièges explains that the Normans had planned an ambush:

When the enemy arrived, the Normans succeeded in drawing away a considerable part of the army and, as if in flight, they led the French into the trap. For suddenly the Normans who seemed to be fleeing, turned around and began violently to cut down the French, so that during that encounter Count Enguerrand of Abbeville among many others was stabbed to death and Hugh Bardulf with many others was taken prisoner.

Here, it would seem, is something slightly different to what we have at Hastings. It is a pre-meditated ruse executed in the open field and not in the heat of a pitched battle. Again the circumstances are not clear, but the idea is one with which the Norman force appears to have been familiar. Perhaps it is also significant that Walter Giffard, the Norman commander at Arques, later fought at Hastings. What is clear, however, is that the manoeuvre requires a degree of discipline. There is no good reason to suppose that the Norman horsemen lacked it.

Another example which bears the same hallmarks as the Arques ambush is that recalled by Amatus (III. 46). In or about 1055, Count Richard (then of Aversa) executed an ambush employing a feigned retreat after suffering an insulting rebuff from Prince Gisulf of Salerno when he approached him for tribute payments:

> On the following morning the prince [Gisulf] rode out in safety and called to the young men with him who were bearing slings and bows. The count's [Richard] knights, when they saw that the prince had left the city, pretended to be fleeing. Those of the city, who were dressed in linen, pursued them to the place where the ambush had been prepared. When the count's men who were laying in wait saw the men of Salerno, they rushed out towards them. The Salernitans were unable to flee. Some of them threw themselves into the sea and others were slain. Thus one hundred and five died.

It is probable that Richard's forces were mounted and that this episode serves as another example of the stratagem being used to bring about an ambush, although quite how that ambush was delivered we are not sure.

One of the first actions in the conquest of Sicily was that at Messina in 1060, carried out by Roger de Hauteville. The enthusiasm of the enemy practically invited the tactic, of which Malaterra says:

> The citizens of that town, of whom there were a huge number, were very angry when they realised that their enemies had invaded their territory, and in particular because they saw how few they were. They hurried from the city gates as fast as they could and went out to engage them. The count, who was most cunning and experienced in battle, at first feigned fear. Then after he had led them some way from the city he attacked, charging them savagely, and put them to flight. Cutting down the stragglers, his fearsome and threatening gaze pursued the fugitives all the long way back to the city gate. Taking the equipment and horses which they had abandoned, he boarded his ships and returned to his brother the duke at Reggio.

Another Sicilian action occurred in 1063 outside the gates of Enna after a newly-arrived African and Arab mercenary contingent had bolstered the Saracen defences. This was another example of a feigned flight deployed to procure an ambush, but it nearly went wrong for Serlo, the nephew of Roger. A small force was sent ahead to entice the Saracens from their battlements. Indeed, the enemy did sally out and as Serlo rode away towards where the ambush was set, he and his men were caught by their pursuers and scarcely one escaped without wounds. Roger's men, however, sprung their trap and succeeded in gaining the victory.

At the Battle of Cassel in 1071, the tactic reappears. This time it is employed as a device to entrap or ambush an enemy, with devastating results for those on the receiving end. Far from being a tactic which was difficult for mounted forces of the Norman era to execute, it was in fact widely practised by the Normans and even had different degrees of employment at both a tactical and slightly wider operational level. It seems utterly unreasonable to suggest that the most feared and renowned cavalrymen of Western Europe should have had little or no knowledge of a tactic which the evidence shows they employed on numerous occasions.

Infantry Tactics: Heavy and Light Infantry

That there were effective infantry forces in the Norman armies is without doubt. Notwithstanding the slow decline of infantry quality in the West after the fall of the Roman Empire, it is important to remember that infantry in the Norman period still played a vital role in warfare, even if cohesion, discipline and morale were somewhat brittle. Infantry were used for a wide variety of tasks, both strategically and tactically, by the Normans. For example, they performed key roles at sieges as both engineers and specialist assault troops. They also provided the garrisons for castles, where roles were further sub-divided. A variety of field engineering tasks were performed by infantry engineers, such as the erection of motte-and-bailey castles and road building.

On the battlefield itself the infantry of the day usually adopted the tactical defensive. As such, they were able to provide adequate defence against cavalry and infantry attack if the circumstances were right. They would suffer greatly if they pursued their cavalry opponents, as the English at Hastings and Dyrrhachium found. The infantryman was variously armed and armoured throughout the Norman world. At the heavier end of the scale, the dismounted Anglo-Norman or (less often) Siculo-Norman knight was equipped with with helmet, mail hauberk, sword, shield and spear and sidearm, in much the same way as his Anglo-Saxon, Danish or Lombard cousins. The spearmen of the fyrd in the north and militia spearmen in the south wore mailcoats or quilted fabric armour, and helmets might often have been worn. Lighter still than these infantry were the skirmishers, whose armour was probably negligible and whose weaponry would have consisted of light javelins and other missile capabilities such as slings.

The heavy infantry most commonly adopted the shield wall formation, with each of the warriors' shields overlapping with the shield of the man next to him, to form a seemingly formidable war-hedge. This formation was capable of limited manoeuvre, being able to move forward as a kind of steam-roller, provided the terrain did not break it up when in motion. However, the loss of shape or cohesion produced by such movement could result in disaster. Any breaches in the shield wall required immediate plugging, lest the enemy exploit the gaps and attack the weak flanks and rear of the units. Once outflanked or surrounded the infantry were in a desperate situation, lacking the mobility to get out of trouble. This happened to the Swabian dismounted swordsmen at Civitate and to the infantrymen of Duke Robert II Curthose's army in 1106 at Tinchebrai.

The phenomenon of the dismounted knight in the northern Anglo-Norman armies deserves special mention. The fyrdsmen who accompanied them were a reasonably capable force, but the presence in their ranks of men heavily armoured and also used to fighting on horseback must have boosted an army's confidence in meeting the mounted charges of an enemy. Even if there were no ranks of fyrd to stiffen, the dismounted knights, fighting in the style of the Anglo-Danish housecarls they had replaced, were capable of defeating enemies in their own right. The reason for dismounting would appear to be that it sent a defiant message to one's enemy. In 1124, before the Battle of Bourgthéroulde, Amaury of Montfort ascribed the dismounting of the knights under Odo Borleng as a sure sign that his enemy were intent on either dying there or winning outright victory. It was a statement of intent. It was just as much a statement to one's subordinates as it was to the enemy. In 991, at the Battle of Maldon, the Anglo-Saxon leader Byrthnoth had dismounted to join his infantry comrades as if to say to them that he would not desert his companions. It is tempting to see Odo Borleng in the same light. The phenomenon was clearly not exclusive to the Normans or even new. The Angevins at the Battle of Alençon in 1118 appear to have dismounted their knights and the Franks had done likewise at the Battle of the Dyle as far back as 891.

Only a generation or so before Bourgthéroulde William of Poitiers wrote of how laughable it was that a Norman knight would dismount to fight. Yet within a few years, the troops of the *Familia Regis* under William II de Warenne were doing just that against Earl Ralph's rebels at the Battle of Fagaduna in 1075. And they won their battle. The Norman ability to take from the stronger military traditions of its conquered foe – in this case the Anglo-Saxons – is perhaps in evidence. In the Anglo-Saxon and Scandinavian worlds there had been a strong infantry tradition. These men were not drilled, could not perform inclines or other complex manoeuvres, but were on the whole useful and robust in the roles for which they were chosen. The Normans in Italy seem to have adopted infantry in a different way than in the north. There were no resolute defensive shield walls as far as we can tell, although the duke of Apulia would have had access to the city militias, which featured so heavily in the wars during the decline of Byzantine control in the early eleventh century. However, there were available to the Normans in the south a variety of infantrymen from their conquered territories, which ranged from these Italo-Lombard militiamen to Sicilian Muslim troops seen in numbers at the siege of Capua in 1098, and other specialist missile and skirmishing troops. So, while it is true that the infantryman of the eleventh and twelfth centuries lacked something in the Vegetian training methods of a bygone age and were perhaps less able to take the offensive to the enemy, there were nonetheless a good variety from which to choose. And of the specialist types available, there was one group of infantrymen whose impact would ultimately have a profound effect on medieval warfare in general.

Infantry Tactics: Archers and Crossbowmen.
During our period the bow and its lethal cousin the crossbow were considered worthy only of the low-born and the mercenary. These weapons were no respecters of class, as Roger of Gloucester found when he was struck on the head and killed by a crossbow bolt at the siege of Falaise in 1106. Neither weapon featured in the feudal arrangements between men. The rather unpleasant attitude towards the men who carried the bows and crossbows is evidenced a little later than our period when sixty archers were beheaded by the future Henry II of England in 1153 after he took the castle at Crowmarsh. This attitude was widespread among the knightly classes, but it did not stop the commanders of the Norman period seeing the true value of archery as part of a combined arms approach to their field tactics. The Normans were simply too pragmatic for that.

Perhaps it was the Norman commanders' personal love of hunting that reinforced their understanding of the military potential of the bow, despite its low status. But it was not the weapon of feudal chivalry. It would be nearly three centuries before the weapon could be seen to belong to a certain 'heroic' class of warrior, enveloped in a new and socially explosive English legend, that of Robin Hood.

As a tactical option on the battlefield and elsewhere, the bow was used widely in both the northern Norman world and in Italy, Sicily and in the Norman campaigns in Illyria. The bow was clearly an ideal and obvious weapon for use by the town militias in Italy for the defence of their walls and fortifications. For example, when Count Richard of Aversa came to Salerno to intimidate the town into paying further tribute, he was met with a hail of both stones and arrows. The bow was also widely adopted by the Saracens, with a composite design heritage which was somewhat different from that of the Western European world. Bows could be used in attack, with some flanking manoeuvres in good evidence, and more commonly in defence as an anti-cavalry counter-measure. They could also be used to provide cover for other specialist troops engaged in undermining fortifications or moving from one part of a siege or battlefield to another. Orderic Vitalis gives us a good example of the posting of both crossbowmen and archers around a Norman camp while the army was on campaign in hostile territory. He says that when William II Rufus came to Coulaines near Le Mans in 1098 the crossbowmen and the archers were posted in the vineyards and explored the pathways to prevent the enemy from passing through. These men frequently used harassing fire on any one coming near to them.

When we talk of tactical options for the archer, the subject of the mounted archer often comes to the fore. Here, we are split between the evidence in the southern regions of the Norman world and that in the north. The mounted archer in the world beyond Christendom was widely known. He habitually fought from the saddle as a horse-archer. Pechenegs and Turks employed them widely against their Byzantine enemies, the former almost exclusively. The tactics usually involved great enveloping movements designed to harass or entrap an enemy. The Byzantines had their own mounted archers and many of the other cultures that the Normans came into contact with in Sicily, North Africa and the Levant used them too. However, the mounted archer in the northern Norman sphere is poorly evidenced, although he is not entirely missing from it. He appears as a lone individual in the closing scenes of the Bayeux Tapestry as an unarmoured mounted archer surrounded by other mounted men. However, these men are in pursuit of the fleeing English infantry and each figure carries a different weapon – here a spear, there a sword. The choice of weapon of our mounted archer may simply have been one of expediency. However, with the evidence from the Battle of Bourgthéroulde in 1124 we are much better off (pages 142-144). Here, the detachment of mounted archers is sent to the enemy right flank to fire into his unshielded side. However, the general opinion is that these men would have dismounted before drawing their bows. The sources entice us again, in Robert of Torigny's mention of Robert of Gloucester's cross-country expedition of 1139, in which he is escorted by knights and mounted archers, but we do not know what they would have done when they came to a point where they had to fight.

For infantry archers we are much better served with the evidence. Wace mentions in his *Roman de Rou* that William the Conqueror's army at Varaville had archers in 1057. They are of course there again in 1066. The reference to bowmen for Hastings is interesting, in that Wace says that the archers came from distinct parts of the duchy, naming Vaudreuil and Breteuil among the recruiting grounds. With William of Poitiers, writing closer to the time of Hastings than Wace, the nature of the employment of the archers becomes clear. They were sent forward to pepper the English line with arrows and were followed by the heavier infantry and then again by groups of mounted knights looking to exploit the weaknesses in the English line, which in this case were very slow to appear due to the superior position of Harold's army. As the archers were withdrawn and the Normans carried out an exchange of ranks, the battle took on another tactical phase until the archers were reintroduced at various parts of the line. Here it is possible that King Harold received his famous arrow wound to the eye, although this is now a somewhat controversial subject. Henry of Huntington mentions that the archers were ordered to shoot not directly at the enemy, but over their heads into the thick mass of infantry behind them. This sort of preparatory fire may have had an important effect on the receiving infantry, which may have included the English king himself. The Bayeux Tapestry also shows the archers in the border of the tapestry firing into the air at a crucial stage of the battle.

The Normans were more used to fighting against cavalry or combined-arms armies than pure infantry armies. The development of their own tactical missile arm can be seen in this context. During the course of the battles examined in this book archery forms a key part of the tactical response to the increasing application of the mounted cavalry charge. This is true of the archers' role at Alençon and Bourgthéroulde particularly.

The role of archery in sieges is well attested, both in attack and defence. It is generally thought that the use of fire arrows in sieges was a matter of the archers wrapping cloth around the arrowhead and setting light to it before firing. However, of particular note is an episode at the siege of Brionne in 1090. Duke Robert II Curthose came to the fortress and, noting that its main stone hall (used by the defenders as a kind of last resort or 'keep') had a wooden shingle roof, ordered the establishment of a forge outside the walls. In this forge were heated the iron heads of the arrows and, on a hot dry day, Curthose's archers shot high into the air, aiming at the shingle roof of the hall. Orderic Vitalis recalls the incident and was impressed by its ingenuity:

> ...the red hot iron of the arrows and darts showered down and was riveted into the dry and crumbly wood of the old shingles...Between the ninth hour and sunset Duke Robert captured Brionne, which his father William, even with the help of Henry, king of France, had scarcely been able to subdue in three years.

Just how archers and crossbowmen were supplied when they came to a siege seems to be made clear by Orderic's recollection of the threat made to Helias of Maine in 1097 by King William II Rufus when he advised him to rebuild his walls against the royal army. Helias was told he would face 'carts laden with bolts and arrows drawn there by oxen'. Clearly the bowmen and crossbowmen were very much part of the logistical organisation of a Norman army.

Conclusion

It cannot be sensibly denied that the Normans were a military success. While it is true that not every mercenary adventurer in Italy was a true 'Norman' (there were many other French adventurers), the martial skills of William of Apulia's 'men of the north wind' were highly valued. What remains is to explain why this was so.

It is apparent from what we have observed that the Normans were not all that different from many of the medieval cultures they came into contact with. We have looked at the celebrated cavalry charge, which was not unique to the Normans, but which certainly impressed. We have looked at the siege capabilities which seem mainly borrowed from antiquity or contemporary Byzantine practice. We have looked at the combined arms approach to battles as well. None of these things provide us with the reason why the Normans prevailed in their time. The answers are not technological, they are human.

What the Normans had in abundance were high-quality men filling positions in the chain of command down to the tactical unit of the *conroi*. What this means is that, for the most part, however small a Norman army might be (such as those in the early days of the conquest of Sicily) there was not a man within it who was not immediately commanded by someone who was close by and knew what he was doing. Only when grand expeditions were conceived such as Hastings (1066) and the Illyrian campaigns of 1081, did the armies become unwieldy. But even here, with good overall generalship William the Conqueror and Robert Guiscard were able to instil control.

It should not surprise us to learn of a degree of sophistication in the Norman approach to warfare. We have evidence for complex recruitment, training, logistics and supply, command, control and discipline, organisation of march, tactical and strategic awareness, fortifications, siege engineering, road-building and troop organisation, the use of prisoners for ransom and the hire of mercenaries for pay. Let no one say these were 'Dark Ages' in military history. This obvious level of sophistication should help us understand the answer to the next question.

Were the Norman war leaders 'Vegetian' in their approach? This is a curious notion, which has absorbed historians in recent years. It is surely clear that the Normans were Vegetian when they wanted to be, but they also showed they could be so much more. William the Conqueror's masterful shadowing strategy against the French king in Normandy is evidence of the Vegetian approach. So too is the strategy adopted by his son William II Rufus whenever he put down a rebellion. Rufus showed no desire to bring about pitched battles, preferring instead to cut his enemies out of the landscape, bringing them either to starvation or surrender.

Nearly all our commanders adopted this Vegetian battle-evasive approach at some stage or other. But to argue that this was all that Norman warfare was about is to simply insult the Normans.

We might remember that, for all that is said about the wisdom of battle evasion, there were in fact many battles in our period. Chief amongst our battle-seekers was Bohemond, prince of Antioch. If we look at what he was trying to achieve (probably nothing less than gaining Constantinople in the first instance) then his military approach becomes clear. The stakes were impossibly high for Bohemond, but he did a fine and very 'un-Vegetian' job. There was nothing Vegetian about his cavalry charges at Arta and Ioannina, and Alexius Comnenus knew it.

We have looked at the main battles of the period and can conclude that the top Norman commanders excelled in forcing their enemies to make strategic and tactical mistakes. At Tinchebrai Henry I completely outwitted his brother with a flank attack and was renowned for fighting only on ground of his choosing. Strategically, at Hastings and Dyrrhachium William the Conqueror and Robert Guiscard succeeded in bringing Harold Godwinson and Alexius Comnenus to battle when in hindsight Harold and Alexius should not have engaged at that time. Only Alexius lived to learn the lesson and save his empire by adopting a more battle-evasive policy, but not before several more defeats.

There is perhaps a little room for a much maligned and discarded notion. The 'Great Man' theory of military history is about as dead now as it will ever be. But it is surely clear that the leadership skills of the Normans are there for all to see. Norman society, like others in the medieval West, was based around bonds of lordship. Inevitably, on the battlefield and on campaign, such ties required a strong central personality to bind men together. The strength of a medieval 'personality' in a position of military command was very important. We are not considering the notion of 'likeability' here. Each of our commanders employed measured cruelty to get his way; a form of psychological warfare unpalatable for the modern observer. Where the strong personality was lacking, the record of success is patchy and in some cases disastrous. Duke Robert II Curthose's career stands testimony to this. So too, with some exceptions, does the later career of Roger Borsa, Guiscard's successor as duke of Apulia, who neither inherited nor learned his father's firebrand leadership skills. Where the strong personality was in abundance the record is remarkable, as the careers of William the Conqueror and Robert Guiscard show. In fact, Amatus's medieval translator says the Normans followed Guiscard more through fear than through love (IV. 32).

Let us take a last look at those leadership skills of our commanders in the military context. William the Conqueror was disciplinarian. He was also a master of reconnaissance, a gifted logistician and a capable strategist. William II Rufus, although exhibiting some personal character defects, was a solid performer, able to crush revolts and wage strategic campaigns to reasonable effect. The Conqueror's son Henry I showed himself to be a master of the political alliance, an accomplished battlefield tactician and an intelligent strategist. Duke Robert II Curthose's unpredictable personality led to military weaknesses. Robert Guiscard, versed in stratagem and boundlessly ambitious, was a master strategist and accomplished battlefield commander. His brother Roger was highly intelligent and ambitious, displaying a propensity to learn from his mistakes. Richard of Capua had shown himself to be a superb fighter and a ruthlessly ambitious leader. Each of these leaders, like their subordinates, demonstrated an extraordinary degree of ambition, which drove their lives forward. Militarily, some were more 'Vegetian' than others. But we leave the last word to perhaps the most archetypal of the Normans, a man who carried the fight to his enemy. Anna Comnena tells of the terror of his name:

> A certain Kelt who had recently made the crossing confirmed that Bohemond was on the point of sailing. When they heard this Kontostephanos' men were struck dumb with fear at the thought of a sea battle with Bohemond (the very mention of his name was enough to scare them). So, they pretended to be ill, claiming to need treatment at the baths.

Bohemond may have died an unfulfilled man, thwarted by a political genius. He may have lost more battles than other commanders. But he fought and won many more. Here was a man whose cavalry could destroy the walls of ancient Babylon, and who could make successful tactical switches in the face of an enemy onslaught. Bohemond of Antioch was the most intriguing and gifted of all our Norman commanders, and yet a serious biography is now nearly a hundred years overdue. As for his squadrons of mounted knights, one has only to imagine experiencing life on the receiving end of these men in action to know how the myth can easily become the reality. If it was enough to make the Byzantine emperor fear it, then it should be enough to elicit modern respect.

In many ways we fall victim to our own modern values when we look at the qualities embodied in our Norman commanders. The ferocity, cruelty, guile and ambition of these men should not be judged in a modern sense. The medieval commentators are better judges in this respect. These leaders successfully led great armies into countless campaigns and established a lasting political legacy in the countries they touched. Militarily, the only 'novel' thing about the Normans was that they were consistently good over a long period of time. This was not a matter of technological development. It was not down to the designs of their castles, or the high-backed saddle, nor was it down to the arrival of the stirrup. The consistent success of the Normans in warfare is attributable to the qualities of the men who led them.

Bibliography

Primary Sources
For the excerpts taken from Malaterra's *Deeds of Count Roger* and William of Apulia's *Deeds of Count Robert I* have used the available English translations at http://www.leeds.ac.uk/arts/info/125040/medieval_europe_research_group/110 2/medieval_history_texts_in_translation (Accessed 17 August 2014). These translations remain the copyright of their author and are listed as works in progress at the time of publication. Translators are as follows:

The Deeds of Count Roger of Calabria and Sicily and of Duke Robert Guiscard his brother by Geoffrey Malaterra, translated by G.A. Loud
Deeds of Robert Guiscard by William of Apulia, translated by G.A. Loud

Other works:
Chibnall, M., 1968-80, *Orderic Vitalis. The Ecclesiastical History*. 6 Vols. Oxford. Oxford University Press.
Downer, L.J., (transl. and ed),1972, *Leges Henrici Primi*. Oxford. Clarendon Press.
Dunbar, P.N., (transl), 2004 The History of the Normans *by Amatus of Monte Cassino. Woodbridge. Boydell.*
Greenway, D (ed.), 1996, Historia Anglorum. *Henry of Huntington. Oxford. Oxford University Press.*
Mynors, R.A.B (Ed.) with Thomson, R.M. and Winterbottom, M., 1998, William of Malmesbury. *Gesta Regum Anglorum: The History of the English Kings. Vol I. Oxford. Clarendon Press.*
Sayers, D., 1957, The Song of Roland. *Harmondsworth. Penguin.*
Sewter, E. R. A., 1969 (transl.), Anna Komnene. The Alexiad. *London: Penguin Classics.*
Swanton, M., (transl. and Ed.), 1998, The Anglo-Saxon Chronicle. *London. Dent.*

Secondary Sources
Aird, W., 2008, *Robert Curthose, Duke of Normandy c.1050–1134*. Woodbridge. Boydell.
Allmand, C.T., 2011, *The De Re Militari of Vegetius: The Reception, Transmission and Legacy of a Roman Text in the Middle Ages*. Cambridge: Cambridge University Press.
Barber, R., 1995, *The Knight and Chivalry*. Woodbridge. Boydell. Revised and updated edition of the 1970 classic.

Bachrach, B., 1971, 'The Feigned Retreat at Hastings'. *Medieval Studies* XXXIII. Toronto. Pontifical Institute of Mediaeval Studies. 344–7.

Bachrach, B., 1985, 'On the Origins of William the Conqueror's Horse Transports'. In: *Technology and Culture* XXVI. Baltimore. John Hopkins University Press. 505-31.

Barlow, F., 1983, *William Rufus*. London. Methuen.

Bates, D., 1994, 'The Rise and Fall of Normandy, c.911-1204'. In: Bates, D. and Curry, A. (Eds.) *England and Normandy in the Middle Ages*. London. 19-35.

Beeler, J.H., 1956, *Castles and Strategy in Norman and Early Angevin England*. Speculum XXI. 581 - 601.

Bennett, M., 1988, 'Wace and Warfare'. In: *Anglo-Norman Studies* XI. Woodbridge. Boydell. 37-58.

Bennett, M., 1989, 'La Règle du Temple as a Military Manual, or How to Deliver a Cavalry Charge'. In: *Studies in Medieval History Presented to R. Allen Brown*. Ed. Harper-Bill, C., Holdsworth, C., and Nelson, J. Woodbridge. Boydell. 7-20.

Bennett, M., 1992, 'Norman Naval Activity in the Mediterranean c.1060 - c.1108'. In: *Anglo-Norman Studies* XV. Woodbridge. Boydell. 41-58.

Bennett, M., 2001, *Campaigns of the Norman Conquest*. Osprey. Oxford.

Bradbury, J., 1983, 'Battles in England and Normandy, 1066-1154'. In: Anglo-Norman Studies VI. Woodbridge. Boydell. 1-12.

Bradbury, J., 1985, *The Medieval Archer*. Woodbridge. Boydell.

Bradbury, J., 1998, *The Battle of Hastings*. Stroud. Sutton.

Bridgeford, A., 2004, 1066. *The Hidden History in the Bayeux Tapestry*. New York. Walker.

Brown, R.A., 1968, *The Normans and the Norman Conquest*. Woodbridge. Boydell.

Brown, R. A., 1980, 'The Battle of Hastings'. In: *Anglo-Norman Studies* III. Woodbridge. Boydell. 1-21.

Carter, J.M., 1988, *The Feigned Flight at Hastings Re-considered*. The Anglo-Norman Anonymous VI.

Chibnall, M., 1984, *The World of Orderic Vitalis*. Woodbridge. Boydell.

Cooke, D.R., 1979, 'The Norman Military Revolution in England'. In: Anglo-Norman Studies II. Woodbridge. Boydell. 94-102.

Davis, R.H.C., 1978, 'The Carmen De Hastingae Proelio'. In: *English Historical Review* 93. Oxford. Oxford University Press. 241-61.

Davis, R.H.C., 1987, 'The Warhorses of the Normans'. In: *Anglo-Norman Studies* X. Woodbridge. Boydell. 67-82.

Douglas, D.C., 1943, 'Companions of the Conqueror'. In: *History* XXVIII. 129-47.

Douglas, D. C., 1964, *William the Conqueror*. Berkeley. Yale.

Gillmour, C. M., 1984, 'The Naval Logistics of the Cross-Channel Operation, 1066'. In: *Anglo-Norman Studies* VII. Woodbridge. Boydell. 105-31.

Gillingham, J., 1989, *William the Bastard at War: Studies in Medieval History*

Presented to R. Allen Brown. Ed. Harper-Bill, C., Holdsworth, C., and Nelson, J. Woodbridge. Boydell. 141-158.

Gillmour, C.M., 1992, 'Practical Chivalry: The Training of Horses for Tournaments and Warfare'. In: *Studies in Medieval and Renaissance History*, Vol XIII. 7-29. New York. AMS Press.

Gravett, C., and Nicolle, D., 2006, *The Normans. Warrior Knights and their Castles*. Oxford. Osprey.

Gravett, C., 1992, *Hastings 1066*. London: Osprey Publishing Ltd.

Green, J. A., 2000, 'Robert Curthose Reassessed'. In: *Anglo-Norman Studies* XXII. Woodbridge. Boydell. 95-116.

Green, J. A., 2009, *Henry I. King of England and Duke of Normandy*. Cambridge. Cambridge University Press.

Hardy, R., 1976, *The Longbow. A Social and Military History*. London. Patrick Stephens Ltd.

Hyland, A., 1994, *The Medieval Warhorse From Byzantium to the Crusades*. Stroud. Sutton.

Lack, C., 2007, *Conqueror's Son: Duke Robert Curthose, Thwarted King*. Stroud. Sutton.

Lawson, M.K., 2002, *The Battle of Hastings*. Stroud. History Press.

Loud, G.A., 2000, *The Age of Robert Guiscard. Southern Italy and the Norman Conquest*. Harlow. Addison-Wesley Longman.

Mason, E., 2005, *William II Rufus, the Red King*. Stroud. Tempus.

Morillo, S. (Ed.), 1994, *Warfare Under the Anglo-Norman Kings, 1066-1135*. Woodbridge. Boydell.

Morillo, S. (Ed.),   1996, *The Battle of Hastings: Sources and Interpretations*. Woodbridge. Boydell.

Morris, M., 2012, *The Norman Conquest*. London. Hutchinson.

Neveux, F., (transl Curtis, H.,), 2008, *The Normans. The Conquests that Changed the Face of Europe*. London. Constable and Robinson.

Norwich, J.J., 1967, *The Normans in the South 1016-1130*. London. Faber.

Payne-Gallwey, Sir R., 1903, *The Crossbow, Medieval and Modern, Military and Sporting*. London. Repr. 1958, Holland Press.

Pierce, I., 1987, 'Arms, Armour and Warfare in the Eleventh Century'. In: *Anglo-Norman Studies* X. Woodbridge. Boydell. 237-57.

Platts, B., 1980, *Origins of Heraldry*. London. The Procter Press.

Searle, E., 1988, *Predatory Kinship and the Creation of Norman Power, 840-1066*. Berkeley. University of California Press.

Sharpe, R., 2004, '1088 – William II and the Rebels'. In: *Anglo-Norman Studies* XXIV. Woodbridge. Boydell. 139-57.

Stanton, C.D., 2013, *The Battle of Civitate: A Plausible Account*. Woodbridge. Boydell.

Strickland, M. (ed), 1992, *Anglo-Norman Warfare*. Woodbridge. Boydell.

Strickland, M., 1996, *Warfare and Chivalry: The Conduct and Perception of War in England and Normandy 1066-1217*. Cambridge. Cambridge University Press.

Theotokis, G., 2010, *The Campaigns of the Norman Dukes of Southern Italy against Byzantium, in the years between 1071 and 1108 AD*. PhD thesis. University of Glasgow.

Van Houts, E., 1988, 'The Ship List of William the Conqueror'. In: *Anglo-Norman Studies* X. Woodbridge. Boydell. 159-83.

Waley, D.P., 1954, 'Combined Operations in Sicily, AD 1060-78'. In: *Papers of the British School in Rome* 22. 118-25.

Yewdale, R., B., 2010, *Bohemond I, Prince of Antioch*. Leonaur Books. New version of original Thesis compiled in 1919.

Index

Æthelwig, Abbot of Evesham 175
Abelard, son of Humphrey de
  Hauteville 28, 103
Acarenza 20
Agrigento 202
Ajello 31, 201
Alberada, first wife of Robert
  Guiscard 27
Alençon, 41
  Battle of (1118) 137–138, 227,
    230
  siege of 41
Alfred the Ætheling, English prince
  11, 120
Alfred the Great (871-900) Anglo-
  Saxon king 7, 38
Alexius Comnenus, Byzantine
  Emperor 26, 29, 103, 112, 160, 164,
  166, 232
  at Battle of Dyrrhachium (1081)
    166–170
Amalfi 16
Amatus of Monte Cassino 3, 14, 16,
  22, 30, 48, 150, 172–173, 190, 195,
  198, 200, 201, 206, 210, 212, 214,
  225, 232
  The History of the Normans 3
Andria 31
Anglo-Saxon Chronicle, the 5, 45, 75,
  120, 127, 197, 207
Anna Comnena 5, 26, 32, 100–101,
  105, 106, 163–164, 166, 193, 218,
  233
  Alexiad 5, 26, 32, 100–101, 218,
    233
Annals of Bari, the 5, 21

Anselm, Archbishop of Canterbury
  65
Antioch, 86
  Siege of (1098) 86, 109
Apulia 5, 16, 17, 19, 29, 31, 33, 58,
  146, 214
Aquino 31, 50, 207
Archery 138, 228–230
  attitude towards archers 228
  effect on cavalry 201
  evidence for mounted archers in the
    west 143, 229
  use of fire arrows 201, 230
Ardouin, Lombard rebel 18–19, 20,
  21, 22–23
Argyrus, son of Melus 19, 21, 22,
  149, 151
Arques 37, 42, 190, 222, 224–225
Arrière ban 32, 178
Ascalon, Battle of (1099) 193
Ascoli 20, 22, 145
Atenulf (of Benevento) 21, 147
Atenulf, Duke of Gaeta 49
Athelstan, King of England (924-939)
  73
Arta, Battle of (1082) 105
Arundel Castle 77, 177, 199, 201
Aversa 17–18, 49
Avlona 164
Avranches 188
Avranchin, the 9
Baldwin of Edessa 112
Ballon 77
Bamburgh (Castle) 74
Bari 16, 21, 29, 32
  Siege of 202–204

Basil II Byzantine Emperor
(972–1024) 16
Basil Boioannes, Byzantine Catapan
16–17
Basil Mesopotamites, Byzantine
commander 165
Battle, Sussex 122
Battles
'typical' battles 172–173
Bayeux 97
Tapestry 120, 122 -123, 127, 185,
220–221, 230
Benedict VIII, pope
Benevento 28, 157, 202
Bessin, the 9
Bohemond, Prince of Antioch 32, 34,
83, 86, 100, 162, 165, 232–233
acquires the name 'Bohemond'
101–102
decisive generalship at Ioannina
(1082) 105
fakes own death 112
second Illyrian campaign (1107)
112
struggles against Roger Borsa 107
Bourgthéroulde, Battle of (1124)
142–144, 180, 200, 209, 217, 222,
227, 230
Brémule
Battle of (1119) 138–142, 214, 217
Bretons 181
Brevis Relatio, the 130
Bridgenorth 182, 199
Brittany 13,
Butrinto 32, 162, 165
Caen 45, 97, 188
Calabria 16, 23, 27, 30, 31, 54–55,
59, 197, 207
famine 55, 207
Cannae, 20
Battle of (1018) 16–17
Canosa 102

Capitulare de Villis 186
Capua 14, 49
Sieges of (1057–1058) 52
(1062) 52
(1098) 62, 202, 227
Cardiff Castle 81, 87
Carlisle 73
Castles 45, 196–199
adulterine castles 197
counter castles 74, 200
role 196–199
Castle Service 178, 179–180
Catalogus Baronum 179
Catapanata 16
Cavalry (Norman/Frankish) 169
Byzantine fear of 105
Ceprano, conference at (1080) 32
Cerami, Battle of (1063) 57, 157–160
Carmen de Hastingae Proelio, the
120, 127, 129
Charlemagne 16, 186
Charles the Bald, French king (840-
877) 7
Charles the Simple, French king (893-
922) 9
Chaumont 75, 78, 201
*Chronicle of the Deeds of the Counts
of Anjou, the* 137–138
Cisternino 31, 215
Civitate 17, 20, 22, 152, 157
Battle of 28, 31, 49, 149–157
Cnut, Danish king of England (1016-
1035) 11, 13
Comino 17
Conrad II (1024-1039), Holy Roman
Emperor 18
Conroi 158, 217, 218
Constantine VIII (1025-1028),
Byzantine Emperor
Constantine IX Monomachus (1042-
1055) Byzantine Emperor 21
Constantinople 107, 203

Constitutio Domus Regis 182
Corato 31
Corfu 32 -33, 164, 165
Cotentin 90
Couched lance 220–221
Cumans 112
Dattus of Bari 17
Destrier (war horse) 180, 184
Dives 44, 121
Dol 41, 44
Domesday survey 38, 177
Domfront 41, 90, 210
Doryleaum, Battle of (1097) 84, 107
Dudo of Saint-Quentin 4, 9
    Historia Normannorum 4,
Drogo de Hauteville 18, 22, 26–27,
    49, 198
Dyrrhachium 32, 107, 112–113, 170,
    202
    Battle of 29, 31, 162–170, 232
    siege of (1108) 205
Eadmer 62, 73
Edgar the Ætheling 45, 73, 75, 91,
    134, 136, 197
Edmund II Ironside, King of England
    178
Edward the Confessor, King of
    England 11, 13, 120, 127
Emma of Normandy 11, 13, 120
Enna, Battle of 30, 61, 187
Ethelred II Unræd, King of England
    (979 -1016) 10–11, 120
Eustace, Count of Boulogne 132
Exaugustus Boioannes, catapan 147
Exeter 200
Exmes 86
Familia 176, 180, 182, 188, 192, 193,
    194
Familia Regis 134, 143, 179, 180,
    182, 188, 194, 217, 227
Feigned retreat/flight 222–226
Feudalism 175

Fécamp 12, 13, 70, 134
First Crusade 82
Flemish Money Fief 96, 180–181
Foggia 16
Fulk Count of Anjou (1068–1109)
    76–77
Fulk V Count of Anjou (1106–1129)
    137
Fyrd 176–178, 227
Gaeta 16
Gaimar III of Salerno (999-1027) 14,
    17
Gaimar IV of Salerno (1027-1052)
    18, 20, 21, 22, 23
Geoffrey of Malaterra 2, 27, 29, 54,
    56, 59, 61, 145, 147, 149, 150,
    158–159, 160, 161, 163, 164, 166,
    179, 181, 187, 192, 201, 210, 225
Geoffrey Martel Count of Anjou
    (1040–1060) 38, 41, 42, 190, 210
Geoffrey Ridel 31
George Palaeologus, governor of
    Dyrrhachium 164–165, 166, 170
George Maniakes, Byzantine
    commander 18–19, 21
Gerace 29, 56, 59, 208
Gerard of Bounalbergo 28, 150
Gerberoi, Battle of (1079) 41, 45, 83
Gilbert Buatère, Norman leader 14,
    16
Gilbert, count of Brionne 37
Gilbert FitzRichard 74
Giovenazzo 21
Giroie family 192
Gisors 76, 97
Gisulf II Prince of Salerno
    (1052–1077) 28, 204–205, 225
Gloucester Cathedral 82, 87
Godfrey of Bouillon 83, 86, 107, 111
Greek Fire (Naptha) 165, 205
Gregory VII (1073–1085) pope 29,
    32, 162

Gundulf, bishop of Rochester 78
Guy, son of Robert Guiscard 32, 113
Guy of Burgundy 37, 117, 120
Guy of Ponthieu 42–43
Harem, Battle of (1098) 109
Harold Godwinson, King of England
   (1066) 44, 75, 170, 207, 232
   at Hastings (1066) 120–133
Harald Sigurdsson ('Hardrada') 18,
   121
Harran, Battle of (1104) 112
Harrying of the North 45, 206, 208
Hastings, Battle of (1066) 120–133,
   209, 211, 222–223, 229, 232
   Malfosse incident 132, 222
Helena, daughter of Robert Guiscard
   32, 57–58
Helias of Maine 76–77, 78, 135, 136,
   198, 199, 206, 209, 230
Henry I, King of England
   (1100–1135) 38, 64, 68, 73, 76, 77,
   86, 88, 177, 178, 180, 182, 183,
   189, 190, 198, 199, 201, 207, 208,
   210, 214, 232–233
   acquires kingdom of England 91
   as a womaniser 89
   at Alençon 137–138
   at Brémule 138–142
   at Tinchebrai (1106) 133–137
   birth 88
   cruelty 90, 92
   death 95
   early years after the Conqueror's
      death 89
   marriage to Edith (Matilda)
      daughter of Malcolm, King of the
      Scots 91
   subsequent marriage
   trains English troops 97
   Welsh campaigns 97–98
Henry II, King of England (1154-
   1189) 95, 189

Henry I, King of France (1031–1060)
   12, 37–38, 42, 43, 190
Henry II, Holy Roman Emperor (972-
   1024) 16–17, 27
Henry IV, Holy Roman Emperor
   (1084–1105) 30
Henry of Huntington 129, 134, 138,
   140, 229
Herman of Aversa (boy) 49
Hermann of Reichenau 5, 149, 151
Hervé Frankopoulos 19
Horses 184–187
   breeding 186–187
   maintenance 189
   management 184
   size 185
   training 193, 218
   value 187
Hugh, Abbot of Cluny (d.1109) 192
Hugh of Chester 76
Hugh of Ivry 12
Humphrey de Hauteville 18, 27, 28,
   30, 49, 149, 150, 151, 154
Hyde Chronicle, the 138, 140
Ibn al-Hawas 61, 158, 161
Ibn at-Timnah 56, 60, 210
Ioannina 105
   Battle of 105
Jersey, island of 13
Jerusalem 86
John of Salisbury 79
John of Worcester 120, 122, 133
John XIX, pope
Jordan, Prince of Capua (1078–1091)
   32
Joscelin of Molfetta 32, 203
Judith, daughter of Henry I of
   England 92 -93
Judith of Evreux 55
Kastoria 103, 106
Kilij Arslan I 107
Knights 178, 180, 192, 227

Knights Templar 219
Lacedonia 31
La Flèche, Battle of (1081) 41
Lanfranc, Archbishop of Canterbury 64–65
La Règle du Temple 219
Larissa 105–106
Latakia 84
Lavello 20, 22, 145
Leges Henrici Primi 177, 189, 194
Le Mans 44, 76, 78, 190, 199
Leo Marsicanus 14–16
Leo IX, pope 28, 149, 152, 154, 157
Lisiard of Sablé 138
Logistics 44, 188–191
London 207
Louis VI, King of France (1081–1137) 92, 93, 97, 98, 190
   at Brémule 138–142
Luc de la Barre 96
Maine, duchy of 44, 76
Malcolm III King of the Scots (1058–1093) 73–74
Malta 62
Mantes 75
Matera 21
Matilda (Empress) daughter of Henry I of England 92, 94–95
Matilda (Edith) wife of Henry I of England 91
Matilda, wife of William the Conqueror 38, 65, 81, 124
Matthew of Edessa 19
Matthew Paris 87
Melfi 17, 20, 21, 22, 23, 27, 54, 145, 147, 208
   Council of (1059) 28
Melitene, Battle of 111
Melus of Bari, Lombard rebel 14, 16–17
Mercenaries 179–183
Messina 31, 60, 212, 225

Michael Doukeianos, Byzantine Catapan 20, 145, 146
Michael IV (1034-1041), Byzantine Emperor 21
Michael VII (1071–1078) Byzantine Emperor 32, 162
Mileto 31, 55
Minervino 20
Misilmeri, Battle of (1068) 57, 161–162
Monopoli 20, 21
Mont-Saint-Michel 73, 90
Monte Gargano 22
Monte Tarantino 57
Montepeloso 20, 22, 31, 198, 214
   Battle of (1041) 149
Montreuil 197
Morcar, Earl of Northumbria 64, 130, 133
Morgengab, Lombard law 49 -50
Mortemer, Battle of (1054) 38, 42–43
Naples 16, 17, 205
Naptha (see Greek Fire)
Newcastle 74
New Forest, England 66
Nicaea 107
   Siege of (1097) 84
Nicholas II, pope (1059–1061) 28
Nigel d'Aubigny 73, 92, 139
Nicephorus Botaniates 162
Nicholas Brenas, Byzantine commander 165
Nikephoros II Doukeianos, Catapan 20
Noirmoutier 7
Normandy
   early history 7–14
   geology 184
Odo, Bishop of Bayeux, Earl of Kent 42, 65, 199
Odo Borleng 142–143, 180, 227
Ofanto, Battle at the river (1041) 147

Olivento, Battle of (1041) 146
Order of march 210–211
Orderic Vitalis 5, 45, 68, 81, 82, 83,
   86, 93, 98, 121, 134, 136, 138, 140,
   174, 183, 189, 192, 193, 196, 199,
   210, 219, 224, 228, 230
Otranto 31, 162
Palermo 31, 203
   Siege of 29, 57, 204
Pandulf IV, of Capua 'Wolf of the
   Abruzzi' 17, 26–27, 30, 49
Pandulf VI of Capua 49
Paternò 197
Pechenegs 19, 112
Perenos, governor of Dyrrhachium 32
Peter of Bisignano 27
Peter, son of Amicus 208
Petralia 55
Pevensey 70, 121, 127
Pontoise 75
Praecepta Militaria (Nikephorus
   Phocas) 136, 170, 173
Pseudo–'Michael', imposter emperor
   165
Radulf Glaber 16
Ragusans 162–163
Rainulf I of Aversa (d. 1045) 17–18,
   22, 48
Rainulf II of Aversa (d. 1048) 48–49
Ralph Tesson 117
Ralph the Red of Pont-Echanfray 98,
   99
Ranulf Flambard 66
Rates of march 212
Ravaging 194, 206–208
Raymond of Toulouse 83, 86, 111
Reading Abbey 89, 95
Recruitment 166, 175–183
Reggio 31, 55, 60–61, 200, 208
   Siege of 59
Richard I, Count of Aversa, Prince of
   Capua (d.1078) 48, 150, 196, 202,

204–205, 207, 219, 228
   appearance 48
   at Civitate (1053) 50, 152, 154–155,
      219, 222
   relations with Duke Atenulf of
      Gaeta 50
   relations with papacy 50, 52
   relations with Robert Guiscard 50
Richard I, Duke of Normandy
   (942–996) 10
Richard II, Duke of Normandy (996 -
   1027) 10, 37
Richard III, Duke of Normandy
   (d.1027) 11
Ridwan of Aleppo 84–85
Robert, Archbishop of Rouen 12, 37
Robert, Count of Eu 43–43
Robert Crispin 186
Robert de Bellême 68, 76, 77, 86, 92,
   134, 136, 177, 180, 182, 198, 199,
   207
   as siege specialist 201
Robert de Comines 45, 196–197
Robert de Mowbray 66, 68, 74 -75,
   177
   rebels against William II Rufus
      74–75
Robert Guiscard, Duke of Apulia,
   Calabria and Sicily 23, 24, 54, 149,
   173, 187, 191, 194–195, 197, 201,
   202, 203, 204, 208, 210, 212, 214,
   215, 231, 232
   acquires the name 'Guiscard' 28
   appearance 26
   at Battle of Civitate (1053) 154–156
   at Battle of Dyrrhachium (1081)
      162–167
   death 30, 33
   first Illyrian campaign 32
   first marriage 28
   incident at Gerace 29, 56
   impressment of troops 166

personality 30
relations with the papacy 29
second marriage 28
trains troops 193
Robert Stuteville 134, 136
Robert I, Duke of Normandy
  (1027–1035) 11–13, 37, 179
  Prepares to invade England 13
Pilgrimage 13
Robert II Count of Flanders
  (crusader) 83, 86, 109, 111
Robert II Curthose, Duke of
  Normandy (1087–1106) 38, 64, 74,
  77, 80, 96, 111, 194, 197, 198, 199,
  208, 227, 230
  acquires name 'curtaocrea' 81
  as crusader 83–84
  at Tinchebrai (1106) 133–137
  criticisms of character 81
  fails to support English 1088
    rebellion 81
  lacks discipline 194
  struggles with brothers William and
    Henry 82
Robert of Meulan 92, 135
Robert of Toringy 142, 143
Robert the Pious, French Capetian
  king (996–1031) 10, 12
Rochester 70, 97, 199
Roger de Beaumont 37
Roger I de Tosny 12
Roger I, Great Count of Sicily (d.
  1101) 28–29, 53, 179, 187, 190,
  197, 202, 203, 208, 225
  at Battle of Cerami (1063) 157–160
  at Battle of Misilmeri (1086)
    161–162
  early campaigns with Robert
    Guiscard 55, 60–61
  falls out with Robert Guiscard 56
  later marriages 58
  marriage to Judith of Evreux 55

political sensitivity and Muslim
  reputation 57–58
psychological approach to warfare
  61, 161–162
supports Robert Guiscard 57–58
supports Roger Borsa 58
surprize tactics 59
temperament 61–62
Roger II of Sicily (1130–1154) 58, 62,
  179
Roger Borsa, duke of Apulia and
  Calabria (d. 1111) 29, 32, 33, 102,
  107, 232
Roger of Montgomery 37, 128
Roger of Wendover 87
Roger Toutebove 32
Rollo, first count of Rouen, traditional
  founder of Normandy 9–10
Romuald of Salerno 164
Rouen 7, 70, 188
Roussel of Bailleul 158, 159, 160,
  164
Saint-Clair-sur-Epte, treaty of 9
Saint George 160
Saint-Valery-Sur-Somme 44, 121, 190
Saint Suzanne 41
Salerno 14, 16, 32, 195, 198, 202, 228
  Saracen raid (999 or 1016) 14
  Siege of (1076) 204–205
Santa Severina 191
Scalea 59
Scouts 210–211
Scribla 23, 27, 197
Scutage 178
Serbs 167, 169
Sergius IV, Duke of Naples 17
Serlo de Hauteville 159, 225–226
Service de chevauchée 178
Service d'host (expedition) 178
Servitium Debitum 176, 178
Ship List, the 123
Sichelgaita, second wife of Robert

Guiscard 28, 169
Sicily 20, 30, 51, 55–57
 Byzantine campaigns in (1038–1040)
  18–19
Sieges 199–205
 equipment 21, 200, 201, 205
 length 201–202
 mining and undermining 200
Siponto 20, 151
Skylitzes, John 18
Slav mercenaries
 in Calabria 27
 at Civitate 150
Spain 12, 184–185
Squillace 55
Stephen of Blois (King of England
 1135–1154) 95, 137, 182, 197
Stratagems 214–215
Strategicon 173
Strategy 196–215
Supply (see Logistics)
Sun Tzu 173
Swabian swordsmen 150–151, 157,
 219, 227
Syracuse 202
S. Marco Argentano 27
St. Philibert 7
Tactics 216–230
 command structures 217
 infantry 226–228
 'shock' cavalry charge 218–220
Taktika (Leo VI) 165, 170, 173, 218
Taktika (Nicephorus Ouranos) 173
Tancred, Lord of Hauteville 18, 191
Tancred de Hauteville (crusader) 83,
 86
Taormina 200
Taranto 21
Tatikios, Byzantine commander 109,
 166
Telese 28
Theobald of Blois 137

Thomas de Saint Jean 133–134
Tinchebrai, Battle of (1106) 97,
 133–137, 232
Tonbridge, siege of 70, 177, 201
Tournament, the 193
Training 192–193
Trani 20, 21, 31, 200, 201
Treaty of Alton (1101) 96
Treaty of Ceprano (1080) 162
Treaty of Devol (1108) 103, 113
Trikala 105
Tristan of Montepeloso 20, 22
Troia 17, 21, 31, 103, 200, 202
Troina, Sicily 55, 56–57, 157
Turcopoles 165, 219
Turks 107, 112, 160, 169
Turold, tutor to William the
 Conqueror 37
Tynemouth 75
Val-ès-Dunes, Battle of (1047) 38,
 117–120, 221
Varangian Guard 16, 19, 103, 147,
 167
 at Cannae 16
 at Dyrrhachium 167–169
Varaville, Battle of (1057) 38, 43, 229
Vegetius 1, 173–174, 194, 206, 211,
 219, 231–232
 De Re Militari 1, 173–174, 194
Venice, Venetians 32, 164–165
Venosa 20, 22, 27, 33, 145
Vexin, the 12, 45, 75 -76, 190
Vignats
 Siege of (1102) 84, 194
Vikings
 Early raids 7–9
Vizier al-Afdal, Fatimid ruler 86
Vlachs 105
Vonista 164
Wace, Master 64, 117, 119, 128, 206,
 217, 221, 229
Waleran, Norman rebel 142–144, 201

Walter Giffard 42–43, 76, 225
Walter Tirel 66–68
Waltheof, English Earl 132
Westminster Hall 78
White Tower, London 66, 78
White Ship disaster, the (1120) 94, 98
William Adelin 91, 93
William Bellabocca 49
William Clito, son of Robert II
    Curthose 92, 94–95, 139, 141–142
William Crispin 140–141
William de Hauteville 18, 22, 29,
    54–55
William de Warenne 42
William I the Conqueror, King of
    England (1066–1087), Duke of
    Normandy (1035–1087) 34–46, 117,
    173, 174, 179, 181, 186, 190,
    194–195, 197, 200, 209, 210, 215,
    229, 231, 232
    appearance 36–37
    avoids battle 172
    brutality 45
    invasion of England 38, 44
    later years 41, 45
    marriage to Matilda 38
    minority years 13, 37
    strategist 43, 44–45, 207
William II de Warenne 134–135, 139,
    227
William II Rufus, King of England
    (1087–1100) 177, 181, 190, 194,
    198, 199, 200, 201, 209, 212, 228,
    230, 231, 232–233
    appearance 63
    campaigns in Maine 76–77
    controversial death 66–68
    faces 1088 rebellion 64, 68
    morality 64
    strategist 74–75, 78–79
    Vexin wars 75 -76
    Welsh campaigns 73, 75

William FitzOsbern 37, 42, 128, 187,
    210
William 'Iron Arm', de Hauteville 18,
    23, 27, 147
William Longsword, Count of
    Normandy 10,
William of Apulia 3, 14, 149, 150,
    152, 154–155, 162, 165, 166, 214,
    231
    *The Deeds of Robert Guiscard
        (Gesta Roberti Wiscardi)* 3, 154–155
William of Conversano 86
William of Eu 74, 75
William of Jumièges 4, 13, 120, 121,
    130, 142, 224
    *Deeds of the Norman Dukes (Gesta
        Normannorum Ducum)* 4, 120
William of Malmesbury 4, 36, 43,
    64–65, 66, 81, 121, 130–131, 223
    A History of the Norman Kings 36,
    64
William of Mortain 134, 136
William of Poitiers 3, 120, 121, 127,
    129, 172, 174, 190, 209, 210–211,
    212, 215, 222–223, 224
    *The Deeds of William, Duke of
        Normandy and King of England
        (Gesta Willelmi...)* 3, 120, 131
William of Saint Calais 65
William of Talou (rebellion against
    William the Conqueror) 38, 42, 190
Wulfnoth Godwinson 64
Yahya, Fort in Palermo 204
York 42